EU ENERGY SECURITY IN THE GAS SECTOR

A fascinating and comprehensive analysis of the major issues at stakes for the future of the EU Energy Security Policy in the Gas Sector. This book offers a detailed assessment of the main achievements by the EU in that field, and soundly highlights the necessary interaction between both internal and external dimensions of the EU energy security policy for gas. It also identifies the right challenges for the EU in the long term.

Sami Andoura, Senior Research Fellow, Notre Europe, France

T0304036

To my parents

EU Energy Security in the Gas Sector

Evolving Dynamics, Policy Dilemmas and Prospects

FILIPPOS PROEDROU

*City College, International Faculty of the University of Sheffield
and DEI College, A Registered Centre of the
University of London Programs, Greece*

Routledge
Taylor & Francis Group

LONDON AND NEW YORK

First published 2012 by Ashgate Publishing

Published 2016 by Routledge
2 Park Square, Milton Park, Abingdon, Oxfordshire OX14 4RN
711 Third Avenue, New York, NY 10017, USA

First issued in paperback 2016

Routledge is an imprint of the Taylor & Francis Group, an informa business

British Library Cataloguing in Publication Data
Proedrou, Filippos.
    EU energy security in the gas sector : evolving dynamics,
    policy dilemmas and prospects.
    1. Natural gas--European Union countries. 2. Natural gas
    reserves--European Union countries. 3. Natural gas--
    Political aspects--European Union countries. 4. Energy
    policy--European Union countries. 5. European Union
    countries--Foreign economic relations.
    I. Title
    333.8'23311'094-dc22

Library of Congress Cataloging-in-Publication Data
Proedrou, Filippos.
    EU energy security in the gas sector : evolving dynamics, policy dilemmas and prospects /
by Filippos Proedrou.
        p. cm.
    Includes bibliographical references and index.
    ISBN 978-1-4094-3804-5 (hbk.) -- ISBN 978-1-4094-3805-2 (ebook)
     1. Energy policy--European Union countries. 2. Energy consumption--European Union
countries. 3. Natural gas reserves--European Union countries. 4. Natural gas industry. 5.
Energy development. I.
Title.
    HD9502.E862P76 2011
    333.8'233094--dc23

                                              2011031610

ISBN 13: 978-1-138-27904-9 (pbk)
ISBN 13: 978-1-4094-3804-5 (hbk)

Contents

List of Figures	*vii*
List of Maps	*ix*
List of Tables	*xi*
Notes on the Author	*xiii*
Acknowledgments	*xv*
List of Abbreviations	*xvii*

1   Introduction   **1**
What is Energy Security?   1
What is an Energy Crisis?   4
Energy Trade-offs and the Interplay of Politics and Economics   11
The Energy Market Today: Security or Crisis?   15
A New Paradigm for Energy Policy and Security   17
The Plan of the Book   20

2   The Global Context and the Strategies of the Main
Importing States   **23**
The Global Context and the Outlook for the Future   23
The Energy Security of the Main Importers: The Cases of the US
    and China   25
Conclusion   39

3   EU Energy Security: Tracing the Main Threats, the Policy
Framework and the Actors   **41**
The Main Challenges for EU Energy Security   41
EU Strategy in the Energy Sector   45
The Framework for EU Energy Policy and Security   48
Setting the Ground: The Gas Sector   53
The EU's Gas Deficit   56
Conclusion   58

4   The Internal Front   **59**
The Liberalization of the EU Gas Market: A Work in Progress   59
Interconnected Europe: Constructing an EU-wide Gas Pipeline
    Network   66
Gas Security Regulation   67

The Missing Link: Promoting the EU's Internal Regulatory
    Model Abroad   69
Conclusion   74

5   Relations with Russia   77
Russian Gas Strategy in the EU   79
EU Energy Strategy Vis-à-vis Russia: The Views from 'Old'
    and 'New' Europe or is Russia a Reliable Supplier or a
    Formidable Threat?   91
Conclusion   103

6   Relations with the Other Producers   105
Norway   105
North Africa   109
The Caspian and the Middle East   114
The Other Suppliers   120
Conclusion   121

7   The Way Forward   123
The EU's Energy Incoherence and the Need for Solidarity   123
The Fading of Gazprom's Threat?   125
The End of (Cheap) Gas   131
A Green Energy Scene for the Twenty-first Century   132

Bibliography   *139*
Index   *167*

List of Figures

1.1   The global energy mix   2
1.2   The outlook for the global energy mix in 2030   2

2.1   The US energy mix   26
2.2   China's energy mix   32

3.1   The EU's energy mix   42
3.2   The EU's gas imports   57

6.1   The EU's projected gas imports in 2030   122

List of Maps

5.1	The Druzhba and Yamal–Europe pipelines	78
5.2	Nord Stream	82
5.3	South Stream	85
5.4	Interconnector Turkey–Greece–Italy	96
5.5	Nabucco	96
5.6	The Transadriatic pipeline (TAP)	97
6.1	Norway–Europe pipeline network	107
6.2	Algeria–Europe pipeline network	110
6.3	Libya–Sicily pipeline	111

List of Tables

4.1   New gas interconnections designed   68

5.1   EU imports of natural gas from Russia (pipeline trade in bcm)   79
5.2   Russia–Europe pipeline network   85
5.3   Main diversification projects   97

6.1   North Africa–Europe pipeline network   111

Notes on the Author

Dr Filippos Proedrou is Lecturer in International Relations in City College, International Faculty of the University of Sheffield, in Thessaloniki, Greece. In 2009 he also joined DEI College, A Registered Centre of the University of London International Programs. He studied Journalism and Mass Media at the Aristotle University of Thessaloniki, Greece (1998–2002), received his MA in International Relations from the University of Warwick, UK (2003), and was awarded his PhD on the EU–Russia energy approach from the Democritus University of Thrace, Greece, in 2009. His research interests and published and forthcoming work focus on energy politics, global governance and cosmopolitan democracy. Besides chapters in edited volumes in Greek, he has published articles in journals such as *European Security, Journal of Contemporary European Studies, Studia Diplomatica – The Brussels Journal of International Relations* and the *Journal of Southeast European and Black Sea Studies*. He is also co-author of the book *The Democratization of Global Politics: An Introduction to Cosmopolitan Democracy* (Sideris Editions 2010).

Acknowledgments

The author would like to express his special thanks to Dr Christos Frangonikopoloulos for his invaluable comments on previous drafts of the book, as well as for his wholehearted support throughout the composition of the book. The author also expresses his thanks to Jérôme Vitenberg for his committed support, guidance and advice, as well as to Nikos Yannakopoulos for his contribution to the graphic design. Many thanks to Michalis Pavlidis for his precious input, as well as to everyone who stood by the author throughout the process.

List of Abbreviations

AGB	Arab Gas Pipeline
AGRI	Azerbaijan–Georgia–Romania Interconnector
APERC	Asia Pacific Energy Research Centre
b/d	barrel per day
bcm	billion cubic meters
BP	Beyond Petroleum
CACI	Central-Asia Caucasus Institute
CASE	Centre for Social and Economic Research
CEPS	Centre for European Policy Studies
CER	Centre for European Reform
CES	Center for Eastern Studies
CGEMP	Centre of Geopolitics of Energy and Raw Materials
CIDOP	Centro de Estudios y Documentación Internacionales de Barcelona
CIEP	Clingendael International Energy Programme
CIR	Centre for International Relations
CIRED	Congrès International des Réseaux Electriques de Distribution
CIS	Commonwealth of Independent States
CITS	Center for International Trade Studies
CNG	Compressed Natural Gas
COMECON	Council of Mutual Economic Assistance
CRS	Congressional Research Service
CSIS	Centre for Strategic and International Studies
CSR	Council on Foreign Relations
CSRC	Conflict Studies Research Centre
CWPE	Cambridge Working Papers in Economics
DG	Directorate General
DIW	Berlin Deutsches Institut für Wirtschaftsforschung (German Institute of Economic Research)
ECT	Energy Charter Treaty
EDC	European Development Co-operation
EDF	Électricité de France
EEA	European Economic Area
EEDP	Energy, Environment and Development Programme

EERP   European Energy Recovery Program
EIA   Energy Information Administration
EKEM   Greek Centre for European Studies
ELIAMEP   Hellenic Foundation for European and Foreign Policy
EMP   Euro–Mediterranean Partnership
ENP   European Neighborhood Policy
EPC   European Policy Centre
EPIN   European Policy Institutes Network
EPRG   Electricity Policy Research Group
EUI   European University Institute
EWEA   European Wind Energy Association

FECER   Fédération Européenne des Cadres de I'Energie et de la Recherche
FEEM   Fondazione Eni Enrico Mattei
FES   Friedrich Ebert Stiftung
FOI   Swedish Defense Research Agency
FRIDE   Fundación para las Relaciones Internacionales y el Diálogo
             Exterior

GCC   Gulf Cooperation Council
GDP   Gross Domestic Product
GECF   Gas Exporting Countries Forum

IAI   Instituto Affari Internazionali
IDEAS   Department of Economics and Liberal Arts Studies
IEA   International Energy Agency
IEP   Institute for Energy Policy
IFP   Institut Francais du Petrole
IFRI   Institut Français des Relations Internationales
IPEEC   International Partnership for Energy Efficiency Cooperation
ISO   Independent System Operator
ITGI   Interconnector Turkey–Italy–Greece

LEED   Leadership in Energy and Environment Design
LEPII   Laboratoire d'économie de la production et de l'intégration
             internationale
LNG   Liquefied Natural Gas

MIT   Massachusetts Institute of Technology

NATO   North Atlantic Treaty Organization
NIGAL   Nigeria–Algeria Pipeline
NYMEX   New York Mercantile Exchange

OECD	Organization for Economic Co-operation and Development
OGEL	Oil Gas and Energy Law
OIES	Oxford Institute for Energy Studies
OPEC	Organization of the Petroleum Exporting Countries
PISM	Polish Institute of International Affairs
PRIO	International Peace Research Institute
SRSP	Silk Road Studies Program
SWE	Stiftung Wissenshaft und Politic (German Institute for International and Security Affairs)
TAP	Transadriatic Pipeline
tcm	trillion cubic meters
TILEC	Tilburg Law and Economics Centre
TSO	Transmission System Operator
UAE	United Arab Emirates
UCWR	University Council on Water Resources
UfM	Union for the Mediterranean
WTO	World Trade Organization

Chapter 1

Introduction

It is the author's conviction that this book should have been written for a previous era, not that of the beginning of the twenty-first century. Energy security should be based upon the extensive use of renewables, primarily solar, wind and geothermal energy and only to a limited degree upon fossil fuels. However, policy-making in general has been quite slow to comprehend the environmental challenge and reshape energy security towards a more sustainable mode. Despite all the innovations towards a green economy and sustainable development, it is widely assumed that no quick switch away from fossil fuels will take place. It is for these reasons expected that they will dominate the energy markets at least for the next few decades and that energy politics and economics will keep on revolving around oil and gas (IEA 2009: 4).

Fossil fuels account for more than three fourths of total global energy consumption. Oil is the basic fuel capturing around one third of overall global consumption, while the share of gas in world energy consumption has risen to more than 20 per cent. Coal is also widely used and accounts for more than one fourth of total global energy consumption. Its damaging effects to the environment, however, create strong grounds for a decreasing share in energy consumption in the mid-term. Moreover, coal is more of a domestic fuel, since only 10 per cent of its global production is being traded (Gros and Eigenhofer 2010: 2). Its weight in the global energy market hence is lesser than that of oil and gas. Renewable sources of energy (nuclear, solar, wind and hydro power and bio-fuels), though on the rise, only capture around 15 per cent of global energy consumption. According to the International Energy Agency (IEA) (2009) and BP (2011) Energy Outlook for 2030, the global energy mix will change within the coming two decades. Oil and coal consumption are set to decrease, while natural gas consumption will further increase. The most important shift regards renewables, whose share will increase to around one third of total energy consumption. Despite this envisaged increase, however, fossil fuels are set to remain dominant in the mid-term. It is for these reasons that when talking about energy markets, energy policy and diplomacy, energy security and energy crises, reference is basically made to oil and natural gas.

What is Energy Security?

Energy is the backbone of all economies and the motor behind growth and development. We burn oil and natural gas to heat our homes, schools and hospitals, as well as light them. Transportation means run predominantly on oil. Coal and

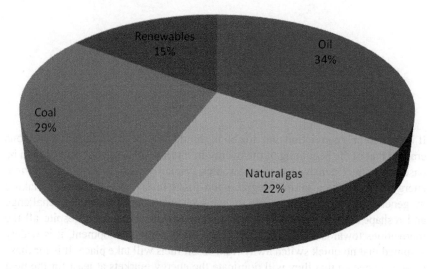

Figure 1.1   The global energy mix
Sources: BP 2010, IEA 2010

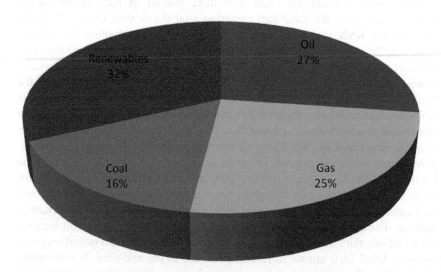

Figure 1.2   The outlook for the global energy mix in 2030
Sources: IEA 2009, BP 2011

hydro power generate electricity and so do nuclear power, bio-fuels and solar, wind and geothermal energy. Without energy economies flounder, growth is suppressed and people will return to more primitive and less efficient and comfortable modes of living. It is for these reasons that energy security has been well incorporated into broader notions and strategies of national security.

At the same time, oil and natural gas reserves are unevenly distributed. While a few states can supply their populations with domestic sources, the majority of countries, including the most developed economies of the world, have to import energy in order to cater for their energy needs. Ensuring adequate supplies then calls for imports from the more well-endowed states. Disruptions in energy supplies inflict grave concerns for growth, development, sustainability and survival. It is under this light that *energy security* is a central issue of global politics.

There is a bias in the literature to deal with the energy security of importers and not that of exporters. This is because most of the scholarly work done deals with the energy security considerations of the West, which is comprised mainly by importing countries. This book reproduces this bias since its aim is to examine an importer's, the EU's, energy security. Nevertheless, we have to sort out the different perspectives behind what exporters and importers perceive as energy security.

Starting with the importers' perspective, energy security refers to that situation whereby states face no energy shortages and meet their energy needs at no excessive cost and without further deteriorating the state of the environment. It is the state whereby states ensure *adequate energy supplies* from *reliable suppliers* and at *reasonable prices*. It can be defined as:

- The guarantee of a stable and reliable supply of energy at reasonable prices (Qingyi 2006: 89).
- Securing adequate energy supplies at reasonable and stable prices in order to sustain economic performance and growth (Eng 2003: 4).
- Being driven by the need to secure energy supplies and deliver clean, affordable energy to combat climate change (Winstone, Bolton and Gore 2007: 1).
- A condition in which a nation and all or most, of its citizens and businesses have access to sufficient energy resources at reasonable prices for the foreseeable future free from serious risk of major disruption of services (Barton et al. 2004: 5).
- The reliable, stable and sustainable supply of energy at affordable prices and at an acceptable social cost (World Economic Forum Global Agenda Council on Energy security cited by Yueh 2010: 1).
- The concept of maintaining stable supply of energy at a reasonable price in order to avoid the macroeconomic dislocation associated with unexpected disruptions in supply or increase in price (Bohi and Toman 1996).

For *importers* energy security means security of supply (that is sustainability of access to energy resources), pursuit of diversified sources of supply, suppliers and routes of supply to minimize risks and vulnerabilities stemming from any kind of dependence, at competitive prices and without harming the environment. *Energy diplomacy*, in this context, embodies the national effort to ensure the availability of energy at affordable prices (Kand 2008: 3). The contrary to energy security is *energy poverty* which can be defined as:

the condition where large swaths of a country's population has inadequate access to energy supplies, suffering in particular by insufficient and unreliable access to electricity that would deprive them of the ability to service basic household needs (IEA 2008).

For *exporters*, on the other hand, energy security equates with security of demand at competitive prices that will guarantee significant profits for the exporter with no extravagant cost to the environment. Parallel interests for exporters include aversion of recession in importing states that will reduce energy demand, as well as aversion of switch to alternative sources and of diversification of suppliers. As Mares (2010: 9) puts it, energy security 'embodies a claim for government action to protect national economic activity from shocks emanating from the international market'.

If we try to combine these two perspectives the most proper definition would be to see energy security as a 'sound balance between energy supply and demand serving the purpose of facilitating sustainable economic and social development' (Zha Daojiong cited by Tonnensson and Kolas 2006: 8) for both importers and exporters. By balance it is meant 'the fit between a variety of energy sources and a complex set of needs'. This broader definition allows us to see the energy field as a system where both exporters and importers are active and satisfy their needs and, most importantly, their interests are not seen under a conflictive, as is usually the case, but under a cooperative prism (Dannreuther 2007: 91–2).

What is an Energy Crisis?

Failure to ensure energy security brings about an *energy crisis*. From the exporters' perspective an energy crisis takes place when the exporter is unable to sell its energy at affordable prices so that it can pay off investment costs and create profits. However, the persisting thirst for energy means that such cases remain limited and marginal. Exporters in most cases find markets to sell their products, even if at times prices were lower than they would opt for. In the beginning of the 1980s, Algeria asked for high prices in order to supply LNG to the US and Spanish markets. The denial of the importers to comply with Algeria's proposals led to the termination of trade for a few years. This led to Algeria sustaining financial damages. However, it still provided energy to alternative customers and one could argue that it was its own initiative to charge extravagant prices that led to these losses (Hayes 2006: 87–8). In the beginning of the 2000s, Russia also found itself in a similar position when Turkey announced that it could not absorb all the gas quantities that were contracted to flow through the Blue Stream pipeline that connects the two countries. As a result, Russia could not attain the profits it was estimating to raise through the function of the pipeline. Russia was, however, able to sell its gas to other consumers, thus facing no energy crisis (although the decision to build this pipeline proved a sub-optimal economic choice) (Hill

2005: 4–5). In the beginning of the 1990s the rise of domestic energy production in Argentina reduced the needs for gas imports from Bolivia. The Argentinean government then renegotiated the contract and secured smaller quantities at better prices. Bolivia was obliged to accept these deteriorated terms in the absence of alternative customers that would absorb its gas (Hayes and Victor 2006: 338).

Despite these incidents, it is far more frequent for importers to be denied supplies for a mix of political, economic and technical reasons. An energy crisis erupts when energy resources are scarce, when producers are (perceived as) unreliable or when the prices rise to an unsustainable level. These three risks are subsequently discussed.

The End of Oil (and Gas)?

Fossil fuels are not inexhaustible. The increasing consumption rates of the last decades have significantly narrowed the lifetime of oil, gas and coal. It is estimated that with current consumption rates oil will not last for more than four decades, gas for no more than seven, while coal will more than outlast another century (Gros and Eigenhofer 2010: 2). The discussion normally centres upon oil and its future availability since it is the dominant fossil fuel. A number of points made for oil, however, are also relevant for natural gas.

There are two schools of thought with regard to the exhaustion of fossil fuels, 'peak theory' and the theory of 'super cycles'. Talk about the inevitability of running out of oil is not recent. The oil peak theorists claim that since oil is exhaustible, we will eventually run out of oil at some point. Oil deposits depletion is continuing at high rates, at the same time that consumption is at its highest with India and, principally, China, multiplying their oil imports in order to cover their mounting energy needs. Even if new deposits are discovered, we are heading towards the end of the oil era. Hence, we have to seek for alternative sources before it is too late (Deffeyes 2001, Checchi, Behrens and Egenhofer 2009: 11–12).[1]

To the contrary, a number of scholars appear much more optimistic about the future of fossil fuels. First of all, the oil price itself at any moment is a crucial factor for oil consumption rates and thus the lifespan of existing reserves. Low prices allow importers to consume further and act as disincentives for exploration schemes and new investments, since they are bound to yield marginal profits for the investors. This in its turn propels a period of tight supply that creates upward pressures to oil prices. Heightened oil prices then push investors to produce more

---

1 Curlee and Sale (2003: 5, 10) even make the point that a further perplexing factor will be the coming water scarcity. Water is extensively used to pump oil and under circumstances of tight water supply oil extraction may well become even more difficult. In another twist of the argument, water scarcity forces a number of states to proceed to water desalination, a rather energy-intensive activity. Due to further projected water scarcity, desalination projects seem likely to substantially increase. Water and energy scarcity seem to impact on one another.

oil to take advantage of higher margins of profit. This boom of oil investments influences the ratio between supply and demand in favour of the former thus serving as a new low prices initiator (Tonnensson and Kolas 2006: 57). The low prices of the 1990s had as a result less investments and thus declining supply for the following decade. For this reason and in combination with the rapid increase in energy demand, mainly stemming from South(east) Asian states as China and India, oil prices rose again and have now once more spurred energy companies to invest in oil exploration schemes in the 2000s.

Secondly, high prices drive importers to turn to a number of defensive measures. When faced with the oil crisis of 1973, an oil embargo and a four-fold oil price increase, importing nations adopted measures such as energy conservation and efficiency, lessening oil demand and switch to other, more economic fuels and suppliers. The use of natural gas was introduced, strategic deposits built up, overall demand for oil decreased and a policy of diversification away from overt reliance on Middle Eastern oil ensued. When in 1979 Iran's Islamic revolution sparked the second oil crisis and new price hikes, importers were in a much stronger position than a few years earlier and withstood the crisis at much lesser cost. In other words, there are cyclical trends in the oil market, rather than a linear line leading towards exhaustion of reserves. This is why despite the century-old prophecies (dating back to 1880), the world still runs on oil (Odell 2004).

The discovery of a number of new fields in the previous years that significantly added to world reserves fortifies the above conclusion. High oil prices since the mid-2000s allowed more difficult and demanding exploration schemes to be realized. Deposits that were considered unprofitable to drill with a barrel of oil being priced at 9 dollars became highly profitable when the price of oil surpassed 100 dollars per barrel. Technological innovations also allow for more difficult, especially offshore and lying at great depth, fields to come on board. Unconventional forms of oil, like sand oil found in great quantities in Canada and heavy oil, create prospects for extending further the lifetime of oil (Odell 2004). Lastly, one also has to take into account that in case global warming keeps apace it may well transform the Arctic, where extensive oil and gas fields are estimated to be lying, into an explorable field (Borgerson 2008).[2] What is even more important is that the drilling capacity does not surpass 30 per cent of overall oil quantities of wells. That means that there is significant space to improve the recovery factor and produce more oil from mature fields through advanced technologies (Pike 2010).

Gas is a newer fossil fuel than oil and takes up a lesser share in global energy consumption. Its lifetime is thus expected to be longer than that of oil. According to the James Baker Institute World Gas Trade Model (Jaffe and Soligo 2006) there is much potential for future gas production that will make up for the increasing gas consumption as projected in the following decades. In his study on

2   To this end, Russia rushed to organize a mission and send a submarine to locate the Russian flag in the bottom of the Arctic sea in order to claim sovereign rights in the promising Arctic area.

European energy security Jonathan Stern (2002: 7) views gas reserves in the wider European area as lasting for more than a century. Besides the above estimations, one can easily apply similar arguments on the exhaustion or persistence of gas. Technological innovations, sweeping climatic changes and price volatility can well provide mechanisms for the postponement into the distant future of the end date for gas reserves. The discovery of significant reserves of shale gas in North America, as well as new gas deposits in the Eastern Mediterranean basin, is estimated to further extend the lifetime of gas (Geny 2010).

Are Suppliers Reliable?

Recent arguments regarding the end of the oil (and gas) era have turned emphasis from geology to politics. Even if, as the 'super cycles' theorists maintain, the end of the oil era is nowhere near, political instability pertaining to the oil market, the function of cartels, such as OPEC (Organization of the Petroleum Exporting Countries) and the strong hand governments retain in the property of oil and gas reserves,[3] create a rather obscure picture for oil trade in the mid-term (Cable 2010: 75–82). One should not forget that both oil crises were provoked by political events in the Middle East, the Yom-Kippur Arab–Israeli war in 1973 and the Islamic Revolution and the subsequent establishment of the Islamic Republic of Iran by Ayatollah Homeini in 1979. In the words of Yergin:

> the major obstacle to the development of new supplies is not geology but what happens above ground: namely, international affairs, politics, decision-making by governments and energy investment and new technological development (2006: 75).

Indeed, a quick glance at the main producing areas reifies this point. The Middle East, which both produces the biggest quantities of oil than all other producers, as well as possesses most of the oil reserves, is a persistently unstable region, embittered by regional controversies of religious, historical, ethnic, economic and geopolitical character. At the same time, it consists of mainly undemocratic regimes with low rates of popular acceptability and raging economic and social problems that in a number of cases follow an opaque foreign policy and provide fertile ground for the nascence of fundamentalism. The ensuing political volatility, together with the function of OPEC, a cartel of producers comprising mainly the Middle Eastern producers (and some Latin American and African exporters), presents a ubiquitous danger for political and economic manipulations against the energy security of importers.

The former Soviet space is also plagued by similar problems. Military and dictatorial regimes form difficult, even if up to now proven reliable, partners. While

---

3   Government-owned companies are estimated to hold 73 per cent of oil reserves and 55 per cent of gas reserves and half of all oil and gas production, see Cable 2010: 79.

the Caspian reserves have yet to be fully discovered and produced in significant quantities, Russia deserves special mention here for a number of reasons. First of all, it possesses one tenth of proven world oil reserves and more than one fourth of total gas reserves thus retaining a critical role in energy markets. Its predominance is especially pronounced in the gas sector bringing many actual and potential implications for the markets it provides. Secondly, it is one of the greatest powers of the world, thus frequently tying energy policy to wider foreign policy goals while also able to back these claims by force. Its 'managed' democratic system and state-capitalistic model of economic development has thwarted early expectations for open market and transparent energy relations and is viewed as problematic and perilous by many states dependent on Russian oil and, most importantly, gas (see Chapter 5).

Latin America is also a well-endowed but problematic region. Relations with the biggest oil importer and consumer, the US, remain opaque, not least because a number of its energy companies were pushed out of these countries. The return of the energy sector to state hands has raised concerns for the politicization of energy trade. In sum, Latin American populous democratic regimes create uncertainties to importing states with regard to the viability of their exports, as well as the rationale, trajectory and ultimate goals of the foreign policy they pursue.

One could argue that the situation in the gas sector is even bleaker. Beyond the predominant role of Russia as a gas exporter, Iran, the pariah state in the eyes of the West, comes second in world gas reserves. Other significant exporters are Malaysia and Indonesia, while small royal Arab states as Qatar and the United Arab Emirates (UAE) capture an increasing share of the market. Any significant increase in gas production can come from Central Asia, Africa and the Middle East, regions mostly governed by autocratic regimes and problematic leaderships (IEA 2010).

In this context, politics frequently jeopardizes the stability of the global market and thus the importers' energy security. The supply of the world market seems to be more endangered by political considerations, rather than by the physical extinction of resources. This, however, is not a new phenomenon. OPEC has existed since the early 1960s, while the Middle East has been problematic since the end of the Second World War. Nevertheless, importing states have cultivated working relations with awkward exporters. Albeit normative disagreements prevail, there is a powerful complementarity of interests between exporting and importing states that works as glue to perpetual energy cooperation. US strategic relationships with the most important exporters, the European Union's low politics approach and mild foreign policy and China's policy to lock up assets from well-endowed states within wider agreement packages are all quite successful strategies that do not minimize the risks, but allow the steady flow of oil and gas from difficult energy partners.

The End of Cheap Oil (and Gas)?

The third element that can lead to an energy crisis is that of prices. Oil and gas must be affordable by consumers. In case prices rise extravagantly, energy trade will significantly diminish. Some scholars argue that even if we are not dramatically running out of oil, we are on the path towards running out of cheap oil, not least because the share of Middle Eastern oil, which is the cheapest to extract, in overall global oil supply is declining. Thus, higher investment costs are bound to yield higher oil prices (Colombo and Lesser 2010: 6, Checchi, Behrens and Egenhofer 2009: 11). Indeed, the price of oil has reached its all-time high within the 2000s and remains at rather high levels since.

The oil market involves a multitude of actors, namely states, cartels, energy companies, speculators and traders. As discussed above, the price of oil is set according to supply and demand dynamics. While some scholars claim that the suppliers retain the upper hand in setting the prices, since they are the ones holding the deposits, others point to the importers' capacity to sustain oil prices at affordable and for years rather low, levels. A more balanced approach would be to scrutinize the impact of producers on supply and importers on demand. The exporters have the capacity to restrain production and thus supply in order to boost prices and increase their profits. The central role of OPEC revolves around fixing the overall supply of its members to such levels that it does not allow a free fall in oil prices. However, exporters need to maintain significant volumes of exports in order to raise profits on which their economies are virtually run. They thus have to be cautious not to provoke *demand destruction*, that is setting so high prices that they bring about a significant cut in consumption and switch to other forms of energy. The consumers, on the other hand, can check upon their demand in order to force lower prices on the exporters. At the same time, however, and despite all the measures taken to curb oil demand, their economies are still predominantly run on oil. Both producers and consumers can influence supply and demand on the margins due to their mutual interdependence (Toyin and Genova 2005: 15–17).

Hence, it would be wiser to say that this is a complex market, rather than nominate it as a suppliers' or a buyers' market. One could argue that while importers had the upper hand in the 1960s, the exporters acquired the capacity to set prices in the 1970s. This, however, as discussed above, led to structural changes in global demand that once more allowed the consumers enough leverage on price-setting. The nationalization of resources, the increase of demand from various centres, especially Southeast Asia and the fact that global refining capacity has been reaching its limits, seem to tilt the balance in favour of the producers once more, albeit the discovery of new fields, the exploration of which is to be encouraged by high oil prices, can once more stabilize the oil market (Liu 2006: 13–14).

It is important here to understand the notion of *spare capacity* and its fundamental impact on the formation of prices. Suppliers do not produce at maximum capacity. OPEC's producing practices assure consumers that oil supply can be boosted in case of an emergency when more supplies may be needed. This is crucial for creating *trust* in the market and the anticipation that short-term mishaps (as, for example, natural disasters) can be withstood. Whenever supply overdoes demand and there is some spare capacity, markets remain at 'normal' levels. It is when demand rises further and the spare capacity shrinks that alarm rings. When we listen that oil deposits will last for another four decades, this reflects the ratio between proven reserves and actual consumption rates. When reserves increase *ceteris paribus,* the expectations for the lifetime of oil is extended. Whenever consumption rates increase *ceteris paribus*, the anticipated lifetime falls. This creates fears for the end of the oil era. This fear is reflected in higher prices (Jesse and van der Linde 2008). In other words, the volatility in the oil market and increased prices reflect worries about the short- and mid-term capacity of supply to cater for overall demand. Prices incorporate the shadow of the future and reflect the extent of trust on the markets to serve the global population (Toyin and Genova 2005: 65–8).

Here is where the role of traders and speculators comes in. When traders anticipate that the price of oil will rise, they rush to buy cheap in order to sell at higher prices and make a profit. This serves as a price hike instigator. To the contrary, when they expect prices to go down they wait until they reach bottom level, thus contributing to declining demand and lower prices. Moreover, hedge funds place a number of bets on the future price of oil (for example, whether the price of oil will be above or under the level of 100 dollars per barrel in one month from now). These estimations, since they are the result of rational calculations through which hedge funds endeavour to raise money, are also taken into consideration by other actors (traders, exporting and importing states) and impact on their actions thus affecting supply and demand patterns. The derivatives market thus forms an integral part of the oil market (Toyin and Genova 2005: 15–17).

Therefore, no government or organization sets the price on its own, albeit OPEC enjoys significant leverage to shape one of the two major dimensions of the market, namely supply (Tonnensson and Kolas 2006: 55). It would be much more precise to argue then that the oil market is rather complex and influenced by a number of actors, with structural characteristics and actors' policies highly influencing and co-determining oil prices. With rising consumption rates worldwide and unless significant new discoveries and/or technological breakthroughs that will allow more oil quantities to be drilled are made, oil prices are going to remain at high levels and may well further increase into the future.

With regard to gas pricing, we find different pricing mechanisms in different regional markets. In the North American market gas is traded freely at the New York Mercantile Exchange (NYMEX) hub. Prices are rather volatile and determined in accordance with supply and demand forces at play each time (Stern 2007). In the European continent, however, gas prices have traditionally been a proportion of and tied to oil prices.[4] The base gas price in Europe is calculated as three fourths of the price of a basket of oil products with a delay of a few months. Natural gas deals have traditionally been conducted through long-term take or pay contracts with small price variations in accordance with the fluctuation of world oil prices (Stern 2009).[5] Nevertheless, the British gas market liberalization since the 1980s and the EU energy liberalization agenda since the 1990s have led to the creation

---

4   The oil price forms the basis of the gas price. Other considerations, such as transportation costs, then add up to the final price.

5   Gas prices in East Asia also follow oil-linked price formulas.

of natural gas spot markets in Europe as well. In these markets the gas price is not linked to world oil prices, but, to the contrary, determined by market (supply and demand) dynamics. The formal contractual linkage with oil prices is this way contested and it is increasingly the case that gas prices break off from formal oil linkages. There is an ongoing debate regarding the gas pricing mechanisms for Europe (see Chapter 4) and it remains to be seen whether these developments will be reversed or whether oil and gas prices will be totally de-linked in the near future (Stern 2007, 2009). If oil prices remain at high levels, this will be a significant incentive for de-linking gas from oil prices. Indeed, it is due to high oil prices and an oversupply of Europe with gas that a partial de-linkage has taken place since 2008 in the European market. High oil prices then will not necessarily mean high gas prices as well. The most possible scenario appears to be that in case oil prices remain high, an independent gas pricing mechanism will be developed in Europe (Stern 2009: 15–16). Even in this scenario, however, it is quite likely that gas will become progressively more expensive in the absence of new discoveries and given rising consumption rates and higher production costs (see Chapter 3).

Energy Trade-offs and the Interplay of Politics and Economics

As discussed above, energy security has three dimensions: security of supplies, economic efficiency and protection of the environment. These goals, however, in a number of cases are not congruent (Röller, Delgado and Friederiszick 2007). Security of supplies or cheap energy can go with more environmental damage. The Chinese economy, for example, is based upon the wide use of coal, the most affordable option, despite its environmental predicament. At the same time, security of supplies frequently calls for a high premium, namely high prices that inflict a burden on the competitiveness of the economy. The US subsidizes domestic production of corn-based ethanol and retains high tariffs on the import of sugar cane-based ethanol to achieve energy security. Security of supplies and potentially lower prices can also be sacrificed for environmental causes. Although offshore gas reserves have been proven in California, they are not exploited, on the basis of safety perceptions and consent against drilling and production activities for fear of environmental pollution. The same is true for Alaskan oil (Mares 2010: 10, 13). The recent oil spill-over in the Gulf of Mexico led the US President Barack Obama to ban the issuance of new licenses for exploration for six months. Moreover, economic efficiency and security of supplies may be at odds. Although Europe, Germany not forming an exception, is dependent on Russian gas, German enterprises disregard the risk dependence poses to security of supplies and pressurize the German government to form deals with Russia so that they can secure gas at competitive prices and keep up their profits. Under the same light, the EU has put in place its rather ambitious 20–20–20 Policy Initiative (see pp. 47–8) aiming to curb carbon emissions by 20 per cent, increase energy efficiency by 20 per cent and raise renewables' share in the overall EU energy mix to 20 per cent by

2020 (plus to increase the share of renewables in all transport fuels at least to 10 per cent by the same year) (European Commission 2007). Since all of these goals are hard to implement by 2020, inevitably a prioritization takes place favouring economic efficiency against environmental protection. Indeed, one significant reason behind the slow penetration of renewables in the EU energy market is the initial high costs such a shift entails.

Besides these trade-offs, energy security is strongly correlated with political issues and economic considerations. The role of energy markets is central. Energy corporations form rather powerful economic entities with much political leverage. Their economic clout (deciding on trade routes and pipelines, contracting quantities and impacting upon the overall energy supply) is matched by their ability to lobby governments in a number of occasions successfully, thus proving themselves the actual powers behind the throne (Jaffe, Hayes and Victor 2006: 468, CIEP 2007). Furthermore, market mechanisms are in place to regulate oil and gas flows, while price increases and decreases form signals to adjust supply and demand (Checchi, Behrens and Egenhofer 2009: 1). Energy markets are global (in the case of oil) and regional (in the case of gas) and thus serve the interests both of producers and consumers for attaining energy security. As Yergin (2006: 79) notes 'large, flexible and well-functioning energy markets provide security by absorbing shocks and allowing supply and demand to respond more quickly and with greater ingenuity than a controlled system could'.

However, markets are not left to operate autonomously. Governments intervene either to avert potential dangers or to improve their national energy security. Although energy security deficiencies can in many cases be dealt with market-based mechanisms (for example, decrease of energy use, boost of energy efficiency, use of alternative sources), responses usually are political. This is understandable, since market solutions in most cases cede fruits within a certain time-frame, while governments in power strive to absorb shocks immediately in order to avert economic hardships (loss of investments, jobs dislocations) and subsequent social turmoil (riots and strikes) with an eye to remain in power (Mares 2010: 9). The close political ties between the US governments and the family of the Sauds breed tight cooperation in the energy field, in the same way ex Russian President Vladimir Putin and ex German Chancellor Gerhard Schröder cemented the Russo–German strategic energy partnership a few years ago with a series of bilateral energy deals (Larsson 2006: 20–21). Russia and China have formed close ties with Hugo Chavez's Venezuela, not least due to his strong anti-US rhetoric and stance and their shared aspiration for a more multilateral world system. In this context, political relations become significant factors that influence energy alliances, strategic partnerships and dividing lines.

Attention, however, must be drawn to the fact that oil is a significant factor in, not the core of, international politics. There is a bias towards explaining all conflicts as wars for oil, when oil may be a decisive factor but not the single or most important one. Although enough is left to speculation and there is margin for subjectivity, the second US war in Iraq in 2003, one could well argue, was not exclusively for oil. Although oil did play an important role in policy-makers' strategy, one cannot undermine the US government's preoccupation with overall political goals, such as getting rid of a brutal and annoying leader of a third country, creating domestic solidarity to distract from internal problems and setting a whole new scene for the wider Middle East region that would cater for the overall US interests (one of which is energy security). Currently, oil production in Iraq remains well below pre-2003 levels and non-US companies appear powerful enough to compete with US multinationals. The Iraqi government's tough negotiating stance and China's competitive bidding has curtailed US companies' margins for profits and led to the first oil deposits exploration rights being allocated, contrary to initial anticipations, to a number of oil companies under tight terms. Only two US oil companies have ensured exploration rights while the corporate portfolio is as diverse to include enterprises from Russia, Japan, Norway, Turkey, South Korea, Angola, China and Malaysia. In another twist of the argument, one could maintain that the Iraqi war helped boost global oil prices and substantially increased revenues for the US oil companies (at the same time, of course, this was to the detriment of US consumers thus imposing an extra burden on the US economy). But is this not the case also for Russian companies that made huge profits out of the oil (and contractually linked gas) price hikes? Most importantly, was this the target of the US energy strategy or was the US aiming at increasing its shares in and control of the Iraqi upstream sector? Did the US achieve this goal? Overall, whether the US energy industry actually gained from this war is contested (Hinnebusch 2007, Schwartz 2008, Business Insider 2010). The Russian wars in Chechnya in the 1990s, also frequently mistaken as wars for oil, were above all wars for defending Russian sovereignty and retaining the Russian Federation intact. In case Chechnya gained independence, a domino effect could follow having as a result the further curtailment of Russian territory. The fundamental preoccupation, thus, was about national integrity, sovereignty and national pride, not about aspects of energy security (Trofimenko 1999: 68, Trenin and Malashenko 2004: 22). One oil pipeline does cross Grozny, the capital of Chechnya, but when damaged in the midst of warfare, a new one bypassing Grozny was briefly constructed.

It is for these reasons that energy security revolves both around politics and economics. Both the function of the market, as well as political strategies and sets of interrelationships have to be studied in order to shed light on the dynamics of energy trade. Markets and governments thus co-decide on the core issues pertaining to the energy sector. These are:

- *Defining the rules of the game:* The rules of the game refer to the core principles and rules of the energy trade. The extent market mechanisms are allowed to work, the level of government intervention, the role of private capital and public-owned and/or public-controlled energy companies, the existence or not of monopolies, monopsonies and cartels, all highly impact on energy trade patterns (Nye 2003: 207–8). These are not pre-given, but depend on the interplay between governments and markets; moreover, they are not static, but dynamic and prone to change. Although the return of resource nationalism,[6] the tendency for the state to resume control of the domestic energy industry, seems to fortify the point that governments manage the rules of the game, one should not undermine the power of global capital and the tight relations markets retain with state apparatuses. Evident as it may be that in a number of cases the role of the government remains central (Russia, China and Venezuela forming the best examples), private enterprises are dominant in a number of other countries (for example, US and Britain). Governments and markets thus co-decide the rules of the game (Müller-Kraenner 2008: xi).

- *Acquisition of resources:* There is an evolving competition for ensuring supplies that will move national economies (Clare 2002). This competition takes place at two levels. States, most prominently among them the US, China, Japan, India and the *sui generis* EU, compete with each other for contracts in order to ensure adequate energy supplies and avoid the economic and social repercussions of energy shortages. Energy corporations (either private or public), on the other hand, have to ensure supplies in order to survive competition and ensure their profitability. In this context, both economic (proximity, technology, low prices), as well as political criteria (cooperation with friendly regimes, conflict with/embargoes on unfriendly ones) are important for the selection of suppliers and markets.

- *Pipeline politics:* Pipelines are of fundamental significance since they determine to an important extent trade patterns and flows of energy. The construction of pipelines creates sunk costs for the investors that can yield returns only on the basis of long-term, steady energy relations. Pipelines thus bind exporters and importers into an interdependent trade relationship and determine that specific quantities of oil and gas will be reserved for specific customers. Hence, the selection of routes and the construction of pipelines are in most cases issues of hot debate and outward conflict since they can fortify the energy security of some states while being detrimental to that of others (Müller-Kraenner 2008: 22–4). Pipelines are far more important in natural gas trade due to its mostly pipeline-bound nature. Gas can also be transported by tankers in liquefied and compressed form, but this is usually more expensive. On the other hand, most of the oil trade takes place through tankers. Thus, flexibility is more easily attainable; the decision on oil pipelines is hence in most cases significant, albeit not determinative (Hayes and Victor 2006, Lesser et al. 2001).

---

6   The substance of resource nationalism lies in that natural resources are considered a property of the nation used for public, not for private gain. Thus it is the state, not private enterprises, that is entitled to exploit these resources. One should note, however, that in some regions of Latin America, it is the tribes that fight to win this privilege over the state on the lines that soil and oil beneath it belong to the traditional tribes, not to modern state structures (Mares 2010: 6–7).

The Energy Market Today: Security or Crisis?

This era is considered to be one of a 'dual crisis' that 'rests on the declining availability of fossil fuels and the restricted ability of the environment to withstand pollution' (Müller-Kraenner 2008: 17). Pertaining to the first element, at the same time well developed states as the US, Japan and the EU are mature consumers, China and India have increased manifold their energy consumption. The projections are that global energy demand will further rise (albeit the global economic recession of 2007–08 seems to have put a hold on energy demand in the Western world) (Stern 2009: 1). The net result is growing demand and competition for resources, while production seems to increase at a much lesser level, the new significant developments offshore Brazil and Israel notwithstanding (*The Economist* 2009, World Oil 2011). Production in the OECD countries is falling by 7 per cent, while in OPEC increases only by 3 per cent; the outcome thus is dwindling oil quantities and augmenting dependence for the importing world (Gregoriev 2010: 3). Moreover, according to current projections, oil production will become even more concentrated in the near future, a development that draws further attention to concerns about overt dependence on a handful of exporters (Yergin 2006). Rousseau (2010) summarizes the problems plaguing security of oil supplies as follows:

> Every day, the world consumes about 85 million barrels. Oil fields that produce that amount of oil are decreasing by about 8 per cent a year, corresponding to around 6.6 million barrels a day. That rate of world oil depletion is equivalent to the daily production of the two Abu Dhabis or the North Sea or more than two Nigerias. The problem in the world energy sector is that there is a rarity of discoveries the magnitude of the North Sea, the Caspian Sea or the newly discovered deep-sea oil fields off the Brazilian coast. The Caspian Sea discoveries, for instance, will add only about 3 per cent to the current world daily production. Most of the various non-OPEC fields coming on stream might add not more than 70,000 to 400,000 barrels per day of production. This situation has to be combined with the fact oil demand is climbing rapidly. The International Energy Agency (IEA) calculates world demand will rise to 86.7 b/d million in 2012, up from 76.8 million in 2001 … Lack of investment in other parts of the intricate global supply web is making a bad situation worse. There are too few tankers, too few gasoline refineries. In North America, the refineries are running at more than 95 percent capacity. In the post-Soviet space, refineries need to be built and soon. The breakdown of a single refinery of any size could send the whole market into a major energy crisis.

High oil prices signal the changing market dynamics and spread further worries among importers. International competition for oil supplies is increasingly seen as zero-sum, with importers aiming to lock-up assets. This creates an *energy security dilemma* where states and energy corporations either allow first bidders to acquire these resources or reciprocate the bidding, a move which will eventually make prices skyrocket (Kang 2008: 1–2). Empowered competition between the importers works to the exporters' interest and seems to tilt the oil market once more to the sellers' side. The depreciating trajectory of the dollar, in which oil is priced, in international exchange markets, is also rather disorientating, as it artificially brings the oil price down and encourages oil consumption even though the supply/demand ratio should pinpoint towards the opposite direction.

Moreover, resource nationalism heightens the risks for energy security. A number of exporting countries have resumed state control of their energy industry, thus meddling political considerations with market mechanisms. This, together with sustained political instability in a number of exporting states, makes the oil market even more challenging for the importing states (Cable 2010: 79). The political landscape is fraught with terrorist attacks, guerilla assaults, nationalist backlashes and ethnic minorities' strive for liberation, autonomy and independence all over the world, as well as with geopolitical rivalries among the main countries. Oil production in Venezuela, up to then a rather reliable exporter, was significantly reduced after Hugo Chavez's successful move to consolidate his power on the energy sector. The war against Iraq also dealt a blow to the global oil supply. Russia contributed major supplies to the oil market throughout the 2000s thus allowing supply to satisfy rising demand, but faces political, regulatory and economic problems that hamper further development of its upstream sector. Iran, OPEC's second-largest producer, has threatened to 'unleash an oil crisis' in the face of threats for its nuclear program. Scattered attacks on some oil facilities reduced exports from Nigeria, which is a major supplier to the United States. Amidst growing political tension attacks on crucial energy infrastructures are always a possibility. Al Qaeda itself has threatened to attack the world economy's critical – comprising energy – infrastructure (Yergin 2006: 70–74). This is not the ideal background for the smooth function of the global oil market.

Secondly, global warming, air pollution and climatic changes make the current energy landscape unviable in the medium- to long-term. Unless global energy consumption does not turn away from fossil fuels, principally coal and oil, global temperature will continue to rise and living standards will deteriorate. Clean air and water will become scarcer, current health standards in the developed world will be jeopardized, while some species will be (threatened to become) extinct, ecosystems destroyed and whole islands and states overwhelmed under higher sea levels (Bordoff, Deshpande and Noel 2010, Diamond 2006). In this context, security of supplies cannot be based upon the improved function of the traditional global energy market. This market has to increasingly turn to renewable sources of energy in order to reverse environmental degradation.

To conclude, while the Third World is persistently faced with energy poverty, the developing states gradually improve upon their energy security, albeit energy shortages are still commonplace.[7] For the West energy security has for long been

---

7   India, for example, still fails to ensure energy security for a significant portion of its population. Shortages remain dramatic in rural areas and main facilities like hospitals and schools (Khandker, Barnes and Samad 2010).

taken as a given. Progressively, however, the risks associated with security of supplies are supplemented by anxiety about the capacity of the environment to endure the cumulative burden of human activity. Although the West is not facing energy poverty, we may not be very far from it, unless we collectively act prudently to avert it (Pascual and Zambetakis 2010). One should bear in mind, moreover, that the challenge is not only to retain and improve the West's energy security, but enhance the energy security of less developed states as well.

A New Paradigm for Energy Policy and Security

For decades, energy politics was based on the assumption of competition and underlying policies of diversification. The division between producers and consumers is reflected in the existence of two opposite institutional frameworks. While OPEC was established to retain a check on supply with an eye to sustain high oil prices for its members, IEA was formed as a counterweight to organize collective responses to exporters' practices and enhance the energy security of importers. IEA focuses on managing and countering exporters-induced crises. To this cause, it has set up strategic oil stockpiles and coordinates their use; it has developed monitoring mechanisms; and it systematically provides analyses of energy markets, country policies and future trends. In this context, the cornerstone of IEA members' policies is the principle of diversification, which boils down to having multiple sources of energy from varied suppliers and through diverse routes so that shortages from one, for any one reason, can be compensated for by other sources/suppliers (Yergin 2006: 69–70, 75).

Nowadays, however, the world system and the world economy are changing fundamentally with the incorporation of the South Asian giants China and India, as well as the progressive significance of other regions, as Southeast Asia and Latin America. The changes in the scale and nature of the energy market create new threats, challenges and problems for both exporting and importing countries and thus call for a new energy paradigm for the twenty-first century. Up to now designated policies only served as means to withstand an energy crisis and to react to short-term supply problems and/or high prices, not to plan ahead of future problems. Nowadays, however, energy policy has to be proactive and lay the grounds for sufficient and secure energy infrastructure, cooperation among importers and exporters and new, environmentally sustainable policy initiatives that will avert a further boost of energy consumption (Verrastro and Ladislaw 2007: 103). The new energy paradigm, then, has to revolve around three core principles/goals:

Transparency, Cooperation and Integration

The globalization of the energy market means that the international energy market expands further to encompass most of the globe. This means that additional players become part of it and the need arises for their full integration (Cherp,

Jewell and Goldthau 2011). Still, however, China, the second biggest oil importer that is projected to surpass the US in the near future, remains outside the importers' institutional framework, IEA. The same is true for India. Albeit its energy imports are not as high as China's, India is a developing country with a population of 1 billion and strategies in place for fast and steady growth. All the above render it a progressively very significant oil importer. India's and China's incorporation into IEA would make importers' cooperation easier and a pragmatically global energy outlook more comprehensive. The flow of information and increased transparency would allow markets to organize better and adjust to supply shortages (Kramer and Lyman 2009: 5). In this context, energy issues should also be on the agenda of international institutions and be discussed as fundamental for the smooth operation of the global economy (Frei 2007, Liu 2006, Kirton 2006, Lesage, van de Graaf and Westphal 2009).

Furthermore, the energy pledges of China and India should not be seen as a potential threat to the West's energy security. Although it is true that China locks up some energy quantities to cater for its own supply, its energy needs have propelled significant investments in the energy sector. China's and India's rising energy needs create challenges, as well as opportunities. While it may seem convenient to designate policies that would aim at out-competing Chinese and Indian enterprises and prioritizing the West's energy security, a more proper and holistic approach would be to see these two countries and their corporations as partners in the energy market. The international community should realize that only if China and India fulfil their energy needs will they acquire a vested interest in the smooth function of the global energy market. In a gradually globalizing environment with transnational networks of interdependence spreading and intensifying, one should look at ways to enhance the proper function of the global energy market, rather than pursue national interests that can easily backfire if seen as isolated from the interests of the global economy. Last but not least, energy security is a necessary prerequisite for human prosperity, a Western-sponsored goal and principle. In case the Western world does not assist developing countries' efforts towards their energy security, it will be seen to go contrary to its declared values of accommodating the needs of people living well below the Western standards and of advancing their welfare.

The globalization of the energy market hence means the proliferation of actors and its subsequent augmenting complexity. All parties share a vested interest in protecting the energy infrastructure in order to avoid abrupt interruptions of oil flows. There are vulnerable hot spots, as the Malacca and Hormuz Straits, through which a significant part of the traded oil passes. The international community should protect this infrastructure from threats of any political, economic and/or technical kind. At the same time, the mismatch between overall production and overall refining capacity has to be bridged in order for the market to function at an era of high demand.

Lastly, besides the entrenched competition between exporters and importers for the level of energy prices, they both share concerns for and interests in a stable market with mutually affordable prices. It is widely realized that deflated oil prices will breed instability in most exporters' economies as well as create hurdles for the sustenance of similar levels of energy production (due to fewer investments as an outcome of less profits stemming from lower prices). At the same time, exporters understand that high prices decrease overall demand and thus also the energy industry's profitability. Balance then is the key (Mares 2010: 10–11, Eng 2003: 47). OPEC (2002) itself 'confirms the broad result that export revenues are not maximized by sustaining extremely high or low prices'.

Deconstructing Energy Independence

At first sight it may seem that it is convenient to be autarkic in the energy sector. Contrary to energy imports that carry foreign policy vulnerabilities, domestic supplies are risk free. While this holds true, only a few states are in a position to be energy autarkic. Even for them, however, this policy option is not unproblematic. Firstly, domestic production may be more expensive than foreign production and/ or bear higher environmental costs. For example, it costs more than 55 dollars to produce a barrel of oil in the US, while it only costs 5 dollars to produce a barrel of oil in the Middle East. Importing oil thus is a preferable option for the US to producing it itself. Secondly, producing states that aim at autarky are not immune from and may suffer costs and hiked prices emanating from shocks that originate in other producing regions and impact on the global oil market (Haghighi 2007: 14). Thirdly, an isolationist energy policy would only serve to isolate politically the states aiming at energy independence. In an era of augmenting and intensifying international and transnational interactions, such a move would most possibly weaken rather than enhance wider notions of security. To the contrary, states should accept that the key to energy security is managing increased interdependence rather than endeavouring to escape it. The fact that the volume of global oil trade is expected to double and that of natural gas trade to triple by 2030 reinforces this conclusion. Moreover, participation in the global market functions as a shield against supply shortages. For example, it was increased imports that allowed the US to withstand any energy shortages, let alone hiked prices, through the Katrina and Rita hurricanes in 2005. For all these reasons, energy independence is very hard to achieve and usually leads to greater costs. It is not uncorrelated that all countries, even the most natural resources-endowed ones, import energy in one form or another. Global energy trade, not least due to the extensive infrastructure already in place that makes it economic and relatively easy to move energy worldwide, provides the mechanisms for energy security for both producers and consumers (Verrastro and Ladislaw 2007: 95–101, Nivola and Carter 2010). As Yergin puts it:

> there is only one oil market, a complex and worldwide system that moves and consumes about 86 million barrels of oil every day. For all consumers, security resides in the stability of this market. Secession is not an option (2006:79).

Energy Conservation, Energy Efficiency and Environmental Sustainability

The more the environmental hazards of energy consumption become obvious, the greater the need to find new pathways towards sustainable development. A key challenge towards this end is to reduce overall energy consumption. Since prices determine the extent of energy usage, subsidies should be terminated and prices should be set at those levels that will encourage energy savings and conservation (Steenblik 2010). Furthermore, the use of renewable resources should be strongly encouraged in order to acquire a much greater share in the global energy mix gradually substituting part of overall coal and oil usage. This, however, can only be achieved if governmental policies shed weight on far-reaching research – governmental spending remains in general too low for the time being – that can lead to technological innovations. These innovations refer not only to production of renewables, but also to ways to shift national economies from industrial to less energy-intensive modes of production. Some steps towards this direction were taken in the West in the 1970s in the aftermath of the first oil crisis. Nowadays, however, the need is even more pressing and calls for a radical reorganization of the energy sector towards sustainable development (Verrastro and Ladislaw 2007: 103, Kramer and Lyman 2009: 7–12, Dannreuhter 2007: 91).

The Plan of the Book

The following chapter sketches out the global context and enumerates the main trends in the global energy market. Thereafter, it examines briefly the energy security strategies of the main importing countries. In particular, it studies how the US and China deal with their energy deficiencies through different policies emanating from their differing perspectives and starting positions. This section introduces the main policy tools they devise to ensure their energy security and paves the way for the analysis of the EU energy strategy.

The next four chapters make up the core of the book. In the third chapter, the energy security of the EU is examined. This chapter focuses on the main challenges posed to EU energy security, as well as on the main policies the EU follows to tackle them. Moreover, it delineates the main actors and explores the ways through which they co-determine the EU's energy security strategy. This chapter also introduces the basic tenets of the natural gas market as well as the EU's gas deficit.

Chapters 4, 5 and 6 examine the EU energy security in the gas sector. The fourth chapter scrutinizes the internal front. In particular, it analyses the liberalization project that has fundamentally transformed the energy landscape and carries critical implications for the state of the EU's gas security. This chapter also studies the EU's plans to create a fully interconnected energy market, as well as the new gas security regulations put in place to facilitate its operation. Lastly, Chapter 4 discusses the EU's attempt to export its energy regulatory model to its periphery as the basis of its external energy strategy and emphasizes the shortcomings of this policy up to date.

Chapters 5 and 6 focus on relations with external suppliers. Russia is spared a whole chapter as it forms the single most important supplier of the EU with a rising share in its gas market. After a short overview of the Russian energy strategy in Europe, this chapter discusses the whole range of open issues between the two entities, the EU's dilemma of diversification vs. enforced interdependence and its limited success in both forming a coherent EU-wide energy policy and in acting in solidarity and providing a shield of protection to its members that feel endangered by Russia's energy diplomacy.

The sixth chapter illustrates the relationship of the EU with the other suppliers, both actual and potential ones. It briefly reviews the energy strategies and interests of the main suppliers and gives a full account of their gas trade with the EU. A significant part of this chapter is devoted to potential suppliers and designated new pipeline projects and their feasibility and potential impact on EU energy security. Thus, the discussion extends beyond Algeria and Norway and encompasses gas-rich regions as the Middle East and Central Asia that carry to differing degrees promises to facilitate the EU's security of supplies.

The last chapter concludes the main risks and dilemmas for EU energy security. It emphasizes the need for the EU to re-conceptualize its energy security, to reframe and re-designate specific political, economic and sectoral interests, to go beyond the rigidities of historical heritage and to move towards a more secure energy landscape. Considering the global energy scene and the need to move towards a new paradigm for energy security that is based upon integration and extended cooperation, it sums up the main challenges for the EU and illustrates a roadway to energy security.

Chapter 2
The Global Context and the Strategies of the Main Importing States

In such a highly integrated global energy market, the global context is a crucial factor that has to be taken into account for the formulation of states' energy security strategy. Moreover, beyond current energy problems and opportunities, future trends are of central importance, not least because the enforcement of policies only yields results in the mid-term due to the long-lead time framework of investments. It is for these reasons that the understanding of the global energy context and the outlook for the future form essential prerequisites for the comprehension of the policies both energy exporters and importers designate. Taking those into account, we analyze the state of energy security of the other main energy importers besides the EU, the US and China, before proceeding to explore the EU's energy security.

The Global Context and the Outlook for the Future

In Chapter 1 I sketched out the basic changes in the global energy mix projected for the year 2030. According to IEA's (2009, 2010) estimations, bio-fuels and other renewables will significantly increase, with the exception of hydropower; demand for coal and gas is set to increase, while demand for oil decreases but does not fade away; the fluctuations in coal's share in the global fuel mix depend on how far green measures are implemented; optimistic scenarios put coal's consumption down, while pessimistic ones project increasing coal consumption. The recent devastating nuclear accident in Japan will inevitably raise waves of scepticism for the use of nuclear power and thus calls into question its projected increase. These estimations are crucial for the energy landscape after 2030. In particular, it is expected that:

- *Import sensitivity and increased competition for supplies will be sustained:* The global economic crisis has left its imprint on the global energy market as well. Energy consumption fell for the first time after around 30 years in 2009, but is gradually on the path to recovering and is estimated to have substantially increased by 2030. In particular, a 40 per cent increase of energy demand is anticipated by that year (1.5 per cent increase annually). Almost all further energy demand originates in developing countries, primarily for coal and gas and only secondarily for oil. This is partly due to the fact that the hybrid car industry is projected to have significantly advanced by 2030–2035. It is important to stress here that all efforts at combating energy poverty, which despite declarations to the contrary remains widespread and extensive, will further put pressure on global consumption. This increase is not only problematic in environmental terms, but also contrasts starkly with the disproportionate estimations for energy production. Unconventional oil may boost overall production, but high supply costs and the fact that this fuel is more of a pollutant than conventional oil speak against extensive extraction. The widening gap between global energy production and consumption creates concerns for enforced competition among importers for the acquisition of supplies. At the same time, while OPEC production is estimated to have peaked by 2010, productivity rates are balanced by other regions with hardly a better reliability record (for example, the Caspian Sea and Latin America). Hence, sensitivity to imports from unreliable suppliers is set to continue. A quite possible scenario for the future then is that further energy demand will not be accommodated from rising production with the effect of sustained high prices, potentially aggravated by instability and the eruption of crises in oil-rich regions that will act as a burden both for developed and developing economies (IEA 2010). This can especially be the case since the economic hardship in the West brings energy investments to a standstill at the same time that the phase of recovery will call for more energy imports (IEA 2009, 2010, BP 2011).

- *The role of states in enhancing energy security will be critical:* In this context, IEA (2009, 2010) highlights the centrality of the role of the state for the smooth function of the global energy market in the next decades. It is estimated that major investments are needed in all levels of the energy chain (exploration, refining, transportation and distribution systems) in order for the market to be in position to satisfy augmenting energy needs. According to IEA (2009, 2010), nevertheless, the market by itself will not create the dynamics for all the necessary investments. Therefore, the public sector has to generate the economic activity that will allow for production to catch up with mounting energy demand and avert an abrupt increase of energy prices. Nevertheless, the latter years the West has witnessed economic turmoil. After the eruption of the world financial crisis of 2007–08, the domino of budget deficits and subsequent deflationary policies in most European states put once more the Western economies under stress. The obvious question that arises is whether governments around the world will be potent and willing to proceed to these investments in the face of their economic hardship (IEA 2009, 2010). This is all the more true for investments in renewables, since green industries are even more capital-intensive. More importantly, only states can cause a significant change in the global energy mix generating incentives for the use of renewables, energy efficiency, conservation and savings, as well as eradicating subsidies to fossil fuels in order to accomplish the fundamental goal of stabilizing the global temperature to the generally acceptable level of two degrees increase (IEA 2010).

• *The gas glut will fluctuate according to supply and demand dynamics and impact consequently upon gas prices formulas*: In the gas sector, demand is likely to grow from 3 tcm to 4.3 tcm by 2035. The main driver of this increase will be high growth rates in Asia, especially China and India, while European demand for gas is also bound to increase as the EU attempts to decrease oil and coal usage and meet its environmental goals. To the contrary, the US is projected to consume less gas by 2035. As far as supply is concerned, it is possible that it will increase in case appropriate investments take place. Many existing deposits will have run out by 2030 and hence investments are needed so that new deposits can come on stream in the following years. Production is projected to come principally from Iran, Qatar and the Caspian. Global gas supply can also be boosted by the exploration of shale gas, primarily in Canada. It is to be stressed that in most regions energy efficiency remains rather low; in case it significantly improves, spare capacity of gas will increase. These developments will retain import dependencies on debatably reliable suppliers. At the same time, however, they may well increase the existing gas glut – the differential between the gas produced and consumed worldwide, which is a factor for lower gas prices. Unless China plays a decisive role to upset such a development, not an unlikely scenario at all, it is plausible that, as a result, gas prices in Europe will be de-linked from oil prices which are projected to remain at high levels and may even rise further (IEA 2010).

The Energy Security of the Main Importers: The Cases of the US and China

In what follows we shed light on the energy security of the most important energy consumers, namely the US and China. We start from a descriptive account of their energy mix. Then we proceed to analyzing these states' state of energy security. The significant variables here are current and anticipated development and growth and hence energy consumption, as well as geographical, historical, economic and political characteristics of trade patterns and energy usage. We conclude with a debate on the policies these states pursue in order to improve their energy security. It is important here to remember that states have three main goals, namely security of supplies, economic efficiency and environmental protection.[1] Both the US and

---

1   For example, the US energy strategy issued in May 2001 set three goals: energy security at a reasonable cost and environmental sustainability. The European Parliament sees energy security as security of supplies, competitiveness and protection of the environment. The British energy review also posits the goal of ensuring cheap, affordable and sustainable forms of energy. Japan's energy strategy revolves around energy security, protection of the environment and economic efficiency, see Mitchell 2002: 3.

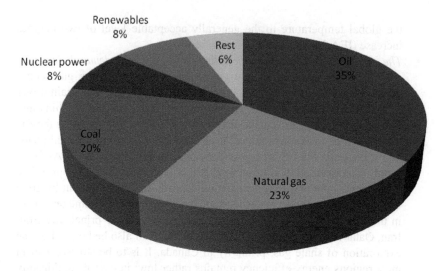

Figure 2.1   The US energy mix
Source: IEA Energy Statistics, EIA 2010c

China endeavours to serve these goals, albeit to differing degrees. For example, environmental protection is far more important for the US than for China; moreover, they aim to achieve economic efficiency in different ways.

The US Energy Security Strategy: Challenges, Policies and Shortcomings

The US is the greatest net importer and consumer of energy worldwide. This position, matched by its central position in the global system and the extensive leverage it entertains, posits that the US energy security strategy has broad ramifications for global energy security.

The US economy is driven by oil. Oil takes up more than one third in the country's energy mix (35 per cent). Natural gas follows with 23 per cent, while coal takes up around one fifth (20 per cent), nuclear power and renewable resources around 8 per cent each (EIA 2010c).

Contrary to what might be assumed due to its dominant role as an oil importer, the US is oil-rich. US companies such as ExxonMobil and ChevronTexaco, among others, have not only been around the world in their quest for oil, but are also active in the well-endowed US subsoil. The US energy strategy, however, is import-oriented. This is so for a number of reasons. Firstly, US indigenous oil production peaked in 1971 and started to decrease since (Nye 2003: 207). Secondly, importing oil from other regions, especially the Middle East, is significantly cheaper than exploring demanding domestic oil fields. Relevant with the latter, as we saw in Chapter 1, the US prefers not to exploit its full production potential due to environmental concerns. Fourthly, imports contribute to the building of significant strategic reserves that can be released in case of emergencies.

US dependence on oil has been rising at fast paces. While at the time of the 1973 energy crisis the US was importing one third of its overall oil consumption, today it imports around two thirds, while its import dependency is estimated to climb to 70 per cent in 2020 (Powers 2010, Yergin 2006: 79). While US imports were no more than 12 million barrels per day (b/d) in the early 2000s, it is estimated that they will approach 21 million b/d in 2025 (Deutch 2004: 9).

US reliance on imports necessitates a strong web of relations with oil-producing countries. Of particular importance here is the committed partnership between the US and Saudi Arabia, OPEC's *swing producer* that retains the biggest oil reserves as well as produces most of the time at the greatest capacity in comparison to all other oil producers. On the one hand, Saudi Arabia interminably contributes to oil availability and global supply, by increasing its quotas within OPEC whenever necessary in order to make up for the rise in energy demand and/or for the reduction of other oil-producing countries' quotas. The US, on the other hand, supports, contrary to its pro-democratic foreign policy posture and rhetoric, the monarchical regime of the House of the Sauds[2] and guarantees its security from potential enemies (Toyin and Genova 2005: 43–61). Saudi Arabia's significance has further increased due to rising tensions in the Middle East. The thirty-year-long dispute between the US and Iran and the subsequent sanctions on the Islamic Republic, has not only annulled bilateral trade, but also diminished overall global oil supply. The Iraq–Iran war (1980–88) devastated much of the energy infrastructure of both states, while Iraq's production capacity has been curtailed by the two Gulf wars. Eight years after the US-led invasion of Iraq, oil production remains well below the pre-war standards. Saudi Arabia's role to sustain global supply at adequate levels has thus become even more critical.

Latin America is the second most important source of oil for the US. Although the US retains amiable relations with a host of Latin American countries, its unrivalled supremacy and ambivalent hegemonic tactics have built up mistrust and in some cases outward hostility in the sub-continent (Young and Kent 2004). Security of supplies is tied with geopolitical alliances and rivalries. A number of producers see in the rise of China the opportunity to sustain high energy-born revenues from exports to US competitors. While, for example, Mexico remains a reliable partner for the US, Hugo Chavez's estrangement with the US has led to reduced US imports and poses a potential threat to US security of supplies from the region (EIA 2011). Venezuela is a prominent example of a country diverting oil supplies to Asia on geopolitical grounds making a strong point against US hegemony. Oil trade with other Latin American states, such as Bolivia, is also prone to similar fluctuations depending on the geopolitical landscape. In such a context, the challenge for the US is to re-shape the international environment in order, among others, to enhance its security of supplies.

A parallel concern for the US is its sensitivity to high oil prices, which raise the costs of most economic entrepreneurships, cause a vicious circle of investment cuts

---

2   Saudi Arabia means Arabia of the Sauds' family.

and demand destruction and thus hinder overall development. Current increased demand from Asia pushes prices upwards thus augmenting US difficulties to escape its current phase of economic stagnation.

Since oil crosses great distances from exporter to importer countries, energy security involves transportation safety. Oil transportation can face multiple threats ranging from modern piracy, to maritime accidents (usually with dramatic consequences for the environment and the subsequent mobilization of civil society against such transportation schemes) and potential terrorist attacks. The US thus takes up the duty to guard specific hot spots and ensure smooth oil transportation. Special reference should be made here to the Malacca Straits in the Indian Ocean, through which the bulk of the Middle Eastern oil reaches the US (Nincic 2009). One should also note here, however, that the US does no more perform the role of global policeman for oil transportation. It focuses on the main hot spots, while it leaves this role to be taken up by other forces, such as the EU and China, in other regions (Colombo and Lesser 2010: 5).

When it comes to natural gas, the US has a well-developed market. Due to the country's own rich gas reserves and Canada's ample gas reserves as well (Caribbean states such as Trinidad and Tobago also are significant gas producers), the US was first to develop a broad gas network. Its mature gas market, however, faces problems of dwindling domestic production and increasing dependence on imports. The US has on a few occasions imported LNG from distant gas-rich countries such as Malaysia and Indonesia to make up for domestic shortages, while the decade-long flirting with Russia for LNG imports recently led to an agreement for the purchase of limited quantities of Russian gas. As Yergin (2006: 70) puts it 'rising demand and constrained supplies mean that North America can no longer be self-reliant and so the United States is joining the new global market'. Overall, however, for the time being security of gas supplies is smoother compared to oil since it escapes reliance on unstable and/or rival regimes. Increasing reliance on gas imports, however, is a worrying trend. Taking into account rising global gas consumption and the prospects for intensified competition, the US may in the mid-term discover that security of gas supplies resembles that of oil with its accompanying risks and uncertainties.

As a result, there is a vivid debate within the US whether it should detach from its global energy policy and revert to domestic sources and isolationism. The main argument the critics of the current US energy policy make is that high dependency on imports exposes the country to all sorts of threats and endangers its energy security. Nevertheless, such arguments miss the point that today's world is a world of interdependence. States form broad webs of interdependence in most sectors. An isolationist policy would thus deprive the US of its very means through which it attains security and predominance, not least in the energy sector, rather than maximize its energy security. Not least, oil imports mean much cheaper prices for the US consumers since the costs for drilling oil in the Middle East and the US are, as we saw before, highly uneven (Verrastro and Ladislaw 2007). We should not forget that the US forbids oil exploration schemes in some of its territories (for example, Alaska and California) for both energy and environmental causes. An isolationist policy would oblige the White House to reverse such policies and exploit this oil potential as well, a potentially disruptive move for the environment.

The other three main energy sources cannot be examined but with close reference to their environmental defects and credentials. Coal is still widely in use for such a developed economy since abundant domestic reserves make this a convenient option, especially in difficult economic circumstances. Since, however, coal is the main culprit for carbon emissions that significantly contribute to the rise of global temperature, the share of coal in the energy mix has to be extensively downscaled. Coal usage is gradually phased off, primarily through its substitution for natural gas. Nevertheless, it is implausible that this policy can reach up to the elimination of coal. Coal industries themselves have applied pressure to the Congress in order to impede legislation that would curb the use of coal. Setting greenhouse gas emission targets and a trading emissions system would create incentives for the marginalization of coal usage. The White House, however, has enforced neither (Jacobs 2010). Furthermore, filtering coal can constrain its environmental damage. Through the coal's processing, its carbon content can be captured and stored and clean coal can be produced. This process presupposes, however, long pipelines and big storage facilities that significantly increase overall costs. This is why it has still not become widespread (Gros and Egenhofer 2010: 3).

In an oil-constrained and highly polluted world nuclear power sounds a fruitful option but for the dangers inherent in its use. It is for this cause that the US policy towards nuclear energy remains rather ambivalent. While its rhetoric is positive, actual measures are lacking. While the US has declared its intent to construct new, modern, safer and more efficient reactors, developments towards this end are rather slow (*The Economist* 2010b). Japan's shattering nuclear accident is certain to cement opposition to nuclear plans with an effect to retard them or annul them altogether. Renewables' percentage in the US energy mix, on the other hand, is on the ascent. This increase is slow but steady. The US subsidizes ethanol sugar cane and other bio-fuels in order to promote environmentally-friendly energy sources and decrease dependence on fossil fuel imports. Federal legislation on the systematic promotion of renewables, nonetheless, is absent. Unless this changes, one cannot expect but modest results (Jacobs 2010).

The challenge for the US then is to tackle dependence and subsequent sensitivity to energy imports in a way that neither sacrifices its developmental goals nor deteriorates the state of the environment. We can discern three main pillars around which the US aims to deliver these goals:

Diversification Washington follows a strategy of multiple, accessible and economically reasonable sources of supply. Its dominant role in energy markets revolves exactly around the facilitation of diversification. The US is dependent on a number of oil-rich countries, most of which it retains good relations with. It is for this reason that persistent animosity with Iran and the war campaign against Iraq, both of which contributed to the fall in overall global supply, as well as friction with Venezuela, have not sacrificed the US energy security. Saudi Arabia, Mexico, Canada and Kuwait, among others, all play a crucial role in supporting global oil supply and ensuring that the necessary oil quantities reach the US market. The US posture as the first among equal great powers in the world serves the goal of ensuring steady energy inflows (Stokes and Raphael 2010: 19).

Decreasing dependence and consumption Despite a successful import diversification portfolio, rising import dependency has alarmed US policy-makers, not least as it intermingles with wider US foreign policy goals, as for example the US overall strategy in the Middle East. In this context, it is an official aim of the US to decrease oil imports. To this aim, the US administration plans to give licenses for offshore explorations in the Gulf of Mexico and the Atlantic. This increase of domestic production can make up for a portion of imports. The second and more holistic goal is to decrease overall energy consumption. One of the measures the US took after the 1973 energy crisis was to significantly constrain energy consumption. This helped it withstand the second energy crisis a few years later much more easily. Nevertheless, the dwindling costs of oil from the decade of the 1980s onwards led to another boom in energy consumption. The 2000s, however, have been marked by the sharp increase of energy prices and another phase of dramatization of the potential end of (particularly cheap) oil. This necessitates new rounds of energy conservation and a cut back on energy consumption. The cornerstone of US industry, the car industry, has responded to these challenges by producing smaller, more energy-efficient cars as well as hybrid cars running on electricity and solar energy. Since oil is dominant in the transportation sector, dwindling oil consumption by vehicles could contribute to the reduction of overall oil consumption. The federal government aims to pose a positive example by introducing similar changes to the federal fleet's consumption patterns. At the same time, an increasing number of both state governments and towns provide tax cuts to construction enterprises that comply with the high energy-efficiency standards set by the Leadership in Energy and Environment Design (LEED). Many federal construction projects also set as a prerequisite compliance with these standards (Diamond 2006).

Initiating a post-Kyoto agreement US unwillingness to ratify the Kyoto Protocol[3] was detrimental in terms of soft power and made the US seem as a culprit for climate change, rather loosely committed to reversing these threatening trends. The Bush administration entrenched these negative policies by demonstrating not only a palpable reluctance to engage in international negotiations and be constrained by internationally agreed targets, but also a parallel inertia regarding

---

3   The Kyoto Protocol was signed in 1997 in Kyoto, Japan. Up to now 191 countries have adopted the treaty that aims to limit carbon emissions with a view to reverse global climate change.

domestic legislation.[4] Barack Obama's election in late 2008 seemed to mark a departure point away from such reactionary and obstructive policies. Obama's initial aspirations centred on introducing a US-wide carbon trading scheme with an eye to significantly cut carbon emissions by 2020. This reform, however, has not yet been implemented, not least due to a rather reluctant Senate that neither shares these environmental concerns nor approves of these measures. Besides this deadlock, Obama's presidency failed to pass federal climate change legislation towards a greener economy (Gros and Egenhofer 2010: 1). Nevertheless, the US administration increasingly commits more sums to carbon capture and storage as a means to cut on carbon emissions. Furthermore and despite the domestic adversities, President Obama was eager to rejoin international negotiations on climate change. The US participated actively in the Copenhagen and Cancun summits for the environment in December of 2009 and 2010 respectively. Despite US willingness to accept bounding limits to carbon emissions, the Copenhagen summit failed to produce global consent and thus was disappointing in terms of actual inputs. A mediocre step forward was made in Cancun with the decision to create a green fund with an emphasis on supporting environmental measures in the developing world (Vaughan 2010). Evidently, the issue of global environmental cooperation has climbed up the US administration's agenda.

The US has vested interests in paving the way for environmentally-friendly collective governance schemes. Firstly, the leading global power cannot be seen to abstain from, let alone resist, collective governance initiatives to ensure global public goods at a time when environmental hazards become all the more evident and the scientific community seems to lean towards an extensive and profound appreciation of environmental problems. Secondly, such global schemes are necessary in order to ensure that no free-riders running on cheaper but environmentally-unfriendly sources of energy maintain a competitive advantage vis-à-vis the US economy's green transition, which seems to be the only panacea to the stagnating US economy. In this context, the challenge that lies ahead for the US is to undertake a leading role in a new, comprehensive environmental treaty.

China's Energy Security Strategy: Challenges, Policies and Shortcomings

While the US economy is oil-driven, China's is coal-driven. More than two thirds of the overall energy consumption in China comes from coal (70 per cent), while less than one fifth (20 per cent) is generated by oil. Hydropower takes up 6 per cent, natural gas 3 per cent and nuclear power and other renewables just 1 per cent (EIA 2010d). Oil dominates the rapidly growing transportation sector, while coal, oil and hydropower dominate the electricity generation sector. The share of gas

---

4 Nevertheless, the US has managed since the 1980s to reduce pollution levels of the six most important pollutants of the atmosphere by 25 per cent, although the US population and energy consumption grew at 40 per cent, see Diamond 2006.

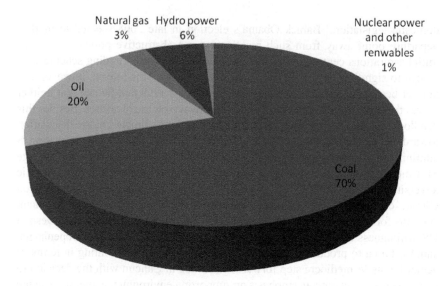

Figure 2.2   China's energy mix
Source: IEA Energy Statistics, IEA 2010

and nuclear power in the country's energy mix is rising fast, but they both start from a very low level.

It is obvious that the first issue pertaining to China's energy security is the predominance of coal and the subsequent damage to the environment. How sustainable this policy is has become increasingly scrutinized. Since Chinese growth is estimated to increase further in the near future – by 2025 China will be using as much coal as all the industrialized countries together (Deutch 2004: 11) – the problem becomes even more serious and calls for drastic solutions. China thus comes under pressure from the international community to burn less coal and to promote clean-coal technologies in order to bring down carbon emissions.

The second issue has to do with China's rising dependency on imported oil. The turning point was 1993 when China became a net oil importer. China is well-endowed with oil resources, which nevertheless are no more enough to cover domestic needs. In the East and South China Seas there lie significant deposits, but territorial disputes impede for the time being their full exploration that could boost domestic supply. Hence, China relies on imports for 40 per cent of its oil needs. This renders the country the largest oil importer outside IEA and the second largest globally (Tonnensson and Kolas 2006: 12–18). The projections are that China's oil imports will rise from 3 million b/d to 9.4 million b/d between 2001 and 2025 making up around 75 per cent of overall oil consumption (Deutch 2004: 9). This high rate of dependency breeds a number of concerns for China, such as sensitivity and potential vulnerability to sudden disruptions of oil that can lead to serious energy shortages and dramatic price hikes. It is also debatable whether China will be able to continue to grow at such a pace in case the price of oil reaches 150 or 200 dollars per barrel.

This is particularly so for Asian consumers since they pay a higher price for the oil they import than consumers in the US or Europe, what is called the Asia Premium (Mitchell and Lahn 2007). In an era of expensive oil, this endangers the country's energy security, especially since China, contrary to the US and the other members of IEA who hold significant reserves equivalent to at least three months' consumption, is short of strategic reserves. Such concerns are also a significant reminder of oil insecurity and reinforce the use of coal despite its environmental repercussions. If you add to the above China's infrastructural problems and the huge size of the country which necessitates the existence of long pipelines, evidently China's energy security faces serious challenges for the mid-term (Kalder 2007).

The problems addressed in Chapter 1, such as instability in producing countries, geopolitical tensions and conflicts that can influence negatively energy trade, transportation accidents, safety of sea lanes and so on are all highly relevant for China's energy security (Tonnensson and Kolas 2006: 19). Furthermore, only 10 per cent of the imported oil comes in Chinese tankers; 90 per cent comes in non-Chinese fleet, while 80–85 per cent comes through the Straits of Malacca. This creates sensitivity and vulnerability to China for two distinct reasons. Firstly, the Malacca Straits are a chokepoint, only one and a half miles wide at the narrowest point and hence prone to maritime accidents and potential acts of terrorism. Secondly, those Straits are militarily controlled by the US, which is perceived to be a liability for Chinese imports. The US has a strong card to play in case tensions with China (perhaps over Taiwan) get out of control (Kalder 2007).

These challenges call for an energy strategy that will enable abundant energy quantities to flow into the country at reasonable cost and without further damaging the environment and accelerating climate change. The main pillars of the Chinese energy strategy are:

Aggressive energy diplomacy   The fact that development rates in China surpass the capacity of indigenous resources to cater for the country's energy needs brings about the need to ensure that enough oil and gas is coming from energy-rich countries. To this end, China has initiated aggressive, multifaceted energy diplomacy (Kong 2009).[5] This is not limited to contracts with exporters, but also involves active engagement in exploration schemes and infrastructure projects (pipelines, LNG terminals, refineries) abroad to facilitate the inflow of energy into

---

5   China has a few big state-controlled energy corporations: China National Petroleum Corporation (CNPC), which was created out of the Ministry of Petroleum Industry in 1988 and is responsible for exploration and production onshore and in shallow, easier offshore fields; China National Offshore Oil Company (CNOOC), which controls most offshore oil business; and China National Petrochemical Corporation (Sinopec), a vertically integrated oil and chemical company, which is China's second largest crude oil producer and a major supplier of refined oil and petrochemical products. These companies have gradually opened up not only to projects outside China but also with regard to their corporate composition. ExxonMobil, BP and Royal Dutch Shell have bought shares in Sinopec and Royal Dutch Shell in CNOOC.

the country. High oil prices may have increased the costs for consumers, but, at the same time, have also encouraged energy enterprises, among them Chinese, to go around the world and operate more complex and demanding oil and gas exploration schemes. Besides beginning to tap oil from some of the disputed sea fields in East China to increase domestic production, China is creating a broad web of trade partners. These include new openings to the Middle East, to Asian neighbours, to African states, to Latin American countries and to Russia and Central Asian producers (Downs 2010).

Energy diplomacy is strongly backed by the government and firmly coordinated with other foreign policy goals. Therefore, it retains a strong political undertone, which is frequently criticized in the West. However, China's international posture as a rising global power that can resist US hegemony as well as offer an alternative to liberal democracy and Western-style capitalism is rather attractive to a bulk of states ranging from autocratic Middle East, African and Asian states to populist Latin American ones. China forms wider geopolitical alliances, with energy partnership being one major component.

Starting with the Middle East, which makes up 40 per cent of China's oil imports, China has fostered significant cooperation with Iran to such an extent that 14 per cent of its oil imports come from the Islamic Republic. In the gas sector, the two countries signed a 70 billion agreement for the purchase of more than 300 bcm of LNG over 30 years (Xuetang 2006: 136). A potential pipeline linkage of Iran and China via the Caspian Sea and Turkmenistan, albeit for the time being seen as remote, could bind the two states into an even closer energy partnership (Liu 2006).

Here we encounter a crucial characteristic of China's energy diplomacy, which we are also going to come across in other regions as well. China approaches energy-rich countries irrespective of their political regime and human rights record (Daojiong 2006: 182). Although a number of Western countries also do business in similar countries, there exist certain limitations in the West (take, for example, countries such as Iran and Sudan, where Western enterprises have not been allowed to do business in). China thus benefits from this Western approach and finds space to sign contracts with such countries.

Furthermore, China has solidified cooperation with Saudi Arabia. From the Saudi Arabian perspective, this is a valuable approach since it offers the country the option to disentangle from overt reliance on the US and may allow it the possibility to play the two powers against each other in order to strike a better deal. Deutch (2004: 10) goes even further and assumes that due to China's dependence and amid fierce competition we cannot rule out a scenario whereby China gives Saudi Arabia nuclear capacity in exchange for securing oil supplies, disrupting this way the strategic ties between the US and Saudi Arabia.

China also opened talks for a free trade area with the Gulf Cooperation Council (GCC).[6] This move aims to broaden trade ties and deepen interdependence with

---

6   The members of GCC are Saudi Arabia, Kuwait, Bahrain, Qatar, the United Arab Emirates and the Sultanate of Oman.

this bloc of states. Obviously, a closer cooperation between the GCC and China can foster China's energy security by ensuring more supplies for China. Moreover, the balanced approach that China holds with reference to the Arab–Israeli conflict averts any confrontation with the Arab world and thus 'makes dependence on the Middle East more affordable' (Daojiong 2006: 181).

Africa has become of major importance for China lately. Around one third of Chinese energy imports come from five African states, namely Tongo, Equatorial Guinea, Sudan, Nigeria and Angola. China is not only the customer, but also actively involved in the exploration of energy in these countries.[7] In general, China offers an attractive package to poor African states. It promises aid in return for lucrative energy contracts (Daojiong 2006: 185). Here, again, we see China doing business in states with unstable and non-democratic regimes, even in the midst of civil war (as in the case of Sudan). The West condemns these Chinese policies, blaming China that in its quest for energy it does not take into account wider political implications in the region and this way fosters dictatorial regimes. Although these allegations may hold true, one cannot disregard the fact that it is Chinese investments that are themselves endangered by prolonged conflicts in these countries.

Houser and Levy (2008: 63–71) make an interesting argument claiming that the guiding principle in these cases is not energy security but serving the sovereignty principle in line with China's entrenched position on Taiwan, Tibet and Xinjiang. In this light, the major preoccupation is with upholding the norm of sovereignty internationally, which is so vital for China's own integrity. Take, for example, Sudan. Resources lie in the region of South Sudan which has long vied for independence and formed a reluctant partner for China. China could have been tempted to court it, negotiate with it separately, bypass the central government and support it against the Sudanese government. China, however, did not act so, as this would undermine the principle of sovereignty. This foreign policy path then seems more to undermine than actually boost China's energy security. In the face of the overwhelmingly pro-independence South Sudanese referendum and the establishment of an independent South Sudanese state, China remains cautious to balance between its foreign policy and energy security interests (LeVine 2011).

Moreover, although the international community criticizes fiercely Chinese practices, it is true that they are contributing to the increase of overall energy supply and hence assist so that prices remain at affordable levels. This is good news for consumers around the world. It has to be underlined that a significant portion of the oil produced by Chinese companies in Africa is, contrary to what is widely believed, not locked up by China but finally bought by a well-respected member of the West, Japan.

Latin American states, especially Venezuela, see in China a potential ally to counter US hegemony. As we saw in the previous sub-chapter, the deteriorating

---

7   It is frequent that such contracts are accompanied by further deals. For example, China is also involved in Algeria's nuclear power programme (Colombo and Lesser 2010: 4–5).

relations between Hugo Chavez and the US and the augmenting oil needs of China form fertile ground for the intensification of the two countries' oil trade. This is a good example of a new tendency in the energy sector, whereby not economic, but political considerations determine flows of energy. China is exploiting long-standing frustration with the US and by offering security of demand becomes a rather welcome alternative to traditional importers.

Asia is also important for China in two ways. The first and most obvious one is that some countries in the region are energy rich and hence suppliers of the Chinese market with decreased transportation costs. Burma, another autocratic regime with good relations with China, exports oil and gas to China (Tonnensson and Kolas 2006: 19–37). Southeast Asia is particularly gas-rich, with Malaysia and Indonesia being traditional LNG exporters for decades. China can take advantage of such potential in its neighbourhood. Secondly, in Asia there is another very big, particularly populous and rapidly developing country, India. Although most analysts focus on the potential for conflict between the two states as they both endeavour to lock up assets for their own energy needs, more emphasis should be given to their cooperation potential. They are already cooperating in the Greater Nile Oil Project in Sudan (China with 40 per cent and India with 25 per cent), as well as in the Yadavaran oil field in Iran (China with 51 per cent and India with 29 per cent) thus increasing overall oil supply (Xuetang 2006: 123, Liu 2006).

Last but not least, China has begun to engage Russia. This is normal, if one takes into account proximity and Russia's particularly rich subsoil. Russia has been supplying oil to China by train for years. An upsurge of agreements between the two sides has lately taken place. Russia is building an oil pipeline that is going to carry around 500,000 b/d from Tayshet to its pacific coast in Nakhodka, from which both China and Japan will be supplied.[8] Russia and China have also agreed on the construction of two pipelines (of a capacity of up to 80 bcm per year) that will bring natural gas to China (Tonnensson and Kolas 2006: 19–37).

Besides Russia, China has turned to Kazakhstan and Turkmenistan for further oil and gas supplies. From the perspective of these two states, China offers security of demand, a lucrative market, higher prices and an alternative to until recently monopsonistic Russia (that takes advantage of its geographical position and buys Turkmen gas and Kazakh oil cheaply in order to supply Europe) (Xuetang 2006: 126). To this end, Kazakhstan and China have constructed the Atasu–Alashankou oil pipeline that will carry 120,000 b/d. This, together with the Russia–China pipeline is especially important if one bears in mind that Chinese imports through the Malacca Straits are, as we saw above, quite sensitive, while pipeline-transferred oil is much safer (Xuetang 2006: 130, Daojiong 2006: 184). Since 2010 China also receives some quantities of Turkmen gas (Pirani, Stern and Yafimava 2010: 23), while it is also negotiating with Turkmenistan the construction of a gas pipeline

---

8   The initial plan was to build a pipeline linking Russia with China, but Russia preferred to build a pipeline running solely through its territory so that it can avoid overt dependence on the Chinese market and supply both lucrative Asian markets.

that will transfer up to 40 bcm per year to China. Lastly, Chinese corporations have been engaged in upstream projects in Kazakhstan, Kyrgyzstan and Tajikistan (Xuetang 2006: 135).

Functional and geographical diversification and environmental protection   The first pillar gives emphasis on the pressing need for China to ensure for itself adequate oil and gas quantities in a world of progressively fierce competition over natural resources. The second one, obviously overlapping at some points with the first, cedes emphasis on the need to diversify the energy mix as well as the sources of supply. Geographical diversification has been achieved since China receives or has agreed to import oil and gas from the Middle East, Latin America, Africa, Southeast and Central Asia and Russia. The challenge, however, for Chinese policy-makers is to achieve functional diversification. This means deliberate changes in the energy mix in order to thwart overt dependence on a single source and encourage supplies of other fuels for economic and environmental reasons.

As depicted above, China is excessively dependent on coal and under pressure to reduce its usage due to the attached environmental risks. Despite the nature of the closed Chinese political system, the Chinese leadership grasps the magnitude of the problem and begins slowly to address it. China's master plan for the year 2050 is for an energy mix of maximum 35 per cent for coal, 40–50 per cent for oil and gas and 15–20 per cent for hydro, solar and wind energy (Liu 2006: 6). Timing is helpful since oil is getting more expensive at the same time that global competition both makes it more difficult to ensure adequate supplies as well as reinforces the end of oil rhetoric. The need to cut down on carbon emissions encourages the further use of natural gas, renewables as well as nuclear power.

Natural gas is especially important here. The Chinese strategy aims to increase gas consumption to 8 per cent up to 2015 (Istock Analyst 2010) and build a wide domestic gas network, a challenging task if one takes into account the size of the country. There are significant domestic reserves of natural gas but they are rather expensive and demanding both in exploration and transportation terms; hence the plans to build gas pipelines from Turkmenistan and Russia to China. There is also a qualitative difference here, since gas contracts are long-term, bind both sides in an interdependent relation and thus provide energy security both to the exporter and the importer; disruptions that may hamper gas trade are considered less likely than oil sea trade and thus gas trade through pipelines is often opted for (Daojiong 2006: 185). Besides, gas imports in LNG from neighbouring Indonesia and Malaysia and even Australia, may be a sound option for the near future. LNG, as well as swap deals, may prove even more beneficial for China, since pipelines will be too long and thus an economic burden for consumers.

Next to all these, alternative ways of energy generation, in particular renewables and nuclear energy, can contribute to functional diversification and environmental protection. China plans to significantly modernize its nuclear reactors in order to boost electricity generation. This however will only take place gradually and evolve hand in hand with rising energy consumption rates. Thus nuclear power is not estimated to acquire a preponderant role in the energy mix (Ferguson 2007). At the same time, the Chinese government already plans to increase the share of hydro in power generation by 2020 (Tonnensson and Kolas 2006: 12–18). Furthermore, China accounted for the majority of new wind energy installations globally in 2009 (Skea 2010). The use of renewables has been rising at more than 25 per cent, which is the fastest rate in the world. Since we start from a very low base, however, this does not amount to that much in absolute terms (Liu 2006). The Beijing municipality authorities have regulated the conversion of car engines so that they can also run on natural gas in order to curb environmental pollution. Moreover, China imposed the use of leadless gasoline in cars only within a year (that is within a much tighter time-frame than attained in the West), while the use of transportation fuels was aligned with the high European efficiency and environmental standards (Diamond 2006). Lastly, China is investing in clean coal technologies and the global community has good reasons to support China's initiatives (Liu 2006). Already Japan and China have set up a joint venture to produce clean coal in the Chinese city of Fushun. Japan has long been the pioneer in clean energy technology and is both able and willing to help China follow its path, not least since Chinese polluted air is the main culprit for acid rain in Japan.

Increase of energy efficiency   China has a very bad record in energy efficiency. For every dollar of GDP produced in China, three times as much energy as the global average is being consumed. It is estimated that average energy consumption is 20 per cent higher than in developed nations. It is hence a priority for China to manage effectively domestic demand and promote energy conservation. The government attempts to reduce coal and oil subsidies that encourage overt use of these fuels and instead creates incentives in order to promote the shift towards less energy-intensive modes of production (Daojiong 2006: 185).

The efforts of China, although being on the right path, seem to be short of energy and strength. China seems to be moving quite slowly towards cleaner forms of energy and towards reshaping its economy into less energy-intensive modes. What creates question marks for the future is China's mid-term ability to ensure abundant supplies at reasonable cost and in such a sustainable way that will at least not further damage the environment. Chinese commitments to increase energy efficiency will be more than evened out by a close to double-digit development growth rate in the following years, which will further boost overall emissions (Gros and Eigenhofer 2010: 1). Contrary to official projections, estimations for 2030 show only limited improvement in China's energy mix with coal decreasing to 62 per cent and oil to 18 per cent, natural gas increasing to 8 per cent, hydropower to 9 per cent and nuclear power to 3 per cent (Wingyi 2006: 89–90).

In contrast with OECD countries that provide low-cost data, analyses, estimations and future scenarios that ensure transparency and form the basis for the designation of policies for the future, China remains secretive and lacks a credible energy information industry. This is one major reason why China should be incorporated into IEA. Since there is one global energy market in which producers and consumers cooperate, such a move would facilitate its smoother function (Daojiong 2006: 187). The key for China then is to engage itself in dialogue, participate in open markets, influence common regulation on energy issues and foster international cooperation, since its national goals can only be served through well-managed interdependence (Houser and Levy 2008: 71). China has a lot to gain from the technologically more advanced West, especially when it comes to cleaner forms of energy and reshaping the economy into more energy-efficient modes of production (Liu 2006: 15).

Conclusion

To sum up, although China and the US both constitute significant importers in the global energy market, their different starting positions, energy needs and policy priorities lead to diverse strategies for achieving energy security. The US aims to retain its predominance in the energy sector and to continue monitoring the smooth operation of the global energy market which allows it a diversified portfolio of imports. Nevertheless, it comprehends that the real challenge for sustainable development in the twenty-first century lies in decreasing external dependencies and energy consumption. This goal is in line with overall efforts to make the US economy less energy-intensive. For this target to be implemented, however, the US also needs to acquire a leading role in regulating new global environmental standards, which will allow US companies to lead the country out of recession and into a sustainable virtuous economic circle.

China, on the other hand, focuses on strengthening ties with exporters in order to increase its imports, at the same time that it is cautious its dependence on any single source does not become excessive. As the most rapidly developing economy in the world, China's energy needs are projected to increase significantly during the next decades. Environmental concerns, nevertheless, amass and China may seriously jeopardize its environmental security in case it does not face up to the challenge. It is in this context that the Chinese leadership has initiated a number of reforms both to improve energy efficiency records as well as to decrease pollution. Despite these measures, however, the situation remains bleak if one takes into account that China will have to further increase energy consumption in order to achieve its ambitious developmental goals.

These energy strategies are devised in the background of tightening energy supply and persisting   of suppliers, increasing global demand and potentially higher energy prices, as well as mounting threats for the environment. While China's preference to increase its imports does not bode well with the overall need for reduction of consumption rates, the US still remains ambivalent how to pursue a more radical agenda on energy and environmental issues. These policies also frame the context within which the EU has to balance its own priorities, conceptualize threats and devise policies accordingly.

Chapter 3

EU Energy Security: Tracing the Main Threats, the Policy Framework and the Actors

Despite the EU's leading role in global efforts to constrain and combat environmental deterioration and climate change, its economy runs predominantly on fossil fuels. Oil takes up 37 per cent of the EU energy mix, while natural gas consumption has increased manifold during the past decades and takes up 25 per cent of overall energy use in the EU. Coal usage has declined, but still takes up 17 per cent; nuclear energy covers 13 per cent of overall EU energy consumption, while renewables have emerged as alternative forms of energy generation. Their share in the EU fuel mix nevertheless remains single-digit for the time being, around 8 per cent (European Commission 2010).

The Main Challenges for EU Energy Security

Europe is not energy-rich, but fortunate enough to be bordering with four regions that are well-endowed with natural resources. Proximity with the Middle East, North Africa, Russia and the North Sea facilitates energy trade between these regions and the EU. The EU's well developed and lucrative market remains attractive for exporters, not least since EU Members pay high prices and in hard currency, while most of the exporters depend for their survival and prosperity on energy-born revenues. On the other hand, however, the particularities of the global energy market, such as transportation safety hazards, hiked prices that may hold growth down, resource nationalism and unreliable suppliers, as well as the monopolistic role of OPEC, are all relevant risks for the EU. For these reasons, although the EU is able to secure adequate supplies, the danger of supply shortages at any time in the future can and should not be downplayed. In addition, it is questionable for how long the EU should remain dependent on fossil fuels in the face of mounting environmental degradation and progressively depleting resources. Taking into account the main tenets of the current energy landscape, as well as the outlook for the future and the trends in the global energy market, we can trace the main threats for EU energy security. In particular, the main challenges are:

High Import Dependency

The main liability of the EU is its high import dependency both on oil and gas. Oil import dependency is approximating 85 per cent, while natural gas import

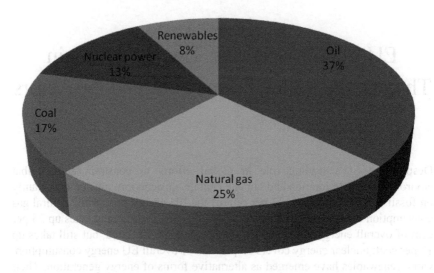

Figure 3.1   The EU's energy mix
Source: European Commission, DG Energy 2010

dependency is lesser but approximates two thirds of overall gas consumption (European Commission 2011). Even worse, projections for the future increase these numbers even further (European Commission 2000, 2006: 3–5 and 2008, European Commission, DG Energy 2011: 3). This might not constitute a grave concern in case suppliers were considered reliable and the smooth function of the global energy market was granted. Reality, however, is quite different. The global oil market is fluid and unstable. The 'pariah state' status of Iran, the turmoil in Iraq throughout the 2000s and the 2011 upsurge in Libya all pinpoint to the instability of the oil market and lead to fluctuations in productivity. Global oil production capacity is already strained and any pitfall in oil producing regions will only serve to aggravate the function of the market even further.

The fact that the majority of oil producing countries retains monarchical regimes with poor governance structures adds to importers' vulnerability. This problem is not limited to the oil sector; most gas-rich states are also unstable and potentially problematic, begging the question whether the EU's energy security strategy has been prudently designed. The recent trend of resource nationalism means that energy is increasingly used as a foreign policy tool as well, a rather disquieting development for the EU.

Increased Competition by the Developing World

The global energy market would be able to operate more efficiently and absorb the shocks emanating from individual producing states in case global energy demand and consumption were constrained. Indeed, for decades the West's energy security was not significantly jeopardized, the two energy crises of the

1970s notwithstanding, exactly because producers eventually needed to sell their energy products in order to raise revenues. As a rule energy supply surpassed energy demand and the West assured for itself adequate energy inflows (Falola and Genova 2005).

The recent impressive boost of energy demand from the developing world, primarily China and India, has significantly squeezed the energy security margin of the West and subsequently of the EU. Supply only marginally surpasses demand and thus any bottleneck in production, transportation or refining can significantly hamper the smooth operation of the energy market. In addition, now oil producing states have more outlets for their energy and can choose markets not only by commercial but also geopolitical criteria.

The nature of EU foreign policy, stemming from its peaceful identity, is a crucial factor here. The EU retains commercial and energy ties with problematic states. This should not be misread as concessions to awkward regimes, but more as part of a more holistic approach which sees low politics and cooperation as a significant first step that can pave the way for further understanding and cooperation in the international system (Keukeleire and MacNaughtan 2008). At the same time, however, the EU frequently links energy deals with compliance with international norms and respect for human rights. In a number of cases, such linkages act as deterrents to enhanced energy cooperation or impact negatively on existing cooperation frameworks. Critics could point to sustained energy cooperation with Russia and Algeria, the regimes of which frequently disregard or act openly against fundamental international norms. On the other hand, however, the EU remains reluctant to engage with a host of dubious regimes (take, for example, Turkmenistan and Uzbekistan).

More importantly, the EU does not enjoy government-backed energy diplomacy; neither does it maintain a strong supranational presence in bilateral negotiations or multilateral energy fora, as is the case in other areas, for example in trade policy with its common stand in the World Trade Organization (WTO). Although certain European governments have played a decisive role behind energy agreements (take, for example, French, Italian and German diplomacy that earned their companies lucrative contracts with Russia), the EU in general does not promote energy projects with the same determinism and effectiveness that the US or China does. China's political system means that all Chinese energy corporations work as arms of the Chinese state (Ferdinand 2007). The US, on the other hand, has since 1979 and the second energy crisis incorporated energy concerns into its national security strategy with the Carter dogma. Since the end of the Cold War, it has zealously and effectively put pressure on energy companies to construct the Baku–Tbilisi–Ceyhan oil pipeline despite its debatable economic efficiency in order to break Russia's monopoly of energy corridors linking the ex-Soviet space and Europe (Cornell, Tsereteli and Socor 2005). To the contrary, the EU's weakness is most pronounced in the Caspian region, where Russia has managed to contract most of the oil and gas quantities that Central Asian states produce, eliminating this way an alternative source of supply for the EU (Socor 2007a).

Increasingly High Prices

The imbalances brought to the ratio of global supply to global demand are one of the central reasons why oil and gas prices have increased manifold the last decade. Many analysts consider that the EU has to learn to live by high energy prices. This is a critical aspect of the EU's attempt to launch a new development and growth round for its economy, especially after the global economic recession of 2007–08, as well as amidst the public sector deficits of a handful of its Members and the growing rates of euro-scepticism within the EU. High energy prices mean that oil and gas imports will act as a burden on the EU economy, estimated to absorb 2 per cent of its GDP (IEA 2009). Even worse, one cannot exclude the possibility that energy prices may further increase in the future (Euractiv 2010), due to rising energy demand from the developing world and potential crises in energy producing regions. Even the consideration that the swing oil producer, Saudi Arabia, might import the domino of revolutions in the Arab world and face internal struggles that will put its production capacity under strain is enough to make prices skyrocket.

How to Tackle the Environmental Challenge

Lastly, the European Commission sees itself as the pioneer of sustainable development and a green economy for the twenty-first century. It is the leading international actor in regulating the promotion of cleaner forms of energy and supporting the passage to less energy-intensive modes of production. Nevertheless, the actual outcomes are for the time being mediocre, while projections for the future do not fare well. There are two main aspects here, the internal and the external. Starting with the internal, the EU has set ambitious environmental goals for its Members, but the most likely scenario is that they will not be able to reach them by 2020 (see pp. 52–3). The European Commission appreciates the difficulties a transition to more environmentally-friendly forms of energy generation and consumption entails and admits that for as long as oil and gas will be available, they will continue to be the main sources of energy (European Commission 2000: 47, 65–6). The EU thus remains firmly attached to conventional forms of energy in order to keep its economy going and not face any energy shortages. Risk aversion, high initial costs and vested interests in oil and gas trade account for the substantial delay in widely introducing greener forms of energy. Sustained high reliance on fossil fuels, however, means that the EU fails to deal with the environmental challenges thoroughly. Supply shortages are averted at a high environmental cost due to the prolonged use of fossil fuels.

Even in case the EU significantly diversifies its energy mix, however, the impact will not be decisive unless other great polluters such as the US and China agree to substantially contribute to the implementation of a global green agenda and reduce their overall emissions. While the internal dimension is of paramount significance both for practical reasons as well as an example-setter, the locus should be on the external dimension and how the EU can broker an international agreement that will successfully contain global climate change and tackle ensuing challenges. This aspect remains deeply problematic. Recent environmental summits are full of symbolism, but have as yet not produced 'binding commitments to reduce global greenhouse gas emission levels' (Ottinger 2010: 411–12). Unless the situation changes dramatically, the EU will suffer the consequences of global inertia on environmental issues.

EU Strategy in the Energy Sector

In order to tackle these challenges, the EU is pursuing an energy strategy that aims to satisfy all three major goals of energy security, namely security of supplies, economic competitiveness and environmental protection. In particular, the main pillars of its energy security strategy are:

Diversification

The EU energy policy is based on the principle of diversification. The European Commission (1995: 21) defines energy security as the state where basic future energy needs will be satisfied through domestic energy resources and strategic deposits under economically acceptable terms and using diversified, stable, reliable and accessible external supplies. Diversification is crucial since it allows importers to withstand supply shortages caused by any supplier, for any political, economic and/or technical reasons, through the contracting of additional supplies by alternative producers. Diversification then works as a shield of protection against high dependency rates on individual producers, as well as discourages exporters from exercising blackmailing policies to exploit asymmetric interdependence.

Diversification has two dimensions, the functional and the geographical. In terms of functional diversification, the EU economy is based on oil, but also runs on natural gas. Nuclear power is a significant source of energy generation, especially in some states such as Britain and France. Coal is still widely in use, while the use of renewables is bound to further increase in accordance with EU international commitments under the Protocol of Kyoto. In other words, the EU energy mix is adequately diversified and does not excessively depend on any single source of energy. It has to be noted here that not all Member-States have a diversified fuel portfolio. Some states are quite dependent on a single fuel. In these cases, the need to further diversify is urgent.

Coming to geographical diversification, the focus here is on oil (leaving natural gas aside for the moment since we are going to explicitly deal with that on Chapters 5 and 6). This is so because both nuclear power and renewables are mainly domestic resources, whereas coal usage follows diminishing trends. A mix of oil imports from the Middle East, Russia, Norway, North Africa and the Caspian allows steady oil inflows covering the EU's oil needs (IEA 2008). What adds to security of oil supplies is the multitude of energy corridors. The EU

Members get most of their oil through tankers coming through the North Sea, the Bosporus Straits[1] and the Mediterranean. In addition, Russia supplies the EU with oil through the Druzhba pipeline system, as well as with tankers from its ports of Novorossiysk, Primorsk and St. Petersburg. Beyond these established trade channels, new oil pipelines such as the Baku–Supsa and Baku–Tbilisi–Ceyhan pipelines bring oil from Azerbaijan (and small oil quantities from Kazakhstan as well) through Georgia and Turkey to EU soil.

Liberalization

In order to deal with overt reliance on external suppliers for its energy security the EU aims at the creation of a unified legal and regulatory framework in energy trade. This framework is based upon market rules and competition and intends to mitigate investment and transit risks and to marginalize the scope for political manoeuvring. It thus serves to bind exporters and importers into a mutually beneficial interdependent relationship, minimize supply risks and enhance the EU's security of supplies. This framework has two dimensions, the external and the internal. While the first aims to regulate relations with external suppliers, the latter aims to regulate the function of the internal market. Since, however, external players operate in the EU market, this also impinges upon external energy relations.

Starting with the external dimension, the fall of the Berlin Wall, the fall of communism and the demise of the oil- and gas-rich Soviet Union transformed the geopolitical map of Eurasia and created fifteen new entities. A handful of them (Russia, Turkmenistan, Kazakhstan, Azerbaijan and Uzbekistan) carried important energy potential as future suppliers of the EU. Russia inherited all the contracts signed by the Soviet Union with European customers, while all newly independent countries inherited these parts of the Soviet-era pipelines that crossed their own territories. However, this infrastructure was quite old and called for modernization. At the same time, all ex-Soviet economies, Russia included, were in economic turmoil and thus unable to invest in their energy infrastructure and resources. The energy production base could thus only be revitalized by foreign direct investments that the West was both able and willing to make in the region. Under this light, the EU, in line with its own interior project of building a single market, devised a liberalization agenda that led to the signing of the Energy Charter Treaty (ECT). This aimed to regulate the energy sector and trade patterns

---

1   The Bosporus has become a chokepoint with frequent delays for tankers and augmenting fears that increased traffic dangerously raises the potential for a dreadful maritime accident. Thus, from both an economic and environmental perspective there is an urgent need to de-congest the Straits. The agreement in 2007 to build the Burgas–Alexandroupolis pipeline and the alternative speculated project Sampsun–Ceyhan aim to achieve this goal, as well as increase transport capacity in accordance with the capacity increase planned by the Caspian Pipeline Consortium operating the pipeline from Kazakhstan to the Russian port of Novorossiysk, see Dellecker 2008 and Nitzov 2011.

between the West and the East according to the rationale of open markets and competition in order to facilitate energy flows from the East to the West as well as financing from the West to the East. All EU Members and ex-Soviet states are members to the treaty. Russia, however, although a signatory member, has refused to ratify it and has made it plain that it does not intend to proceed to ratification anytime soon. The main issues of discontent revolve around the reform of the energy sector and the mandatory break-up of monopolies, as well as the transit protocol that forces all states to allow third party access (TPA) to their pipelines. Russia's interests are more contrary to than congruent with these regulations, since Russia enjoys political control over Caspian oil and gas and over the Soviet-era pipeline system to Europe, as well as ensures for itself higher revenues by means of buying those states' energy and re-selling it to Europe at higher prices. In case it ratified the treaty and complied with TPA regulations, Russia would lose these privileges. Hence, the international liberalization package promoted by the EU brought only restricted results pertaining mostly to technological cooperation between producers and consumers (de Jong 2008: 60–61, Energy Charter Official Website, Haghighi 2007, European Commission 2004: 2).

Although the EU failed to spread this liberalization agenda to Eurasia, however, it went on with the liberalization of its own gas and electricity market (the domestic oil market was already liberalized). The electricity and gas directives achieved the break-up of state-owned monopolies and allowed the entrance of new private players into the market (European Commission 1996, 1998, 2003). Although competition is still wrought with problems, the EU energy market is on the path to full liberalization and increasingly applies pressure on foreign players to adhere to such rules (see Chapter 4). This liberalization program is intended to achieve lower prices for EU consumers, multiple suppliers and more flexibility that will add to EU energy security (Jaffe and Soligo 2006: 462).

Sustainable Development

The EU comprehends that diversification and liberalization are necessary, albeit not adequate policy measures for tackling import dependencies. They more serve to mitigate short-term risks, rather than pave the way for a more secure energy landscape in the mid-term. Depleting resources and the urgent need to protect the environment means that energy security cannot for long be based upon the consumption of fossil fuels. It is for these reasons that the European Commission has devised the 20–20–20 strategy to achieve its dual goal of energy security and environmental protection. This entails three concrete targets:

• To bring down its greenhouse gas emissions by 20 per cent by 2020 in accordance with the Kyoto agreement, in which it has sustained a leading role throughout the negotiation and enforcement processes. This goal presupposes a drastic decrease in the use of coal and the promotion of clean coal technologies.

- To increase the percentage of renewable resources in energy consumption to 20 per cent by 2020 (to 10 per cent in the transportation sector). In accordance with this goal, the EU provides a series of incentives for the further increase of wind, solar, biomass and geothermal energy.
- To increase overall energy efficiency by 20 per cent by the same year, in order to significantly cut down on overall energy consumption. Such a move will have as a parallel result the loosening of oil and gas import dependency (European Commission 2010).

The Framework for EU Energy Policy and Security

Since its inception, the European Union's policy-making procedures are based upon a consensus approach. Member States attempt to agree, together with supranational organs, on common policies and joint actions that will respect the preferences and legitimate concerns of all Members (Cameron 2010: 1). The downside of this political mentality is that more frequently than not either no decision is taken when not viewed as urgent or policies of the lowest common denominator prevail (Jupille 1999, Meunier 2000, Nugent 2010). As a result, EU policy-making often fails to satisfy high expectations for efficient action. This also holds true in the energy domain, where internal disputes and difficult relations with powerful external suppliers, matched with the decisive impact of market dynamics, present the EU with mounting challenges.

Tracing the Main Actors

There is ample literature regarding the complexity of the European Union, the mosaic of European institutions and the hybrid, path-dependent mode of policy-making within the EU (Staab 2008, Wallace and Wallace 2000, Richardson 2001, Hix and Høyland 2011). In this complex political environment, it is normal that there is obscurity with regard to where authority lies, who undertakes policy initiatives, who gets decisions on the energy mix and pipeline projects and so on. Member States, the European Commission and the energy industry are the principal actors that co-determine the EU energy policy.

In what follows, we analyse their main functions, competences, powers and weaknesses:

Member States   Since its inception the European Union consists of, is based upon and rests its power and legitimacy from its Member States. According to the neo-functional logic, states have been locked into a process of surrendering part of their sovereignty to supranational institutions, which have risen in significance and have seen their authorities substantially increase (Haas 1958, Alexander 1998). Although this holds true and in a number of cases states find themselves in difficult positions and have to accept decisions they would themselves not have taken, states remain critical actors within the EU policy scene. In a number of cases and particularly in the most strategic sectors, states prefer to retain full sovereignty (Nugent 2010, Moravcsik 1999, Rosamond 2000). This is the case also with regard to energy issues. There has been a debate, both in academic and policy-making circles, on whether the EU should proceed to more supranational forms of governance and form a coherent, truly EU-wide common energy policy supervised and run by its executive organ, the European Commission (European Commission 2007, Andoura, Hancher and van der Woude 2010). Despite declarations and concrete small steps taken towards better coordinated policies, this appears a too far-fetched prospect. Member States remain intent to retain their sovereignty with regard to determining their energy mix, as well as choosing their suppliers. All proposals for a supranational authority that will regulate and monitor the energy mix, overall consumption and imports in the EU have been dashed. States prefer not to transfer any further authorities to the executive branch of the EU, the European Commission (de Jong 2007: 58).

The main argument that national officials bring to counter the voices calling for more supranationalism in energy policy is Member States' diverse state of energy security. For example, Cyprus and Malta consume no gas while the Baltic states are excessively dependent on Russian gas. Nuclear reactors cover a significant part of France's energy needs, while other countries remain sceptical to the use of nuclear power for electricity generation. Portugal is supplied by North African gas, while Lithuania is only supplied by Russia. Member States face different threats and challenges and thus hold different approaches towards energy security. Supranational schemes, the argument continues, would thus be inappropriate for dealing with so diverse problems (Butler 2009: 137). Furthermore, besides the obvious reason that governments prefer to retain competences rather than disseminate them, there is an additional reason why they persist to treat energy security at a national level. Energy issues are closely intertwined with wider foreign policy considerations. States thus are enmeshed into energy diplomacy as part and parcel of their overall foreign policy.

Energy enterprises The advent of liberalization throughout the last decades paved the way for a far more critical role for the energy industry. The most fundamental changes have been under way in the gas and electricity sectors since the oil sector is long privatized. A few years ago it was monopolistic, state-owned energy companies that contracted gas and electricity from external suppliers. A number of ministers and government officials sat on the executive boards of these enterprises and decided on their strategy and the ways to ensure security of supplies. The interests and strategies of governments and their energy companies naturally converged and hence the companies' strategies could analytically be treated as pillars of their states' foreign and energy policy. Since the liberalization of the gas and electricity field, however, governments were forced to sell (most of) their shares in these companies and to allow the entrance of new players in the market. Therefore, their role has since been limited (Finon and Locatelli 2002: 3).

The private energy companies that have emerged cannot be treated analytically in the same way as state-owned and state-controlled companies. These new actors are autonomous players in the market, driven foremost by their interests in survival and economic profitability. Since they have to serve their shareholders' interests, their policies, interests and strategies frequently deviate from those of their governments (Schmidt 1995, Strange 1996, CIEP 2007, Youngs 2009).

In this new economic environment, their relations with their home countries and other governments are much more complicated. First of all, these corporations have become significant partners for the governments. States need to cooperate with energy enterprises to ensure their energy security. This is so because it is energy companies, not governments that operate in the energy field, sign supply contracts, form joint ventures, invest money on exploration and transportation schemes and provide energy to industries and households. Energy security thus depends on the performance of these corporations (Jaffe, Hayes and Victor 2006: 468). German officials have acknowledged that the German energy industry manages the country's energy security with the state retaining a back-seat, supportive role (Sander 2007: 23). Indeed, Germany's gas security is served by its main enterprises' strategic partnership with Gazprom, while the Italian company ENI's strategic alliance with Gazprom has enforced Italy's security of gas supplies (Stern 1999, Sander 2007, Geden, Marcelis and Maurer 2006: 18).

At the same time, since national governments give directives and design the basic framework within which corporate actors will function, corporations need to comply with governmental regulations, court with governments and retain channels of pressure and influence. Furthermore, since energy trade takes place within the contours of international politics and is thus significantly influenced by geopolitical factors, energy companies seek political support from states in order to earn lucrative contracts. Such backing is of critical importance especially when dealing with state-owned or state-controlled energy companies as is the case with Russia's Gazprom or Algeria's Sonatrach. For this reason, energy companies are also cautious not to upset or alienate governments (CIEP 2007).

The European Commission   Although no common energy policy managed by a supranational authority has been formed and no one is anywhere near, the role of supranational organs is also critical in the framing of energy policy within the EU. We focus here on the role of the European Commission since the European Parliament retains a largely discursive role; it has limited powers to significantly influence decisions taken by the European Commission and Member States with regard to energy security. The European Commission, on the other hand, has a specialized Energy Directorate that 'establishes and monitors a set of energy policy objectives, publishes detailed energy statistics and forecasts and suggests guidelines for national policy making' (Weyman-Jones 1997: 545). In particular, the European Commission enjoys four main competences:

- First of all, utilizing the right of initiative that the founding treaties endowed it with, the European Commission has been the pioneer for the establishment of a single market since the signing of the Single European Act in 1986. To this aim, it has issued a number of directives for the reform of the gas and electricity sector that would create a unified European energy market. Those reforms are constitutive of a differentiated energy field in which there are no more fragmented national markets with monopolistic players, but a single market in which multiple corporate actors operate. The Commission thus co-decides the rules of the game that are critical for the state of EU energy security.
- Secondly, it is the Commission's task to monitor that all states implement the liberalization of their gas and electricity markets. Corporate actors' strategies and policies are ruled by EU-wide competition regulations also supervised by the European Commission.
- Thirdly, the European Commission is responsible for overseeing the penetration of foreign enterprises in the EU market and for monitoring whether they meet the terms to operate in it. This gives it crucial leverage with regard to relations with export behemoths like Gazprom, Sonatrach and Statoil.
- Fourthly, it participates in international energy fora. It has established the INOGATE energy program[2] and is an active participant in all institutional structures binding the EU with external suppliers (for example, the EU–Russia energy dialogue). Hence, it is in a position to propose and apply pressure for the construction of new pipelines and energy facilities that will improve the EU's energy security.

A breakthrough has been achieved in the Lisbon Treaty, which turns energy policy from a national into a shared competence between the EU and its Member States, openly fortifying the role of the European Commission. This constitutes a significant development since it will facilitate more collective modes of decision-making on energy issues (Egenhofer and Behrens 2008: 3, Braun 2011).

Lastly, the Gas Coordination Group was established in 2006 with the aim to facilitate the exchange of information and the definition of joint actions between Member States, the Commission, the gas industry and consumers. The Group is monitored by the Commission and has a central role in enhancing coordination, solidarity, cohesion and security of supplies in the internal gas market (European Commission 2010b).

While these actors agree on the need to facilitate energy security, they diverge on the aspects of energy security that hold priority. As we saw in the first chapter, energy security has three main dimensions, security of supplies, competitiveness and affordable prices and environmental protection and security. Member States

---

2   INOGATE is an international energy cooperation program between the EU, the littoral states of the Black and Caspian Seas and their neighboring countries. It aims to cement their cooperation in the energy sector and enhance their energy security.

prioritize the first two components while incorporating as much as possible the third dimension. Energy enterprises' operations also are chiefly driven by the competitiveness and security of supplies rationale in order to sustain their profitability. This does not mean that they disregard in general the need to cater for the environment; only that this aim falls back in relation to the first two. The European Commission, to the contrary, as the key institution that monitors the internal market, places emphasis on competition and the proper function of the single energy market. Together with a proactive green agenda that aims at a de-carbonized economy and a cleaner and safer environment, it considers that security of supplies can only be achieved on the basis of a truly competitive market.

This is to a significant extent the result of differing competences. Governments have to ensure that their people enjoy steady flow of energy to cover their energy needs and that the national economy will further develop. They thus insist on retaining a central role in key negotiations with external suppliers in order to secure supplies and avoid energy shortages. As a result, external relations remain basically intergovernmental in nature. To the contrary, the European Commission enjoys a leading role in supervising the common market. This is a community, not a national competence and thus market regulations retain an intense supranational flavour. The same is true, albeit to a lesser degree, for environmental policy. Although the Commission and the Member States remain open to inter-institutional pressures and deliberations and at times proceed to policy compromises, in general one could argue that Member States determine the external front of energy policy, while the Commission orchestrates action with regard to the common market regulations and environmental policies. This dichotomy, however, is rather artificial and the lines between the external and internal dimensions are blurred. For one, the EU environmental policies are in line with commitments undertaken in international conventions. Moreover, while internal energy regulation bears an impact on external suppliers' operations in the common market, existing interdependencies have to be taken into account in all deliberations concerning the function of the internal market (Haghighi 2007). The case of Russia and the future role of Gazprom in the EU energy market is the most prominent example (see Chapters 4 and 5). Energy security thus is determined in both fronts through the interplay between Member States, the European Commission and the energy industry.

Empirical evidence pinpoints towards the dual conclusion that the three dimensions of energy security are not pursued in an equiponderant way; and that Member States retain a pivotal role in designing, implementing and monitoring energy security. These traits are not self-evidently positive. The point is increasingly made that the EU has to find a better balance both between the three aspects of energy security, as well as between the main actors. For example, environmental issues lag behind because they are seen as detrimental to economic efficiency at a time when the EU economy is underperforming and faces fierce external competition not only from established economic powers such as the US and Japan, but also from new rising centres, as, for example, China, Brazil and India. Increasing renewables in accordance with the 20 per cent target is an expensive option and thus seems to become gradually marginalized and substituted for by more mediocre goals. Indeed, renewables are estimated to increase only to 9 per cent of the total energy mix by 2030, well below the initial goal (Larsson 2007b: 17–18). To take another example, in the absence of alternatives to diversify away from Russian oil and gas, Poland reverted to increased coal use, thus going against EU-wide environmental goals of carbon emissions decrease. Furthermore, projections for 2015 are that gas consumption in the EU will be around 600–680 bcm (CIEP 2008: 66). The James Baker Institute World Gas Trade Model estimates that it will reach 700 bcm by 2020 and 770 bcm by 2030 (Jaffe and Soligo 2006: 441–4). Larsson (2007b: 9, 40) then has a valid point when arguing that emphasis is wrongly set on the increase of supplies rather than on energy efficiency and decrease of demand. 'Obsession with finding new inlets of gas overshadows the more important concerns of fuel switching and energy conservation.' Competitiveness and sustainable development seem to be sacrificed for enhanced security of supplies.

Coming to the predominance of state actors, the view that energy policy should become more of a shared than a national competence is widespread (Aalto 2006: 101–2, 121, Smith 2006: 2, Röller, Delgado and Friederiszick 2007: 25–7, 39–42). Indeed, the oxymoron for all scholarly work done on EU energy security is the contested character of the very term. The notion of EU energy security is a contradiction in terms since there are no supranational competences to decide on EU energy security. Member States retain a primary role, while it is national, not EU, energy security that is a national interest of Member States. This point is crucial since it carries important ramifications for EU solidarity in the energy sector (see Chapter 5). There is ample rhetoric on European energy security, but as yet not enough substance to it (Auer 2007). Although supranational institutions have acquired a significant role in the decision-making process, this is only true for some dimensions of energy security. As we saw above, others remain the exclusive province of Member States.

This, however, does not pose problems for our analysis, since in all systems of policy-making we find conflictive elements and approaches between the constituent parts. The discourse on EU energy security thus expands to the action undertaken by all stakeholders both at the national and supranational level that aims at ensuring security of supplies, economic competitiveness, affordable prices and environmental security.

Setting the Ground: The Gas Sector

Most economies, including that of the EU, are still based more on oil than on gas. The question then naturally emerges: why focus on gas? Initially, natural gas was given a boost by the first oil crisis of 1973 that revealed the Western world's sensitivity to oil imports from the Middle East. It served the need to hedge against unreliable oil producers and as a partial response to mounting fears for the end of oil. Contractual linkage of gas prices to those of oil was a means to retain gas prices at a lower level than oil and thus competitive. Within four decades natural gas has acquired a one fourth share in the EU gas market and according to estimations it will have jumped to 32 per cent of overall EU energy consumption by 2030 (Larsson 2007b: 17–18). Importantly, natural gas is much less of a pollutant than oil. In a world that has no choice but to face up to global climate change and substantially reduce carbon emissions, this asset is rather critical (Stern 2009a: 2). For these reasons, the importance of natural gas in energy security is set to further increase.

Oil vs. Natural Gas: Explaining the Locus

One cannot understand gas trade dynamics simply by reference to oil. According to Checchi, Behrens and Egenhofer (2009: 43), although natural gas and oil share some economic features, 'the concept of security of supply for natural gas is significantly at odds with the one used for oil'. IEA (2004, quoted by Checchi, Behrens and Egenhofer 2009: 14) defines security of gas supply as the 'capability to manage, for a given time, external market influences which cannot be balanced by the market itself' including 'the capacity to mobilize investment to develop supply and infrastructure as well as the insurance to ensure reliable supply'. We can discern six characteristics that make gas politics and economics deviate from those of oil (Hayes and Victor 2006, Helm 2007, Lesser et al. 2001):

- *Mostly pipeline-bound trade:* Contrary to oil trade that is mostly carried out through tankers crossing long distances, natural gas runs principally through pipelines. Less than 10 per cent of traded gas is shipped through tankers in LNG (or CNG) form.
- *Shortages more difficult to make up:* This creates limitations to the options of importers and exporters. Pipeline trade cultivates the dynamics of mutual dependence of the trading parties, rather than diversification and flexibility. While oil comes from multiple sources and through multiple corridors, gas comes from fewer sources and through a limited number of pipelines. When for any political, economic or technical reasons there are cuts on exports or imports, it is difficult for trade partners to find alternative sources to make up for these shortages.
- *A regional rather than a global market:* The result of the above is that there is as yet no unified global gas market, but a number of mainly regional markets. We can discern four main regional markets:
  - the Eurasian gas market spanning from Russia and North Africa to Norway and the westernmost country of the EU, Portugal;
  - the North American gas market of the US and Canada (comprising also Mexico and the Caribbean states);
  - the East Asian gas market with Indonesia and Malaysia supplying Japan and South Korea, and
  - the South American market embracing the sub-continent.

There are certain interconnections between these markets through LNG trade. Indonesia and Malaysia, for example, have occasionally supplied the US market as well; Nigeria is also an LNG supplier to the US; small LNG quantities from the Middle East have reached Britain; Russia, the traditional gas supplier of Europe, has agreed to send LNG to the US market. Nevertheless, gas trade remains primarily regional, rather than global.

- *Concentration of gas resources:* Oil reserves are unevenly allocated with the Middle East being the most endowed region. This is all the more true with regard to natural gas. Only one country, Russia, retains around one fourth of the total gas reserves. Iran comes second with 14 per cent. This high concentration of gas reserves makes diversification policies difficult to pursue and raises hurdles to the establishment and function of a global market.[3]

- *Contractual differences:* Oil is primarily sold on spot markets and negotiated on a day-to-day basis. Contracts are short-term usually spanning from three to six months. As we have already seen, on the other hand, gas trade takes place principally through long-term contracts (Müller-Kraenner 2008: 8). While in the North American gas market gas is sold in spot markets and contracts are quite short-term (spanning maximum a few years), in East Asia as well as in Europe gas trade is basically conducted on a long-term contracts basis. The duration of such contracts used to surpass two decades. The rationale behind such long-term agreements is that the exporter should enjoy security of demand for its gas in order to be able to invest both in exploration schemes and pipeline projects. These take-or-pay contracts define quantities and prices irrespective of whether the consumer will need all the gas quantities contracted. The contracts were signed by monopolistic companies of the exporter and importer countries. Contrary to the liberalized oil market, no new entrants were allowed into the market and no competition was at work (Egenhofer and Behrens 2008: 2). As we are going to see in more detail in the next chapter, the neo-liberal approach of the 1980s and 1990s has challenged this type of agreement that obstructs competition and allows no room for flexibility to adjust to changing energy needs. These changing perceptions have led to the reduction of the average duration of such contracts in Europe from 25 to 15 years (and gradually even less) and the progressive emergence of spot markets. At the same time, monopolies within the EU had to be dismantled thus allowing space for new companies to enter the market (Locatelli 2010: 2). While gas markets

---

3   One could, however, argue that with the most important supplier, Russia, stretching to two continents (the gas-rich eastern coast of which is not very distant from the western coast of Canada and the US), there is enough potential for a future global market. This, however, is only a prospect for the future; and one difficult to materialize if one takes into account domestic production considerations (see Chapter 5).

are being liberalized, however, gas trade still remains more regulated than oil trade. National champions retain a central role and entry barriers persist, not least due to problematic access to gas grids (Finon 2008, Buchan 2002: 108). The fundamentals of gas and oil trade thus still deviate.

•   The diverging economics of gas and oil trade: European gas prices have traditionally been contractually linked with those of oil. At the same time, however, gas sold in spot markets is priced autonomously from world oil prices. Hence, with the emergence of spot markets in Europe two distinct price mechanisms co-exist for gas-pricing in the EU market. A combination of developments[4] has brought gas prices down in contrast to soaring oil prices. Starting from late 2008 spot gas prices have been around half of those in oil-indexed long-term contracts. The main EU gas supplier itself, Gazprom, agreed to include up to 15 per cent of the spot gas-based prices in long-term contracts prices, beginning from 2010, in order to bridge this differential. Thus, a significant shift in market dynamics has taken place with gas economics increasingly determining gas prices (Stern 2009a: 6–12, Pirani, Stern and Yafimava 2010: 24, Holz, von Hirschhausen and Kemfert 2008). This double-pricing anomaly opens the discussion as to whether gas prices will continue to be oil-indexed, a double pricing mechanism will emerge or a move away from oil-linked to independent gas pricing will be established (as is long ago the case with the North American, but not the Pacific, regional gas market) (Stern 2007, 2009).

The EU's Gas Deficit

The European Union in general is not well-endowed with natural gas. Netherlands is the most important EU producer. The discovery of the Groningen fields in the early 1970s has led to the development of a vibrant Dutch gas market and export industry. Britain and Denmark also produced and exported gas to other EU Members. The former, however, has seen its production dwindle and now is a net importer of natural gas. Denmark, despite its small production base, has limited domestic gas consumption and thus exports gas to Sweden, Germany and the Netherlands (CIEP 2008: 42–4). Except for the promising recent discoveries of gas deposits offshore Cyprus (The Economist Intelligence Unit 2011), the other Member States have a very narrow gas production base. While the EU consumes more than 600 bcm of natural gas per year, less than half of them come from indigenous production.

---

4   These developments are the oversupply of Europe with LNG partly due to demand reduction in the Pacific and partly due to the surge of shale gas in the US that released more quantities for other markets, the increased regasification capacity in Britain and the falling demand for gas in Europe since the world economic recession in 2008.

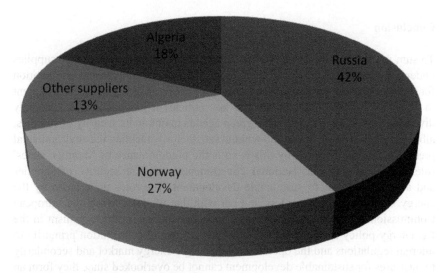

Figure 3.2   The EU's gas imports
Source: Ghiles 2009

For the rest of the gas it consumes, the EU is dependent on imports from foreign suppliers. Russia exports the lion's share to the EU with more than 150 bcm per year, which accounts for more than 40 per cent of total gas imports. Norway comes second with around 80 bcm per year capturing more than one fourth of the EU gas market. Algeria approaches a 20 per cent share of the market with exports of more than 50 bcm per year. Nigeria, Libya, Egypt, Qatar, Oman and Trinidad Tobago contribute together less than 50 bcm per year accounting for 13 per cent of total EU gas imports (Ghiles 2009).

Hence, an overarching concern of the EU is its overt dependence on external suppliers. This dependence is estimated to climb to extravagant numbers within the next two decades. IEA foresees that the EU will import 70 per cent of the gas it consumes by 2020 and more than 80 per cent by 2030 (Birol 2009). According to the James Baker Institute World Gas Trade Model, the EU production is set to decrease to around 150 bcm until 2030, while it will need more than 750 bcm of natural gas at the same year (Jaffe and Soligo 2006: 441–4). Although the global economic crisis and the subsequent stagnation of the European economy have put these estimations in different perspective, the EU is on the path to increasing its gas consumption and thus also its dependence on gas imports in the mid-term.

It is reasonable then that the EU retains a good network of relations with external suppliers in order to satisfy its gas needs. As we are going to see in more detail in Chapters 5 and 6, there is an established pipeline network linking producing countries with European markets and a number of new pipelines are already under construction or negotiation. The sheer size of the EU, around 450 million citizens that import more than 300 bcm per year, are a very attractive option for exporters.

Conclusion

To sum up, the EU faces the challenge how to secure adequate energy supplies under the adverse conditions of tightening global supply, increasing competition for resources, resource nationalism and the progressive inability of the environment to withstand further degradation. The key policies it has put in place, namely diversification, liberalization and a green agenda maintain its security of supplies, albeit at relatively high prices and without satisfactorily tackling the environmental predicament. One reason why this is so is the predominance of Member States' role in the energy field. National governments prioritize security of supplies and affordable prices to sustainable development. The roles undertaken by the energy industry are more or less in a par with that of states, while the European Commission has failed to significantly engender further supranationalism in the EU energy policy arena. Nevertheless, its fundamental contribution primarily to internal regulations and the operation of the single energy market and secondarily to measures for sustainable development cannot be overlooked since they form an integral part of overall EU efforts at achieving energy security.

The gas sector significantly deviates from that of oil and thus cannot be analysed under its umbrella. Since the EU is poor on gas, the EU's high import dependency rate and its increasing trends are rather alarming. For this reason, relations with external suppliers are of paramount importance. Before meticulously analysing EU relations with Russia, Algeria, Norway, the Middle East, the Caspian and more distant producers, we turn to profoundly examine the internal regulations of the EU gas market. This is crucial for three reasons: firstly, these regulations create new opportunities as well as threats for EU energy security in the gas sector; secondly, they (are intended to) serve as a shield of protection against existing and potential threats posed by the high import dependency rate; and, thirdly, they highly impact upon the EU's external energy relations.

Chapter 4
The Internal Front

In the previous chapter we elucidated that EU energy security has two dimensions, the external and the internal. This is also the case with gas security. While the external dimension refers to relations with third countries, principally gas suppliers and transit states, the internal includes the set of measures the EU undertakes to ensure the smooth function of its internal gas market. Once more, this distinction cannot but be artificial, since there is an obvious overlap between the two spheres. Internal regulation impacts upon relations with external suppliers, while developments originating outside the EU have serious ramifications for the function of the single energy market. Nevertheless, this distinction helps us categorize the main factors that determine EU energy security. We thus tackle the internal front in this chapter, while the external dimension is mainly covered in Chapters 5 and 6.

Since the 1990s the EU has been very active in reforming its gas market. Indeed, few of its pre-1990s characteristics have remained untouched. The progressive liberalization of the gas market, the establishment of multiple interconnections among national markets, the increased emphasis on common solutions to energy threats and the creation of joint crisis resolution mechanisms has brought significant changes in relations with suppliers, as well as with regard to gas volumes imported and prices charged to EU consumers. These changes are not finalized and the trajectory towards their implementation has all but been smooth and linear. Despite the shortcomings in their accomplishment and the missing links in the EU energy strategy in the gas sector, these developments have significantly altered the EU gas market. In this chapter, we also discuss policy proposals that have not translated into concrete action. However, they are important for ceding light to minority voices within the EU policy-making circles. Moreover, they may resurface providing significant roadmaps for action in the near future in case circumstances turn conducive. In sum, understanding the complexities of the EU gas market is a necessary prerequisite in order to appreciate the state of EU energy security in the gas sector. Moreover, it is an integral part of our understanding of the multifaceted relations the EU retains with external suppliers. This is especially so since the EU aims to project its internal regulatory model to its peripheral states with the intent to form a wider European gas market.

The Liberalization of the EU Gas Market: A Work in Progress

The neo-liberal economic orthodoxy has been dominant in Europe since the 1980s. The Single European Act re-launched European integration and set in motion the merging of national markets into a single one operating under the same rules. This also carried critical implications for the development of the EU gas market.

Röller, Delgado and Friederiszick summarize the main setbacks of natural gas markets underlining that (both oil and) gas:

> have a tendency towards regional fragmentation and a concentration of market power. This is due to ... the reliance on a physical network and low demand elasticity, together with product homogeneity and high entry cost ... these translate into the emergence of significant market power' for suppliers. 'Consumers cannot easily switch to alternative energy sources and supply is constrained by long lead times for planning and construction or access to network infrastructure (Röller, Delgado and Friederiszick 2007: 3–4).

In the pre-liberalization era, natural gas was exclusively sold at the border. State-owned national distributors signed contracts with external suppliers and enjoyed a monopoly in the supply of domestic customers. National distributors thus were in charge of ensuring security of supplies for the domestic population. Liberalization challenged these traditional market patterns. In particular, the term liberalization is rather broad and entails three parallel but not identical processes. The first is *deregulation* meaning that rigid rules set by the governments are removed and market dynamics, supply and demand, gain centre stage and determine gas volumes and prices. The second process is *privatization,* that is selling out (shares of) state-owned energy companies. This has extensively taken place as a means to increase efficiency. The third process, namely *liberalization,* refers to opening up entry to private corporate actors to operate and compete freely in the market. State enterprises can still operate in the market, but they can no more hold a monopoly as was the case beforehand (van Damme 2004: 1–20, 35–8).

In the 1990s and the 2000s the European Commission issued three directives for the liberalization of the gas market. These aimed a) to dismantle monopolistic forces that wrought competition and retained fragmented national gas markets, which were in favour of strong monopolistic distributors but worked to the detriment of final consumers and b) to create a single, unified gas market with multiple interconnections that would ensure security of supplies and affordable prices. The Third Energy Package, approved in 2009, aimed to deal with the shortcomings that resulted out of the patchy liberalization of some national markets and to further mitigate subsequent market distortions (European Commission 2009b).

In accordance with these reforms, new distributors were allowed into the market, including foreign suppliers that beforehand sold their gas exclusively at the border. Liberalization also enabled Member States' distributors to expand their operations beyond their national markets to those of other Member States as well. The operation of multiple distributors introduced the critical issue of access to the distribution networks. While in the pre-liberalization era national distributors filled the pipelines exclusively with their own gas, the new regulations resolved that all distributors should have access to the distribution networks, as well as to storage facilities. This would ensure that no market player is handicapped vis-à-vis its competitors. Non-discriminatory TPA thus became a distinguishing feature of the liberalized EU gas market (IEA 2000: 75–9).[1]

The reform of the gas market is based upon the idea that markets are efficient and more conducive to energy security. In this mindset, competition forms a shield against monopolistic structures and allows the smooth function of the market for a number of reasons:

- It ensures security of supplies since there are many providers operating in the market.
- This multiplicity of providers adds flexibility to the market, which is crucial in cases of emergency to withstand supply shortages.
- It normally brings prices down. It is important to remember here that affordable energy is a prerequisite for positive rates of growth, and
- It renders politically-motivated acts more difficult to materialize (Jaffe and Soligo 2006: 462, Finon and Locatelli 2007: 3).

Internal Controversies

Liberalization proposals have met with ambivalent responses. Although the market orthodoxy is widely shared within the EU, specifying the function of the gas market proved much more problematic. While the European Commission reform packages have been enthusiastically endorsed by some Member States, others are keen on retaining a semi-liberalized market (Wright 2006, Schmidt-Felzmann 2008: 67, Leonard and Popescu 2007: 26–50, Lohman 2006). The northern Members, such as Britain, Sweden and Denmark, have been among the most fervent supporters of liberalization. Indeed, Scandinavian states and Britain have liberalized their (electricity and) gas sectors and regulated TPA rights even before the European Commission issued the first directives after the mid-1990s (Heather 2010). This allowed new companies to enter the market boosting competition. This, in its turn, brought prices down and gave flexibility to the market. Especially since 2008 customers in these states have entertained much lower prices than in continental Europe. Due to increased supply and lesser demand there was abundant gas traded in spot markets with the effect of depressed prices, at the same time that in continental Europe long-term contracts signed by a few oligopolistic companies with external suppliers reflected oil prices that remained at high levels throughout that period (Stern 2009a, Helm 2007).

On the other hand, a handful of Member States, such as Germany and Italy among others, are reluctant to fully sanction liberalization and remain thus slow

---

1   Third party access can be either regulated or negotiated. While in the first case strict regulations exist *a priori* and determine all relevant issues (as, for example, the level of tariffs to be paid by the user to the operator), in the latter it is up to the participatory parts to agree on them.

to adjust. This is so for a number of reasons. In the case of the Baltic states, for example, it is feared that liberalization may give a free hand to Russian energy enterprises to operate in their market, a development running adversely to these states' fundamental interest of minimizing dependence on Russia and thus Russian leverage. Other Member States prefer to retain strong state-backed corporations to ensure energy security. According to this mindset, energy is a strategic public good and thus the market cannot be relied upon to ensure energy security; the state should remain involved in the market in order to ensure that no significant supply shortages arise. Customers, it is argued, should be protected by considerable fluctuations in prices, which are to be expected in unregulated gas markets. Relying exclusively on market mechanisms may mean lower prices at some periods but also higher prices in others, as was the case for some time in the North European states (Checchi, Behrens and Egenhofer 2009: 22–4, Wright 2006). Moreover, liberalization means the existence of a number of medium-size energy corporations. However, these have to negotiate contracts with behemoths like Gazprom and Sonatrach and this asymmetry of size and power can prove detrimental to the EU's energy security (CIEP 2010). The strong opposition of a number of Member States to full liberalization reflects their faith in the value of state-backed national champions that have the leverage to attract contracts from the main suppliers and to regulate efficiently the supply of their domestic market (albeit usually at higher costs for the consumers than is the case in thoroughly liberalized gas markets) (Röller, Delgado and Friederiszick 2007: 39–40).

This opposition raises the critical issue whether markets should be relied upon to determine energy security and what happens in case of failure. A number of scholars stress the point that market failures in the energy supply are frequent and harsh. In the actual world, 'when the assumptions of a perfectly competitive world break down', competition and efficiency are in friction (Weyman-Jones 1997: 565–6). While energy companies are now called upon to operate already existing infrastructure – that was financed by the public sector – it is debatable whether they will proceed to investments on further pipelines or prefer to free-ride expecting others, possibly once more the state, to construct them (Locatelli 2010: 10, Stern and Honore 2004). Since infrastructural capacity and investments are not guaranteed in a liberalized gas market, it remains vague where the blame will rest and who is going to act to reverse the situation, in cases of supply shortages or excessively high gas prices. Market liberalization is at odds with traditional notions of democracy and accountability (Checchi, Behrens and Egenhofer, 2009: 22–4; Egenhofer and Behrens, 2008: 5).

Contrary to this approach, the European Commission sees the predominant role of national champions as a great impediment to competition. Its antitrust services revealed in 2006 that a handful of them proceeded to secret agreements allocating among themselves market shares to the exclusion of third companies. Moreover, they were found guilty of illegally depriving other market players from access to the pipeline networks they owned and of monopolizing their use, despite their entrenched obligation to cede TPA for part of the pipelines' capacity. These violations are of paramount importance since in an increasingly interconnected market TPA is essential so that competition distortions and *de facto* oligopolistic structures are eclipsed.

These disclosures led the Commission to 'unbundling proposals to off-set the conflicting interests between energy generation and transmission' (Auer 2007). In particular, the Commission proposed the ownership unbundling of the companies that are both network owners and energy distributors in two totally independent economic entities. The one would operate the system and the other would trade energy. Alternatively, it has proposed the establishment of a totally independent system operator (ISO) (European Commission 2007, Deutsche Bank 2010, Cottier, Matteotti-Berkutova and Nartova 2010). A group of eight Members, however, under the leadership of France and Germany,[2] remained loath to these proposals and thus promoted a third alternative. Companies would be allowed to retain full ownership of their networks while a transmission system operator (TSO) would undertake investments for the modernization of the networks and monitor fair access to the pipelines. This operator, contrary to the second option, would not be independent but could remain under the same ownership structures, albeit being bound to comply with EU-wide regulations pertaining to TPA and modernization investments (Pollit 2008). The Commission eventually acquiesced to these proposals and incorporated them in the Third Energy Package in 2009 (European Commission 2009b). The end result was a softer version of unbundling that retains a significant place in the gas market for national champions (Haase 2008: 36, Goldirova 2008, Lohmann 2009).

As a result, liberalization has not been implemented uniformly. The European Commission's gas directives as to now remain incompletely enforced; competition is still distorted and state-controlled enterprises seem intent to continue to hold a major (albeit no more absolute) share of their domestic markets (Auer 2007). The 2007 Council of the European Union (2007: 16) statement that due to the non-implementation 'of the letter and spirit of existing Internal Market legislation relating to the opening up of the gas and electricity markets … a truly competitive, interconnected and single Europe-wide internal energy market that will have major benefits for competitiveness and EU consumers as well as increasing security of supply has not yet been achieved' is still more pertinent than not to the EU gas market.

As a result of the deregulation of the EU gas market, the price linkage of oil to gas is increasingly disputed. Although termination of oil-linked prices will not in itself induce more competition (and lower prices), increased competition has created the dynamics for different pricing mechanisms. The more competitive a market becomes, the more irrelevant oil price indexation becomes and the harder energy utilities will find it to forego market dynamics and force arbitrary prices. The opening up of the EU gas market to global LNG competition further refutes the oil-linkage rationale since LNG prices are determined by market dynamics.

---

2   The other six Members are Austria, Bulgaria, Greece, Luxemburg, Latvia and the Slovak Republic.

Retaining high oil-linked gas prices hence is futile since it guarantees destruction demand, a development running to the detriment of all parties involved in gas trade. This constitutes an important driver for de-linkage from oil (Stern 2007: 23–34).

The dilemma then for the EU is whether to scrap or maintain the contractual linkage between oil and gas. While North European Member States view competition as a panacea and oil-linked prices as an absurdity in a liberalized gas market, other Member States praise the low fluctuation rates of oil-linked prices. Most energy utilities in Central, Eastern and Southern Europe are comfortable with the current pricing system as they retain their market power and high margins of profits (Stern 2009, Utility Week 2009). They also cite the danger of further liberalization resulting in export giants like Gazprom and Sonatrach controlling prices. Even worse, in the case of the formation of a gas OPEC (see Chapter 5) this would mean arbitrary prices set by a gas cartel (Stern 2007: 22, 2009: 4–5). While today's double-pricing mechanism is problematic, the EU is hesitant to form an alternative gas-based pricing system.

Alternative Voices beyond Liberalization

As absurd as it may sound, the deregulation and liberalization of the gas market have been accompanied by protectionist plans. These developments cannot be understood but with close relation to Russia's domineering stance as the principal supplier, its reluctance to fully comply with free-market regulations, the inadequacies of the liberalization project to deal with the threats Gazprom is perceived to set for the energy security of some Member States, as well as the potential of liberalization to become a means for Gazprom's further penetration into the EU gas market (see Chapter 5). In this context, the European Commission, after deliberations with East European Members, has designated and presented a new, rather protectionist plan for relations with exporters. Crucially, this plan aims to exclude the European energy sector from the domain of the free market and to define it as a strategic sector. This framing enables the enforcement of measures that run contrary to the EU's neo-liberal mindset, but are considered necessary and effective in thwarting external threats that may impinge upon the EU's energy security (Goldirova 2007).

According to the Commission's proposals, the EU would follow a protectionist policy in order to forbid Gazprom to acquire a greater role in the EU gas market. Russian energy companies would be allowed to buy into European ones only if they open up their own assets to European firms (Buchan 2007). Reciprocity, not free-market regulations would become the cornerstone of their energy trade. The plan aimed to push Russia to instigate the reform of its domestic gas sector as a prerequisite for being allowed to compete in the lucrative European gas market. The application of this regulation would not be limited to Gazprom, but would apply to any non-EU firm does not follow the rules of the game within the EU gas market.

Nevertheless, this plan is difficult to materialize for a number of reasons. Northern Member States will never accept protectionist measures, if only as a matter of principle. They hold a deeply-embedded belief in the orthodoxy of open markets and the defects of protectionist economic policies. Furthermore, Gazprom entertains the support of core EU Member States and powerful European energy companies that closely cooperate with it. For these reasons, although Gazprom's energy strategy creates fertile ground for the development of protectionist policies, it seems that they remain a remote scenario for the EU gas market. The EU's concerns about Gazprom's preponderant role are much more plausibly going to be projected through the advent of free-market regulations that alter the rules of the game in the EU gas market and hence raise obstacles to Gazprom's operation in it (see Chapter 5).

A further proposal for ensuring energy security in the gas sector refers to the creation of an EU-wide gas operator. This suggestion reflects concerns for full liberalization and utilizes insights for the need for powerful market players, but situates them at the supranational, not the national level. In particular, the underlying assumption is that while national champions may be potent to provide energy security, this is not always the case since not all national champions carry the same weight. While German and French national champions, for example, are powerful, Polish and Lithuanian ones are not. This is so due to their diverse political might and leverage and the non-equiponderant size of their domestic market. As a result, the current EU gas regulatory framework is more conducive to German and French, but not to Polish or Lithuanian energy security.

This liability can be tackled with through the substitution of national champions with an EU-wide operator that would equally cater for the energy security interests of all EU citizens. Proponents of this option make the argument that the EU's market power is its strong card and should be fully exploited, especially since in its gas trade it has to deal with giant, vertically integrated companies. For the time being this card is underplayed since contracts are negotiated at a national, not EU level. A number of advantages spring from such an approach (de Jong 2008: 58). In particular:

- First of all, an EU-wide authority would not be bullied by any supplier as has been the case, for example, with Gazprom's blackmailing policies vis-à-vis Lithuania and Poland (Aalto 2006: 101–2, 121, Orttung 2006: 29–30, Smith 2006: 2, Pleines 2006: 58–9). It would be rather audacious for any supplier to attempt to play political games vis-à-vis an authority that represents the energy security interests of a single market comprising 450 million consumers.
- This authority would be much more efficient in negotiating gas volumes, thus facilitating security of supplies.
- It would also be in a position to achieve better prices due to its quasi-monopsonistic role. This is a crucial point because lower energy prices act as a boost for the industry and will serve to improve the European economy's global competitiveness, especially under current circumstances of economic hardship (Röller, Delgado and Friederiszick 2007: 25–7, 39–42).

• Finally, it would allocate resources efficiently. This would facilitate EU solidarity in the energy sector, in the same way that structural funds have contributed to the cohesion of the EU.

This top-management model is quite adverse to EU economics and runs contrary to the liberalization project of the last decades. It hence stands little chance of being enforced. Needless to say, beyond the former communist new Members that feel energy insecure and thus support such collective schemes, the majority of Member States refuse to contemplate this option. This is so because they are loath not only to reverse the liberalization scheme, but also to surrender any further competences to supranational authorities. The critics of the proposal make the point that states stand only to lose by the creation of such a central mechanism to manage the EU's energy security since national policy-makers have a much clearer perspective of the issues at hand than would some bureaucrats in Brussels. Whenever Member States' interests are congruent or they face identical threats, the argument continues, they can coordinate their policies in the European fora, the Council of Ministers and the European Council, in order to devise collective policies. In this mindset, an ad hoc supranational mechanism is not only unnecessary and difficult to materialize, but might also negatively impact upon the EU's energy security (de Jong 2007: 58).

Interconnected Europe: Constructing an EU-wide Gas Pipeline Network

A fundamental prerequisite for the function of the single market is its interconnectedness. Nevertheless, the emphasis has been foremost on regulatory issues rather than on enhancing the technical interconnection of national grids. The most important existing interconnections are those linking the British market with the Belgian and the Dutch ones. While further interconnections exist between Member States, these are few and limited to Central Europe. There is hence an urgent need to build an EU-wide gas network. The problem of inadequate interconnections was especially highlighted during the Russo-Ukrainian crisis of 2009 that led to the suspension of supplies of Russian gas to a number of European Member States (see Chapter 5). As a result, most of them suffered supply shortages since they were not connected to alternative infrastructure that would allow them to be supplied by other exporters (European Commission 2011c).

The EU has recently moved to respond to these shortcomings. It has set the goal to establish a well-interconnected market by 2014 with no national market forming an energy island by 2015 (European Commission 2011c, Tindale 2011). The global economic crisis and the ensuing adverse investment climate have prompted the EU to inaugurate an ambitious plan to finance interconnectivity itself in the fear that market forces will fail to deliver such goals. To this cause, the European Energy Recovery Program (EERP), with an initial budget of 200 billion Euros, has been devised calling for 'coordinated national action, complemented by direct EU action, aimed at injecting purchasing power and boosting demand in the economy' (European Commission 2010c). Sixty per cent of the total financing is devoted to the interconnection of the EU gas and electricity market. The goal is 'to build the infrastructure needed to allow gas from any source to be bought and sold anywhere in the EU, regardless of national boundaries. This would also ensure security of demand by providing for more choice and a bigger market for gas producers to sell their products', thus enhancing EU energy security in the gas sector (European Commission, DG Energy 2011: 13).

In particular, the following projects have been decided upon:

- Ensuring reverse capacity in existing pipelines in Portugal, Romania, Austria, Slovakia, the Czech Republic, Hungary, Latvia, Lithuania and Poland 'to allow cooperation and gas trading in both directions with adjacent countries and, by extension, with more distant countries' (European Commission 2010c: 4).
- The construction of new region-wide interconnector pipelines, as well as the modernization of older ones. The main pipeline networks targeted are the Iberian one, linking Portugal, Spain and France in a bi-directional capacity; the Central–Northern European one, linking Germany, Belgium and the UK also in a bidirectional capacity; the Balkan–Central European one, linking Romania, Bulgaria, Greece, Italy, Slovakia and Hungary also in a bi-directional capacity; and, lastly, the Baltic one, linking the Baltic countries, Poland, Denmark and Germany also in a bidirectional capacity. This last interconnection is highly critical, since Poland and the Baltic states are among the most dependent Member States on a single source of gas. Its accomplishment would finalize one of the main priorities of EU energy security, the integration of the Baltic states into the EU energy market (European Commission, DG Energy 2008).
- In addition, the program targets to enhance the EU's overall import capacity by 50 bcm by means of co-financing import pipelines and storage facilities. Priority is given to the construction of the Nabucco pipeline that is designed to bring natural gas from the Caspian and the Middle East to Turkey and from there to Balkan and Central European Members; to the construction of the Interconnector Turkey–Greece–Italy (ITGI) that will bring Azeri gas through Turkey to Greece and Italy; to the construction of the GALSI pipeline linking Algeria to Italy; and to the establishment of new LNG terminals in Poland and Cyprus (see Chapters 5 and 6) (European Commission 2010c, European Commission 2011b).

Gas Security Regulation

As analysed in Chapter 3, Member States retain a pivotal role in determining their energy security strategy. It is within this framework that they long remained

Table 4.1   New gas interconnections designed

Pipeline	Countries involved
Iberian	Portugal, Spain and France
Central–Northern European	Germany, Belgium and the UK
Balkan–Central European	Romania, Bulgaria, Greece, Italy, Slovakia and Hungary
Baltic	The Baltic countries, Poland, Denmark and Germany

Source: European Commission 2010c

reluctant to cede to the Commission the management of their national energy strategic reserves that they (as members of IEA) hold in case of an emergency. When in 2007 the European Commission suggested the creation of an EU-wide energy policy on securing and diversifying energy supplies, as well as a crisis response mechanism, the European Council thwarted the proposals and instead promoted measures of more efficient coordination within the EU. As Egenhofer and Behrens (2008: 5) put it, 'the European Council stripped the European Commission of its more ambitious aspirations beyond better coordination'.

Nevertheless, Member States have belatedly adopted a more holistic approach towards energy security in the understanding that the more the single gas market is cemented, the greater the need to bolster supranational monitoring. The functional logic thus slowly works in favour of the transfer of more competencies to supranational institutions. In this context, the gas security regulation adopted in 2010 is a significant step forward towards both strengthening the supranational level, as well as fortifying the state of EU energy security (European Commission 2010b, Tsakiris 2011).

In the pre-liberalization era, Member States could only respond to reduced gas supplies through diversification, namely contracting more supplies from alternative providers (and switching capacity). Nevertheless, due to the rigid nature of gas infrastructure this was not always possible. The gradual function of a single, interconnected EU gas market, as we saw in the previous subchapter, will allow a further policy tool to come into play. Member States facing supply shortages will be able to be provided within the common market through alternative suppliers. Indeed, in accordance with the solidarity principle, Member States have the obligation to channel extra supplies to any Member State facing supply shortages. In this sense, liberalization serves as a facilitator to EU energy security.

On a twist of the argument, however, national markets now become more interdependent meaning that supply problems in one country may impact upon the security of supply of other Member States as well and, by extension, act to the detriment of the common gas market. The fact that Member States retain ample leverage to determine their energy strategy also means that national actions may have adverse consequences for EU-wide energy security. In order to allay that risk the European Commission has initiated legislation that will monitor security of supply providing 'for solidarity and coordination in response to supply crises' (European Commission 2010b: 2). In particular, this new legislation aims at improving coordination between Member States and the Commission, facilitating the optimal function of the EU-wide gas network and bringing more reliability and security to the EU gas market (European Commission 2010b).

In this context, national regulatory authorities of Member States are mandated to draw national plans assessing their state of energy security. These plans, starting from 2012, will have to be renewed every two years and are subject to the approval of the European Commission. The Commission retains the right to ask from states to review them in case it does not agree with their assessments. At the same time, these plans should provide reliable data for the capacity of the pipeline networks to cater for the needs of the single market, thus allowing the Commission to monitor and coordinate its function. In these plans caution is also taken that gas holdings equivalent of 30 days of consumption are reserved in case of an emergency.

Moreover, national plans sketch out existing and potential threats and devise various crisis preventive and emergency mechanisms to tackle with imminent challenges. In particular, depending on the estimated seriousness of the threat, these mechanisms operate at the early warning, alert and emergency level:

- The early warning mechanism is activated when there is the need to draw attention on the serious possibility that certain events may infringe upon security of supplies.
- The alert level is activated when supply shortages take place either due to supply disruptions or due to exceptionally high gas demand or both. In this case, however, market mechanisms are considered adequate to respond to the threats at hand.
- The emergency level is activated in a similar case to the previous one but only after the implementation of market measures has failed to tackle the deteriorating state of energy security and non-market mechanisms have to be brought into play (European Commission 2010b, Tsakiris 2011).

These mechanisms, albeit devised at the national level, have to be congruent with the state of play in the other national markets. The European Commission bears the responsibility to coordinate national plans so that they do not contradict each other and contribute to EU gas security. Furthermore, depending on the situation, regional or EU-wide plans are devised under the auspices of the European Commission to deal with challenges operating at the corresponding level. In other words, a joint security regulation mechanism has been established and the role of the European Commission has been significantly advanced reflecting the changing needs of the unified EU gas market.

The Missing Link: Promoting the EU's Internal Regulatory Model Abroad

The EU has also been at pains to project its internal regulatory model as the cornerstone of its external energy policy (Youngs 2007, Haghighi 2007). This translates into concerted action to embed its own values, norms and legal regulatory regime to peripheral states, as well as to strengthen institutional structures at the global level and, by extension, solidify cooperation with both importing and exporting countries. This is seen as an essential step to mitigate the risks emanating from the diverging interests and values of third states in the energy sector.

Starting with the global level, the European Commission (2006b) suggests that the EU should integrate its energy policy into a more holistic framework and project its energy interests in wider global fora. It thus proposes to integrate the EU's goals in the energy sector and the means by which these are to be pursued, into its well-developed trade policy and to link them to the WTO. Another forum that could be put into good to the same cause is the G8. Of particular importance here could be the G8+5 mechanism that includes the rising global actors Brazil, China, India and South Africa, as well as energy-rich Mexico. This forum could enhance deliberations among these actors and the EU and hence contribute to a more profound mutual understanding of the interconnected energy and environmental challenges the world faces. In the same context, the EU should also facilitate China's and India's incorporation into IEA, so that it becomes more representative and more potent to monitor the energy markets. Lastly, the endorsement of an international agreement on energy efficiency, energy conservation and savings and a greener fuel mix would also be an initiative towards the right direction.

Going to the regional level, the EU aims to implant its market-based energy regulatory framework on its periphery. The goal is the creation of a well-interconnected wider European area, where energy can be produced, traded and consumed freely according to well entrenched market rules. This constitutes a good

> example of the EU reproducing its own constituent norms – now widely recognized as central to the EU's international identity. It would be exaggerated to say that the aim is a wholesale export of the internal market, but the logic is to extend as many of its rules as are political and economically feasible outside EU structures (Youngs 2007: 2).

The unbundling regulation also has an essential external component, namely to discipline exporters into acquiescing to internal EU regulation and thus pave the way for the reform of their energy sector.

In this context, in 2005 the EU signed with Albania, Croatia, Serbia, Bosnia and Herzegovina, Montenegro, FYROM and the United Nations Interim Administration Mission acting on behalf of Kosovo the Energy Community Treaty that established the Energy Community. Its goal is to create a stable energy framework that will eventually lead to the formation of an integrated market in Southeastern Europe (European Commission 2011d). This did not constitute an especially problematic development, if one bears in mind that these states hold the target of eventually entering the EU and are thus not reluctant to incorporate the EU *acquis*. The EU also aims to expand the Energy Community Treaty to the European Economic Area

(EEA)[3] and European Neighbourhood Policy (ENP)[4] countries. Moldova and Ukraine acceded to the Community in 2010 and 2011 respectively. Before this target is accomplished for the whole region, however, a lot of work is needed upon regulatory convergence so that competition is ensured, the investment climate significantly improves and environmental protection and safety standards are harmonized. In particular with regard to the southern members of the ENP, the Commission's Mediterranean aid program up to 2013 defines as central goals the integration of the North African regional energy market into that of the EU and the extension of the Energy Community Treaty to the region (Wyciszkiewicz 2008).

Going to the ex-Soviet space, since 2007 and the incorporation of two Black Sea countries into the EU, Bulgaria and Romania, the EU has developed its Black Sea Synergy (European Commission 2007d), a multifaceted policy framework with a distinct energy pillar. This new framework has the goal to instil the EU regulatory model in this region and integrate it into the EU market. In 2004 the EU had inaugurated the Baku initiative, which aimed to bolster energy sector reform in the Caspian and Central Asian region. The aim was to create the necessary interconnections between these regions and the EU market and, once more, to integrate their markets. In return for proceeding to market reforms, as well as guaranteeing supplies to the EU market, the Caspian states were to attract significant sums that would allow them to invest in their natural resources. Complementary to the above, the EU devised in 2007 a new strategy vis-à-vis Central Asia with two main goals, to expand the regulatory framework of the internal market to the region and to support the implementation of new pipelines that would carry natural gas to the EU (Youngs 2007: 3–4, Wyciszkiewicz 2008).[5]

Lastly, the EU has also established the goal for the African markets to move towards its own regulatory model. Nevertheless, progress towards this goal is rather slow in the understanding that priority should be given to the eradication of energy poverty in the region. To this aim, emphasis is given on promoting interconnections that will enhance the supply of the most deprived regions and will thus ameliorate energy poverty. Finally, provisions for energy security are incorporated into overall poverty reduction programs (Youngs 2007).

Relevant not only to Africa, but also to the Caspian and the Central Asian regions is the Extractives Industry Transparency Initiative, undertaken in 2002

---

3 The EEA countries are Iceland, Lichtenstein and Norway.

4 The ENP group comprises countries in North Africa and the Middle East, as well as ex-Soviet states, namely Algeria, Armenia, Azerbaijan, Belarus, Egypt, Georgia, Israel, Jordan, Lebanon, Libya, Moldova, Morocco, Occupied Palestinian Territory, Syria, Tunisia and Ukraine.

5 Besides these interregional initiatives, the EU has also signed bilateral energy agreements with Ukraine, Azerbaijan and Kazakhstan in 2005–2006 and has offered similar packages to Algeria and Egypt. Some progress has been noted in Azerbaijan, which agreed to the adoption both of an independent energy regulatory authority and independent transmission system operators in line with EU regulations, see Youngs 2007.

by then British Prime Minister Tony Blair at the World Summit for Sustainable Development. The initiative aimed to introduce transparency in the operations of energy companies and specifically in their deals with state officials with the proclaimed goal to reduce bribery. It signals a significant link between energy policy and good governance structures and aims to combat resource-linked corruption in energy-rich states (Ocheje 2006).

Shortcomings and Policy Proposals

The project of exporting the internal market model, however, clearly has its limits. It is inherently inadequate since not all states are like-minded and believe in the capacity of the market to regulate most efficiently the energy sector. To the contrary, energy is a public good and thus many peripheral states view it as essential to retain it under strong public auspices, rather than allow the market utter freedom. Another contesting view is that market liberalization is mostly conducive to importers' interests, since it maximizes production and ensures the security of supplies for consumers at the same time that it is likely to reduce prices; to the contrary, exporters are more likely to entertain lower profits from lower prices, face fiercer competition and have thus to produce at greatest capacities accelerating this way the pace of their natural resources depletion (Bradshaw 2006: 151, Fredholm 2004: 5, Gorst 2004: 8, Chufrin 2004: 18, CIEP 2004: 15–16).

The patchy development of the ECT and Russia's persistent reluctance to ratify it pinpoint toward the different rationales and highlight the difficulties the EU faces in promoting its regulatory model abroad (European Commission 2004: 2, Hirman 2001: 91). The EU now endeavours to persuade Russia to accept as many of the provisions of the ECT as possible in a new Partnership and Cooperation Agreement. This begs the question to what degree the EU can compromise its regulatory standards to accommodate difficult but essential energy partners.

While one could argue that Russia poses a special case due to its status both as a predominant supplier as well as a great power, it is evident that EU attempts to spread its regulatory model to the other peripheral states have met with extensive resistance, thus vindicating the more general observation that the EU's persuasive power dwindles when not matched by the carrot of integration. Contrary to the Balkan states that are welcome within the EU in case they fulfil the relevant criteria, most other peripheral states comprehend that admission to the EU is a far-fetched, if not altogether implausible, prospect. It is not uncorrelated that little progress has been achieved in the adoption of the EU legal energy framework by non-Balkan states. EU deliberations with the OPEC group have proliferated, as is the case with the GCC as well (Nonneman 2007). While discussions between the EU and the GCC on the establishment of a free trade arena have been ongoing for eighteen years, however, little progress has been achieved. Espousing the energy acquis thus also remains a remote possibility for these states (Echagüe 2007). Caspian exporters are also quite hesitant to embrace the free-market rationale. Indeed, they can hardly see the point in initiating costly energy market reforms, since they are already significant suppliers with much leverage in energy-hungry markets. Instead of yielding to liberalization reforms, they ask for more solid strategic ties with the EU, coupled with guarantees for security of demand and specific contracts (Gault 2007).

In parallel, as we saw in Chapter 1, energy politics is tightly interconnected with wider political concerns. This implies that the EU external energy policy would stand to benefit by its politicization (Gault 2004). Nevertheless, the EU foreign policy structure, albeit symbolically fortified by the establishment of a position for the Minister of Foreign Affairs of the Union and of the European External Action Service, does not seem well placed to tackle these issues. Foreign policy remains an essentially national competence, with only coordinative action of an intergovernmental character taking place at the EU level. Cohesion, solidarity and a single voice are in many cases absent from the EU's foreign policy even twenty years after the creation of the Common Foreign and Security Policy (Sjursen 1998, Hoffmann 2000, Peterson and Sjursen 1998). In this context, the EU foreign policy in the energy sector is an amalgam of the projection of its common market regulatory framework backed up by the individual priorities, interests and initiatives of Member States. The EU thus seems to 'hover ineffectively *between* markets and geopolitics, where it needs more effectively to *conjoin* these two necessary strands of energy security' (Youngs 2007: 1).

The reluctance of the EU to back its energy diplomacy with well entrenched foreign policy proposals and actions pinpoints to the EU's eagerness deficit to proceed united. While what the EU is in dire need of is a single European voice in global and regional energy and environmental governance structures, Member States remain firmly attached to their own seats in the international institutions where significant energy issues are discussed (Cameron 2010: 3). At the same time, many analysts make the point that the EU should review its lightly securitized agenda in energy issues. Some even suggest that the EU should follow the example of the US that views any impingement upon its energy security as a threat to its national security and thus reserves for itself the full range of policy instruments to tackle with it. The French proposal for the creation of a position of an Energy Special Representative was a move towards this direction and would give flesh to a more dynamic EU external energy policy. Such a development, nevertheless, runs the danger of contradicting the Commission's free-market rationale and of leading to an emphatically geopolitical approach that would hamper the EU's positive image abroad as a pacifist entity (Youngs 2007: 5–7).

In this context, it is not obscure that the EU external energy policy is predominantly based on bilateral deals and that the EU has as yet failed to create a wider open regional market (Haghighi 2007, Youngs 2007, Wyciszkiewicz 2008). What seems to be the missing link is a more holistic framework that will integrate the economic, political and developmental dimensions into the EU energy strategy. Firstly, issues such as stability and peace-making, democracy and human rights should be thoroughly and consistently linked with energy policy goals. Political stability is a necessary prerequisite for energy supply and the smooth function of the energy market. It should thus be pursued in close conjunction with more specific energy goals. Caution, however, should be taken that foreign policy in energy issues remains within the normative framework of the pacifist, compromising and conciliatory nature that distinguishes the EU and does not involve military instruments that may act as a boomerang to overall EU goals. Furthermore, the EU should enhance its economic cooperation with peripheral European states. Developmental policies and goals should be integrated in the EU's external energy policy. Many of the energy-rich countries are underdeveloped economies with poor economic (as well as political and social) governance structures. The role of the EU in boosting their economic performance and living standards is critical for both normative and practical reasons. The target should not be solely improvement of the investment climate; it would be much more prudent for the EU to aim both at strengthening broad economic ties, as well as at upgrading the welfare level of energy-producing states. This would enhance their capacity to proceed to investments in the energy sector, thus contributing both to their own energy security as well as to the EU's. The EU should operate in the understanding that its energy security depends to a significant extent upon the development and well-being of the peripheral states and their populations (Haghighi 2007: 381–417).

In order for these bits and pieces to be put together, however, a necessary prerequisite is that the EU appreciates

> the necessity of genuine investment ... in the goal of regional integration. While not always politically expedient, national governments would be wise to put the long-term goal of cooperation above more immediate domestic priorities. More importantly, if integration is to succeed, governments and publics should believe that it is in their vital national interest (Cameron 2010: 5).

Conclusion

To sum up, liberalization has been a dominant process of reforming the EU gas market with the aim to add flexibility, facilitate security of supplies through the operation of multiple providers and bring gas prices down. Nevertheless, this neo-liberal orthodoxy is not equally shared by all Member States and thus progress has been patchy. Competition remains at times distorted, while national champions retain an important share of the market and thus substantial leverage. The EU's plans to create a well-interconnected gas market until 2014 is a necessary complement to the deregulation and liberalization of the gas market, will facilitate diversification of supplies and will contribute to the smooth function of the single market.

This development has created the need for gas security regulations at the supranational level. According to the new legislation, national regulatory authorities of energy have to draw national plans that are to be approved by the European Commission. The Commission retains responsibility for coordinating national actions and for monitoring the operation of both the gas market and the distribution networks. At the same time, preventive and emergency mechanisms are put in place to signal in time and avert any supply shortages through both market and non-market instruments depending on the seriousness of the danger posed.

Finally, the EU comprehends that due to its already high import dependency rate, which is projected to further rise in the near future, relations with exporters are of paramount importance. To this cause, it aims to export its energy regulatory model to its periphery with little, however, success up to now, the establishment of the Energy Community Treaty notwithstanding. Unless energy policy is integrated with the wider political, economic and developmental policies of the EU, it is hard to see how the EU will be able to create a wider open gas market that will facilitate its own energy security. In the absence of a holistic EU energy policy framework, bilateral relations between EU Member States and external suppliers figure prominently in the energy security equation. It is to this we now turn to, starting with the preponderant gas supplier, Russia.

Chapter 5
Relations with Russia

Russia is the single most important supplier of the EU. In 2008 it exported more than 155 bcm to the EU,[1] accounting for around half of total EU gas imports (Chyong, Noël and Reiner 2010: 26). Although these quantities have declined during the last two years due to economic recession in Europe, Gazprom remains by far the most prominent EU supplier. This trade cooperation goes back to the 1970s. The Soviet Union constructed long pipelines in order to bring gas to its communist allies of Eastern Europe, namely Poland, Czechoslovakia and Hungary (the Baltic states were at that time integrated in the internal Soviet pipeline system). As a result of their Soviet heritage, these countries nowadays have an overt dependence on Russian gas that in some cases reaches 100 per cent. These pipelines were gradually extended up to France in the west and up to Greece in the south enabling Gazprom to become a supplier of most European states (Wybrew-Bond 1999: 7). After the fall of the Soviet Union, Russia inherited the contracts with European states and the obligation to fulfil them. The fall of domestic demand within Russia and the former Soviet states allowed more gas to flow into the core EU states. At that point Russia was no more seen as a Cold War enemy and even US concerns as to dependence on Russian gas were significantly relaxed. Switch to gas was considered a positive functional diversification to reduce dependence on the volatile Middle East, cheaper and much more environmentally-friendly than oil (Campaner 2007: 2, Stern 1999: 141–53, 172, Wybrew-Bond 1999: 7).

The bulk of the Russian gas is transmitted to Europe through the Druzhba pipeline (Map 5.1). The capacity of the pipeline is 175 bcm per year, albeit for technical reasons it carries around 135 bcm annually. An internal pipeline system brings gas mainly from the Nadym–Pur–Taz region and supplies a number of pipeline branches: from the Ukraine to Poland; from Belarus and the Ukraine to Slovakia and Hungary; and from the Ukraine towards Moldova, Romania, Bulgaria, Turkey and Greece. The northern branch brings gas to the Baltic states and to Northwestern Europe through Belarus.

The availability of Russian gas in the 1990s and the rising demand in Europe led to the construction of a new pipeline, linking Russia and Europe through Belarus. The Yamal–Europe pipeline was named after the gas-rich region of Yamal, from which this pipeline would be supplied. Nevertheless, exploration schemes are significantly delayed and the pipeline still carries gas drilled from mature fields in Western Siberia. The Yamal pipeline (Map 5.1) has an annual capacity of more than 20 bcm and brings

---

1 These data are only for the EU27, not for Europe in general. Hence supplies to Turkey, Serbia, Croatia, Bosnia-Herzegovina, FYROM and Switzerland are not included.

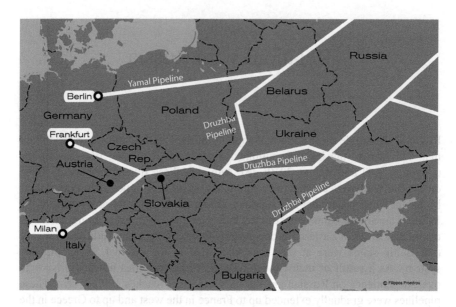

Map 5.1   The Druzhba and Yamal–Europe pipelines
Source: Author's map

gas to Poland and Germany. It was constructed in late 1999 and forms a significant source of route – not source – diversification for both the EU and Russia.

This decades-long cooperation between the EU and Russia is mutually beneficial for both. Russia has ensured high revenues that allowed it to repay international lenders well before due time and brought economic stability in the country. The EU, on the other hand, covers its energy needs and avoids a dangerously excessive dependence on the Middle East. Their relation thus is one of interdependence. This is so because while the EU is dependent on Russian gas for a bit less than half of its total gas imports and a number of EU states are overly dependent on Russian gas, Russia is also dependent on the EU market since two thirds of Russian gas exports are absorbed by the EU market (the rest supply the non-EU Europe as, for example, Ukraine and Belarus) (BP 2008, EU Energy Commissioner 2006). This absence of viable alternatives for both sides forms the cornerstone of their gas trade.

Although this mutual dependence creates the ground for steady cooperation, the liabilities of overt dependence remain. Former Soviet satellites now within the EU, as well as a series of other states (such as Austria, Greece and Slovenia) depend extravagantly on Russian gas. This dependence constitutes a potential threat than can undermine their energy security. Hence the EU–Russia energy relations are characterized by an *energy security dilemma*. The fear of both entities that one might diversify its imports/markets pushes the other to follow the same logic. Thus, a rupture in their energy cooperation may become a self-fulfilling prophecy, although this is the least optimal outcome for either of them. The challenge for the

Table 5.1   EU imports of natural gas from Russia (pipeline trade in bcm)

	Imports from Russia (in bcm)	% of overall imports
Austria	5.6	75
Belgium	0.5	2.5
Bulgaria	3.1	100
Czech Republic	6.4	80
Finland	4.3	100
France	7.6	22
Germany	35.5	40
Greece	2.8	82
Hungary	7.8	75
Italy	23.8	35
Latvia	1.6	100
Lithuania	3.4	100
Netherlands	2.3	13
Poland	6.2	66
Romania	2.5	48
Slovakia	5.8	100
Slovenia	0.5	50

Source: BP 2008, Losoncz 2006

EU and Russia is to regulate efficiently their energy relations and build up trust so that they can evade mishaps in their gas trade. Before discussing the main policies of the EU vis-à-vis Russia, we first have to shed light on Russia's energy strategy, tactics and main interests in Europe.

Russian Gas Strategy in the EU

Russia's economy is heavily dependent on fossil fuels, both oil and gas. Around one third of its growth can be attributed to the immense oil and natural gas price hikes since the early 2000s. Oil and gas production accounts for more than 20 per cent of Russia's current GDP, while more than half of total export revenues since 2003 came from these two resources. Russia's significant foreign exchange reserves have been built up mainly by energy-born revenues (Rousseau 2010). All the above make clear that profits from energy exports are of fundamental importance for Russia's economic survival and prosperity.

Gazprom is Russia's gas export monopoly.[2] Hence, the Russian gas strategy in Europe is formulated and carried out by Gazprom. Since the Russian state has

---

2   Itera was the only Russian company that was allowed to sell gas to foreign markets. However, it seems that Gazprom officials were behind Itera and transferred illegally Gazprom's assets to the company in order to acquire high revenues for themselves, see Shelley 2003.

a 51 per cent in the company and six out of the eleven members of its executive board are state officials, it is the Kremlin that has a first say in the formulation of the corporate strategy. Former President and current Prime Minister Vladimir Putin (quoted in Gallis 2006) has acknowledged that Gazprom is an important lever of Russian political and economic influence in the world. That means that foreign policy considerations are incorporated in Gazprom's strategy and must be complied with. Indeed, some of Gazprom's actions may seem obscure and irrational unless we take into account their political rationale and underpinnings (Wenger, Orttung and Perovic 2006). Gazprom applies a multifaceted strategy in Europe with the following tenets:

Different Logics in 'Old' and 'New' Europe

Russia's strategy in the EU is driven by different rationales in 'old' and 'new' Europe. On the one hand, Russia considers Western Europe a lucrative economic zone with which gas trade is indispensable for the country's economic fortification. Particularly important in this context are the German, Italian and British markets due to their big populations that import significant quantities of Russian gas. Rising demand for Russian gas in these countries reinforces Gazprom's eagerness to retain amiable trade relations with them. Moreover, these customers pay higher prices than the ones charged to the Commonwealth of Independent States (CIS)[3] and provide the Russian cashiers with hard currency (Victor and Victor 2006, Geden, Marcelis and Maurer 2006). This economic cooperation is cemented by Gazprom's strategic partnerships with a number of energy utilities not only in Germany and Italy, but also in other EU Members, such as Austria and Greece (Stern 1999).[4] Besides these economic reasons, Russia faces the core EU Members as important, responsible and powerful partners in the global system that co-manage together with the other great powers the principal issues and challenges of global politics. Gas trade then has to evolve within the framework of easy-going relations and must not negatively affect wider political relations.

On the other hand, Russia approaches 'new' Europe in a neo-imperialist way, since it continues to view the former communist world as its (to-be) sphere of influence. The fact that the market of the new EU Members is not so important for Russia allows it to follow such a stance. Although these states have been incorporated in the Western structures and have escaped Russian control, energy offers the most efficient lever for Moscow to punish these countries for their anti-Russian stance and to create hurdles to their prosperity (Larsson 2006a). Indeed,

---

3   The CIS was created in 1991 as the successor organization to the Soviet Union, but only remains a loose organization with limited potential.

4   Gazprom's main customers are German EON Ruhrgas and Wintershall, Italian ENI, French Gaz de France, Austrian OMV, Austro-Hungarian MOL, Dutch Gasunie and Danish DONG. In 2006 Gazprom renewed its contracts with its German, Italian and French partners ensuring gas sales for the next two to three decades, see Baran 2008: 160, Stern 1999, Finon and Locatelli 2007.

'new' Europe has suffered from Russian aggressive energy diplomacy. A number of contracts have been breached upon on the basis of political and/or commercial issues. To take an example, within the period 1998–2000 Russia ceased nine times oil supplies to Lithuania to dissuade it from selling Mazeikiu Nafta, its port that also comprises a refinery and a pipeline to the port, to a US energy company (Aalto 2006: 101–102, Orttung 2006). Russian oil pipeline monopoly Transneft enforced these cuts in order to pressurize Lithuania into selling the port to Transneft. Moreover, in 2006 Transneft terminated oil supplies to Lithuania. The official reason given was that there were technical problems in the pipeline's function. No oil has run through the pipeline since and these quantities have been diverted to the Russian interior pipeline system leading to the port of Primorsk. As a result, Lithuania and Poland now receive oil at a higher price due to higher transportation costs (Nies 2008: 39). Since Gazprom, as Transneft, is a state-managed enterprise, there are fears that it may use the energy lever against them as well (Pleines 2006, Baran 2008: 159). Although these moves do harm Russia's reliability as a supplier, Russia seems to treat such incidents as 'affordable collateral damage' (Larsson 2007b: 46) for the satisfaction of important foreign policy goals.

This bifurcated approach is reflected in Russia's initiative to build the Nord Stream pipeline (Map 5.2). Nord Stream was inaugurated in September 2011 and will link Russia with Germany directly under the Baltic Sea. Its capacity will be 27.5 bcm per year, while a second leg may be situated in parallel with the first doubling the pipeline's annual capacity. Nord Stream's construction ensures Gazprom a vital presence in one of the most lucrative European gas markets (Larsson 2006b, Loskot-Strachota and Antas 2010). The shortcoming for EU gas security, however, lies in the fact that the unified pipeline system that links Russia with Europe does not allow Gazprom to supply exclusively one Member State or another. For Gazprom to supply Germany, gas has to cross Polish (and Slovak) territory. This way these states have a counterweight to potential Russian blackmails to inflict unilateral supplies cut-offs, since Gazprom cannot afford to cease supply to its most affluent customers. Now that Nord Stream has come on stream, Gazprom will be able to supply 'old' Europe and, at the same time, play political games against 'new' Europe. Furthermore, new Members stand to lose the revenues they enjoy from the transit of gas through their territory. Therefore, 'new' European states oppose fervently the Russian initiative. They instead suggested the modernization of the existing pipeline system through Ukraine or, alternatively, the construction of a shorter land pipeline through Latvia. Both options are much cheaper, but were bluntly rejected. This group of states thus hails Nord Stream as a project short of any economic logic, driven exclusively by geopolitical interests (Larsson 2007a, Baran 2008: 158).

Elimination of Transit Dependency

Russia turned down such accusations as unfounded bringing two important counter-arguments into the discussion. The first is that dependency on transit states

Map 5.2   Nord Stream
Source: Author's map

– 85 per cent of the gas destined for EU countries has to cross Ukraine, while the remaining 15 per cent has to cross Belarus – creates vulnerability in the most important sector of the Russian economy. Since Russian exports have suffered due to the obstructionist policies of these transit countries, Russian energy security can only be solidified if transit dependency is eliminated. This calls for supplementing or substituting for Soviet-era pipelines with direct Russia–EU ones.

Russian relations with both Ukraine and Belarus, while amiable in the 1990s, have come under friction in the 2000s. This sharp deterioration in overall political relations has had a dreadful impact on their energy approach as well. Ukraine and Belarus not only used to purchase Russian gas at very low prices, but also retained (and still do) huge debts to Gazprom. Gas subsidies to allies and tolerance to their unpaid bills followed a certain political rationale. Through the subsidization of fellow countries' industries and economies Russia ensured their loyalty and support to its foreign policy goals. Since the 2004 Orange Revolution in Ukraine, however, it became irrational for Russia to support financially the unfriendly Yuschenko regime. Tensions with Belarus are not so far-fetched, since Belarus did not follow a pro-Western foreign policy. The Kremlin, however, grew increasingly impatient and frustrated with Lukaschenka's regime and the stalling of bilateral cooperation in a number of sectors.[5] For these reasons, Gazprom has been demanding both debts repayment and a substantial increase of the gas price. Ukraine and Belarus were paying four times less than Western Europe, an economic practice that generated high costs for Gazprom. Seen from a market rationale, which Moscow increasingly adopts in its deliberations with the EU, the setting of market prices was not only an acceptable demand, but also necessary for Gazprom in order to boost its revenues and be able to invest further in new deposits and infrastructure projects. This would enhance both its own energy security, as well as that of its principal customer, the EU (van der Linder and de Jong 2009, McFaul 2006, Pirani, Stern and Yafimava 2010: 1–3).

The amply covered gas crises with Ukraine in 2006 and 2009 and Belarus in 2007 and 2010 reveal Gazprom's transit-related problems. The story in these crises is in general similar. Neither the Ukrainian nor the Belarusian economy could afford a fourfold increase of gas prices. When Gazprom cut off supplies (allowing only the gas quantities destined for the rest of Europe to cross the pipeline) in order to enforce debt repayments and higher prices, Ukraine and Belarus siphoned off the gas that was destined for Western Europe, thus creating problems in the Russia–EU gas trade.[6] These transit-related episodes have incurred high costs for Gazprom at both economic and reputational level (Kramer 2006, McFaul 2006, Pirani, Stern and Yafimava 2010, van der Linde and de Jong 2009, Yafimava, 2010).

It is in this light that Nord Stream serves Russian gas interests. Transit avoidance will allow Russia to control its export trade and suffer neither any economic losses nor any further damage to its reliability. Ensuring independence from transit countries is thus a legitimate interest of Gazprom, albeit one can hardly overlook how this increases Russia's leverage in its dealings with 'new' Europe (Larsson 2007b).

Pursuit of Security of Demand

The second argument has to do with Gazprom's vision for its presence in the EU market. In the same way that importers seek security of supply, exporters pursue security of demand, that is markets that can absorb their exports. Thus, Gazprom endeavours to lock up demand in the EU for its gas through the construction of

---

5   While Russia and Belarus had signed an agreement to form a Union, which practically meant that Russia would absorb Belarus, this agreement was never implemented. In addition, although Russia and Belarus experimented with closer economic cooperation and the establishment of a customs union, cooperation remains rather shallow and partial, see Bruce 2005, Karaganov 1997, Zaiko 2006.

6   Russia's machinations did not seem to aim at a conciliatory approach, but at a conflictive one that would force Ukraine and Belarus to accept Gazprom's pledges. Nevertheless, the principal point made here is that Russia had both the political and economic reasons to act as it did.

direct Russia–EU pipelines. While Nord Stream provides direct access to one of the most lucrative national gas markets within the EU, South Stream will cater for the augmenting gas needs of Southeastern Europe. The Italian energy company ENI, which aims to lock up more Russian gas and broaden its customer base within the European gas market, has embarked upon agreement on an equal footing with Gazprom to build the South Stream pipeline (Map 5.3).[7] South Stream, estimated to have a capacity of 30 bcm per year, will cross the Black Sea to Bulgaria. From there, the pipeline will have two branches supplying Romania, Austria, Hungary, Slovenia, Greece and Italy (and non-EU Members Croatia, Serbia and Bosnia-Herzegovina).

South Stream is seen as a competitor to the Nabucco pipeline (see pp. 95–6) since they both aim at the market of Southeastern Europe. Gazprom aspires to build South Stream before Nabucco in order to make the alternative project more unlikely to materialize. Indeed, in case South Stream comes on stream first, it is debatable whether the non-Russian gas carried through Nabucco will be absorbed (especially since Russian gas will be cheaper than the one alternative producers will offer). A number of scholars view the two projects as mutually exclusive and consider that the first one built will outrival the other and postpone to a much later date, if not altogether cancel, its construction (Grigoriadis 2008). Crucially, Gazprom announced plans to build this pipeline after its proposal to participate in ITGI (via the Blue Stream pipeline that brings Russian gas to Turkey) was rejected. The Russo–Ukrainian crisis of 2009 that lasted for more than two weeks and caused the harshest breakdown of Russia–Europe gas trade pushed Russian officials to announce plans for the doubling of throughput capacity (to 63 bcm). No resolute decision on the matter, however, has up to now been taken. South Stream, besides having an EU-wide character in contrast to the divisive one of Nord Stream, further avoids transit-dependency risks emanating from Ukraine and Belarus and adds another route to EU–Russia gas trade, enhancing this way security of demand for Russian gas (Larsson 2006b).

Exploitation of the Opportunities of Liberalization within the EU

Furthermore, Gazprom aims to take advantage of the EU's liberalization project. This takes three forms: firstly, liberalization creates chances for Gazprom to buy out shares or whole companies that are traditional distributors in the EU gas market. Secondly, Gazprom is entitled to set its own daughter retailing companies in EU soil or to form joint ventures with other companies, as is the case in Germany,

---

7   Gazprom and ENI are planning to incorporate EDF (*Électricité de France*) and Wintershall in the corporate structure. The first is anticipated to acquire a 10 per cent stake, while the latter a 15 per cent stake in the pipeline. Both will be deducted from ENI's share that will be brought down to 25 per cent. There are also talks for the inclusion of EON Ruhrgas in the corporate structure.

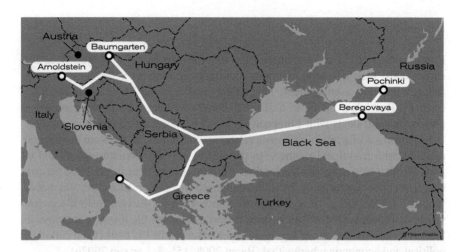

Map 5.3   South Stream
Source: Author's map

Table 5.2   Russia–Europe pipeline network

Pipeline	(Estimated) Annual capacity (in bcm)
Druzhba	135
Yamal–Europe	20
Nord Stream	27.5–55
South Stream	30–63
Total	**212.5–273**

Austria and Greece among others,[8] it is no more obliged to sell its gas to European distributors at the border. For example, Gazprom now sells directly 3 bcm per year in the Italian market. Such penetration of the downstream sector is crucial since it entails higher margins for profits and a potentially higher share of the EU gas market (Locatelli 2008, Pleines 2006, Stern 2002). Thirdly, Gazprom has become a player in the EU spot markets, where margins for profits are even higher. To this end, it plans to expand overall storage capacity in European soil (that today total 2 bcm) to more than 6 bcm (Dempsey 2006, Ria Novosti 2010). Liberalization seems to serve as a vehicle for Gazprom's further penetration into the EU market and thus as a means to further augment its market power (Locatelli 2008).

---

8   Gazprom and Wintershall have established Wingas, Wieh and WIEE to distribute gas to the German and Central European market. To the same aim Gazprom and OMV have established GWH Gas Warenhandelsges. Gazprom also has a 50 per cent share in Prometheus gas, a gas distributor in the Greek gas market.

Bilateralism vs. Multilateralism

Russia and the EU have established the EU–Russian energy dialogue since the early 2000s. Despite early ambitions, the dialogue remains a largely discursive forum with weak competences. This reflects not only the EU's inertia but also, crucially, Russia's aversion to deal multilaterally with the EU. To the contrary, it prefers bilateral deals with European states. This allows Gazprom to court some EU Members while retaining hostile relations with others, to promote contractual relations with traditional partners, to proceed to new infrastructure plans and to play Member States against each other. All these are evident in the Nord Stream case. Even more importantly, by following *divide et impera* tactics Gazprom makes it harder for the EU to form a common stance vis-à-vis Russia. Such a scenario would be problematic for Russia since it would diminish the leverage it enjoys in bilateral relations, expose its aggregate dependence on the EU market and curtail its political and economic wherewithal (Baran 2008: 155–8, Larsson 2007b).

Dealing with the Domestic Gas Deficit

Although it may sound absurd in the face of its vast gas resources, Russia faces a looming gas deficit. One has to distinguish here between reserves, thus potential for future production, and production capacity, which is how much gas can be drilled on current investments (Paillard 2007, Gaddy and Ickes 2008). A number of reasons explain this deficit. First of all, Russia's main gas deposits are quite mature. Production from the gas fields of Urengoy, Yamburg and Medevhze has started to decline and hence there is growing need to explore new fields. Most of them, however, call for enormous investments and advanced know-how, especially if one bears in mind that they lie offshore, at great depth and in difficult geological environment. Moreover, as a result of the Soviet exploration strategy, the more well-endowed deposits in the western part of the country have been exploited, while a high number of small scattered ones remain unexploited. This makes production from these fields less profitable (OECD 2004: 13). Gas from the Yamal region has to start flowing in great quantities, a joint venture has been formed to explore the giant Stokhman field in the Russian Arctic region (estimated to hold 3.7 tcm), while a number of fields in the Sakhalin island in the eastern part of Russia are currently under exploration. Nevertheless, Russia needs a comprehensive plan of investments in the energy sector in order not to see its production decrease dramatically in the following years (Stern 2005, Monaghan and Montanaro-Jankovski 2006: 18–19, Stern 2009b). Unless enormous investments take place in the next years, Russia will likely face difficulties in fulfilling its commitments towards its main customer, the EU. This is so in the face of mounting domestic demand in accordance with Russia's growth, rising gas demand in the CIS states, which Russia traditionally supplies earning significant political leverage in the region, as well as Russia's intention to increasingly supply the Asian market (Pirani 2009, Götz 2005b).

To make matters worse, the structural problems of the Russian gas sector hold back economic efficiency and impede its further development. First of all, Gazprom's monopoly in both gas exports and the domestic pipeline system, together with its predominant role in the upstream sector, are not conducive to competition. There are hardly any incentives for new private companies to enter the gas market and enhance competition. When they do, they have to use the Gazprom-controlled pipeline network to supply domestic suppliers and, most importantly, they are forbidden from selling abroad, where prices are much higher than within Russia. This cuts profit margins and acts as a grave disincentive against their corporate expansion (Victor 2008: 10–16). Nevertheless, the Russian government has belatedly turned to encouraging production from private gas companies, which can be tripled in the following years thus significantly contributing to overall gas production (Henderson 2010).[9] Even more important, it has announced the intention to grant independent producers access to Gazprom's network (Ria Novosti 2011b). Such moves are necessary if one takes into account that Gazprom's economics are in a mess, not least due to gas subsidies to a number of states and *de facto* statelets (as, for example, Moldova, Transnistria, Armenia, Nagorno-Karabakh and South Ossetia), unpaid debts incurred by non-reliable trade partners as Ukraine and Belarus have built up and Gazprom has absurdly expanded its reach into third sectors. All these severely hamper Gazprom's ability to invest in new exploration schemes (Vahtra and Liuhto 2004: 42, Olcott 2004: 26, Bank of Finland 2005: 47, Stern 2009b).

Furthermore, Gazprom is obliged to sell its gas to domestic customers at prices well below market levels (Monaghan and Montanaro-Jankovski 2006: 13).[10] Gas is seen as an indispensable public good that has to be offered to Russian citizens at affordable prices. Cheap gas also offers Russian industries a competitive advantage vis-à-vis their foreign competitors. The fault line is that Gazprom's activities in the domestic field are thus not profitable. There has been a lot of pressure by the European Commission and the WTO on Russia to increase domestic prices. Although Gazprom has made it clear that prices will not reach market levels, it agreed to a moderate gradual increase of the price. The bottom line is that Gazprom's profits mainly emanate from exports to Europe and are set to remain so (Paillard 2007). Last but not least, Russia's energy efficiency record remains poor. A lot of gas is wasted in an outdated pipeline network, while the affluence of gas encourages excessive spending rather than saving. Energy efficiency programs have started to develop in Russia, but remain in an elementary stage. In case Russia substantially improves its energy-efficiency record, significant gas quantities will be saved. It should be noted here that it is less than five years that gas companies in Russia committed themselves to eradicate the costly and environmentally-

---

9   Still, however, Gazprom remains averse to any plans to allow non-Gazprom gas to enter Europe in order to avoid Russian gas-to-gas competition.

10   According to Gazprom, the gas prices that domestic customers paid in 2008 were 4.7 times less than what the Europeans pay.

unfriendly habit of flaring gas. The gas that was difficult to extract or that remained unsold due to the rigidity of the domestic gas market was burnt into the air, a rather unadvisable practice from every perspective (Kupchinsky 2009).

Gazprom then, let alone other domestic producers, seems unable to significantly invest in the upstream sector and increase Russian gas production. What could achieve this goal are foreign investments. Due to Russia's rich subsoil, a number of foreign enterprises have shown a vivid interest in acquiring (oil and) gas exploration rights, despite Russia's rather obscure institutional and legal framework. Nevertheless, Russia views energy as a strategic sector and does not welcome badly needed foreign investments. To the contrary, the Kremlin has scrapped production sharing agreements, which facilitate foreign investments and orchestrated a reduction in foreign enterprises' shares in the Russian upstream sector.[11] The Russian federal law that came into force during the 2000s forbids foreign firms from acquiring a share that surpasses 50 per cent in any exploration project (Victor 2008: 55–61). As a result, currently all gas projects are led or exclusively run by Russian enterprises, principally Gazprom (Bradshaw 2006: 145, Poussenkova 2004: 17). Russia still admits junior partners due to lack of capital and, crucially, know-how (Kryukov and Moe 2008, Baghat 2004: 139). It should be stressed, nonetheless, that in those cases that foreign corporations are admitted as junior partners, geopolitical factors seem to hold a significant role in the final decision.[12]

Finon and Locatelli (2007: 13) present an interesting argument here. What is seen as a liability, namely Gazprom's difficulty to maintain current production levels, suits Gazprom's price-setting interests. Producing and selling at the margins makes manipulation of prices easier and allows Gazprom high benefits from sales to Europe, both when negotiating long-term contracts prices, as well as in spot markets. This is not to argue that Gazprom is dragging its feet to invest on new deposits for this reason. Nevertheless, a high rate of investments would boost Russian gas production, amplify the availability of gas and potentially push gas prices down. This is not the optimal strategy for Russia and thus should be regarded as an unlikely scenario for the future.

---

11   BP had to relinquish a majority share in the Kovykta field, while Royal Dutch Shell was forced to decrease its share in the consortium operating the Sakhalin 2 field as a prerequisite to remain a partner. In both cases Gazprom undertook a leading role.

12   For example, Russia rejected US companies' proposals to participate in the exploration of the Shtokman field amid hostile bilateral relations and admitted France's Total and Norway's Statoil instead. Besides the close ties between Vladimir Putin and the French President Nikola Sarkozy, Russia preferred these two companies due to the state's dominant role in them. Russia prefers to make deals with state-backed, rather than private enterprises, promoting thus state to liberal capitalism. The recent agreement between Russia's Rosneft and the US ExxonMobil for the joint exploration of oil and gas fields in the Black Sea may signal a shift in Russian policy in accordance with improving US–Russia relations after President Obama's rise on power.

A Gas Alliance with Central Asia and Relations with Third Producers

The oxymoron is that while Russia does not invest on the upstream sector, it does invest on joint ventures for the distribution of gas and, much more crucially, to build the ambiguous Nord Stream pipeline. The Russian energy strategy obviously prioritizes transit independence and direct access to the EU market to maximization of export potential. It is the import of Central Asian gas that allows Russia to follow such a prioritization.

Due to the deadlocked geographical position of Central Asian producers, their gas can only reach Europe either via Russia or through the Caspian. The second option is difficult to materialize if one takes into account the unresolved legal status of the Caspian,[13] subsequent disputes between the five Caspian states as to the delimitation of the sea borders, environmental concerns as well as the high costs that the construction of an undersea pipeline entails (see Chapter 6). These states then are forced to use the existing Russian pipeline network. Russia does not allow access to its pipeline system, since that would create competition with Russian gas, reduce Russia's share in the EU market and potentially bring prices down (Seliverstov 2009). For these reasons, Russia has contracted most of the gas these states produce at relatively low prices and sells it to the EU market for much higher prices. In return, it commits sums to the development of the upstream and downstream sectors of the Central Asian states' energy industries. This gas alliance dates back to 2002 and includes, besides gas contracts, cooperation on the modernization of the existing infrastructure linking Central Asia with Russia, as well as the construction of a new pipeline that will run across the Caspian and bring Central Asian gas to Russia. This move is of crucial importance since it locks up assets for Russia and allows it to maximize its export potential, at the same time that it deprives the EU of valuable alternative sources of supply. Close relations between ex-Soviet officials and Russia's aptitude to court non-democratic regimes and conclude lucrative contracts with them were detrimental to this development (Chufrin 2004: 18–20, Perovic 2006: 98–101, Olcott 2006: 224, Fredholm 2005: 15–16).

Besides this gas alliance, Gazprom has approached other gas producers as well. First of all, it has contracted small gas quantities from Azerbaijan (also a Caspian state, whose geographic position nevertheless allows it to send its gas to Europe without transit through Russia), an alarming development if one keeps in mind that the EU's hopes for drastic diversification centre upon Azeri future production. Secondly, it has signed a framework agreement with Algeria's Sonatrach. This agreement includes deliberations and joint bidding for the acquisition of shares in third countries, assets swaps and cooperation in the LNG sector (Twining 2006, Buckley 2008).[14]

---

13 There is a dispute whether the Caspian should be considered a lake or a sea. International law has different provisions for the delimitation of borders of seas and lakes.

14 LNG has been the focus of an agreement between Egypt and Gazprom as well. The Russian monopoly is also interested in acquiring assets in Libya and Nigeria.

Furthermore, Russia has played a leading role in the creation of the Gas Exporting Countries Forum (GECF). The forum was established in 2001 and its members hold around two thirds of total gas reserves. GECF serves as a forum for consultation among the main suppliers with regard to volumes produced, technological innovation and price controls. It has thus raised fears both for Gazprom's expansionist intentions, as well as for the potential formation of a cartel similar to that of the OPEC (Socor 2008). Iran's zealous participation has also raised eyebrows for political reasons. Nevertheless, this institution only serves as a forum for discussion for the time being and it most probably will remain so for a number of reasons:

- There is as yet no global gas market. There are only few interconnections between regional markets acting quite autonomously one from the other. Although LNG technology is reducing this drift, this only happens at a slow pace and with indeterminate results. Proximity still remains crucial. Only if LNG trade becomes more competitive will there be a strong incentive for the globalization of the natural gas market.
- Around 30 per cent of total gas reserves remain outside the control of GEFC. Countries like Norway and the Netherlands are quite improbable to join the institution as they are averse to such manipulative mechanisms and committed to an open market philosophy. Some North African and Middle East producers have also shown little enthusiasm for participation in a gas cartel.
- The cartelization of gas will mean higher prices and a market largely controlled by the producers. These will provide strong incentives to consumers to shift away from gas. Therefore, such practices seem self-defeating for the producers, most of whom rely on energy-born revenues to sustain their growth. Such a prospect then does not seem to hold much potential for the future (Jaffe and Soligo 2006, Hallouche 2006).

Diversification to the East

All these moves have strengthened the Russian presence in the EU gas market. Nevertheless, the EU rhetoric on diversification (see pp. 94–9) has intensified Gazprom's insecurity and has driven it to devise alternative policies. Even if it was not for the EU rhetoric and declared goal to marginalize dependence on Russia, though, Gazprom would be prudent to search for alternative markets in case they present better terms than the EU does. Diversification is also a sensible policy *per se* since it hedges against overt dependence on specific markets, offers alternative options and averts potential crises. Indeed, a number of parameters point towards this direction. Russia borders with the fastest developing country in the world, China, whose energy needs are increasing rapidly. Another neighbour, Japan, has no indigenous energy sources and is overly dependent on imported oil from the Middle East and LNG from Indonesia and Malaysia. Japan has repeatedly vied for

Russian supplies that will enhance its energy security and seems willing to pay high prices to this cause. In addition to achieving security of demand and diversification of markets, there is a concrete economic logic behind such trade deals with the East. Most new gas fields lie at the eastern part of the country. Logistics and low transportation costs make trade with China and Japan very attractive. As we saw in Chapter 2, when discussing China's quest for energy security, two gas pipelines are already under construction to bring Russian gas to China. Last but not least, China and Japan, contrary to the EU that creates regulatory hurdles in the EU–Russia gas trade and recurrently stresses the need to diversify against Russia, are zealous to get Russian gas and pose no impediments to and prerequisites for their energy trade (Morozov 2005: 7).

EU Energy Strategy Vis-à-vis Russia: The Views from 'Old' and 'New' Europe or is Russia a Reliable Supplier or a Formidable Threat?

From an EU point of view, Russia is both an indispensable and valuable partner, as well as a formidable threat. There is a broad dichotomy between what scholars call 'old' and 'new' Europe (Larsson 2006a, 2007b, Smith 2009). The former communist European states were integrated in the energy infrastructure of the COMECON (Council for Mutual Economic Assistance) and thus were supplied exclusively by Russian (oil and) gas (besides some indigenous energy production). This communist heritage of 'new' Europeans, overt dependence on Russian energy, is problematic, not least due to their tense relations with the big eastern neighbour. The rationale behind their drive to join the EU (and NATO) was to solidify their stance as a non-Russian sphere of influence and disentangle from the Kremlin's stronghold. Subsequently, the enlargement of 2004 also imbued into the EU arena a deep concern for Russian policies, not least in the energy sector (Valasek 2005: 24). These former Soviet satellites still view Russia as their number one threat and have as their foreign policy priority to eradicate Russian influence (Larsson 2006a, 2007b).

This anti-Russian bias, although understandable through the East European[15] states' perspective, is not shared by 'old' Europe (the EU15). These states see Russia as a valuable partner that has never cut energy supplies to them (with the exception of the Ukrainian and Belarusian crises of the previous years, for which

---

15   One of the first things these states attempted to do after their communist regimes' collapse was to persuade the outer world that they do not belong to East, but to Central Europe. This identity issue referred to their perception of belonging to Europe and to the belief that half a century under communist domination was an aberration. This strategy also enhanced their quick integration into the Western institutional structures, both the EU and NATO. This point is well taken. We use here the term East Europe in geographical terms, so that any confusion with central European states as Germany (whose energy policy contrasts sharply with that of its eastern neighbors) is avoided.

however the blame does not rest solely with Russia). It is significant to note here that these states (with the exception of Greece, Austria and Finland) do not depend on Russian gas for more than 40 per cent of their overall gas usage. As a result, they do not see in Russia an actual threat to their energy security; to the contrary, they view Russia as an indispensable partner that contributes to their balanced and diversified import portfolio and hence to their energy security (Geden, Marcelis and Maurer 2006). Due to its significant energy wealth, Russia is considered as a necessary, if at times awkward partner. As we saw above, in addition, a number of energy companies in Western Europe have formed strategic partnerships with Gazprom and thus have a legitimate interest in furthering amiable ties between Western Europe and Russia. These companies put pressure on their governments not to proceed to any actions that may hamper this smooth business relationship and this way promote steady energy cooperation with Russia (Götz 2005). Furthermore, states like Britain, France and Germany which comprise, together with Russia, the leading powers of world politics are rather hesitant to disrupt friendly relations with Russia at their East European partners' will. East Europeans, on the other hand, consider it unacceptable that their stronger EU partners not only do not back them in their intricate relations with a much mightier neighbour, but that they also prefer bilateral deals and cordial relations with third countries that further deteriorate their own energy security (Smith 2009).

The dividing lines between 'old' and 'new' Europe on the role Russia should play in the EU gas market propels a wider debate on which strategy is optimal, namely diversification or interdependence: for East European Member States, diversification is the key in order to thwart dependence on Russian imports. Despite that, these states only hold flamboyant diversification rhetoric and do not proceed to contract quantities from alternative suppliers. This is so because the options are few and usually involve higher costs, especially if one takes into account that they presuppose the construction of costly infrastructure (pipelines, compressor stations, LNG terminals). The existing Russia–Europe gas infrastructure, to the contrary, puts costs down and creates a forceful economic logic for the maintenance of their energy trade.

While for 'new' Europe there is the need to diversify against Russia, 'old' Europe sees Russia as a means to diversify from Middle East oil and North Sea gas. Even more important, these states tend to see mounting cooperation as a pro rather than as a liability. Increased trade only furthers the benefits of cooperation, builds up trust and makes any exit out of this mutually beneficial relationship even more costly and hence unlikely for both sides. This pattern is captured better by the term interdependence rather than the one-sided term dependence that 'new' Europe continually employs. Interdependent relations with the most important supplier can ensure long-term security of supplies, an overarching interest of the EU. A crucial parameter here is that 'old' Europe does not carry a heritage of Soviet (or tsarist) domination. East Europe, however, does and is therefore in most cases loath to engage in any such discussions and cooperative approaches with Russia, which it still perceives in negative rather than constructive terms. This 'old' versus 'new' Europe dichotomy then runs too deep. Both material interests and ideational factors diverge considerably, create friction between 'old' and 'new' Europe and put EU solidarity in test.

This duality is reflected in two sets of principal, albeit antithetical, pillars of the EU gas strategy, namely enforced interdependence vs. diversification and liberalization vs. protectionism. While enforced interdependence and diversification coexist, even if uneasily, liberalization is an enduring principle and is only marginally countered by protectionist voices that remain in minority. The reason for such a complex and often contradictory EU energy strategy is the multiplicity of actors and their frequently diverging interests and approaches to energy security. In what follows we discuss the three main pillars of the EU energy strategy vis-à-vis Russia and evaluate the strength and potential of the protectionist path.

Enforcing Interdependence

A number of European Member States, Germany and Italy being the most prominent among them, opt for strong cooperation with Russia as a means to facilitate their energy security. The rationale behind this policy is that the more Russia becomes embedded in the EU market, the more EU energy security is enhanced, not endangered. In an era of fierce competition for energy resources, such agreements bind EU Member States and Russia in a network of mutual benefits and fight back Russia's plans for diversification towards other markets. The EU's principal supplier, it is argued, should be courted with, not treated as a rival and a threat (Cameron 2009, Geden, Marcelis and Maurer 2006: 16–17).

Investments on the network infrastructure and expansive trade are crucial for enforcing interdependence. Starting with the former, pipelines are crucial for gas trade since they create stable relations and the anticipation of enduring trade. Agreements on infrastructure schemes signal commitment from contracting parties to engage in long-term cooperation and hence embed them in an interdependent relationship (Lesser et al. 2003). European willingness to proceed with the construction of two new Russia–Europe pipelines testifies to enforced interdependence. Nord Stream is a Russo–German project[16] cultivated by the amiable relations between ex-Russian President Vladimir Putin and ex-German Chancellor Gerhard Schröder. Germany's dominant energy companies EON Ruhrgas and Wintershall applied significant pressure on the German government to back the deal. Not only did they get shares in the pipeline, but they also signed new supply contracts with Gazprom that will allow them to remain preponderant distributors of gas to the German and wider Central European market (Sander 2007). Germany sees in this agreement the opportunity to ensure supplies for

---

16   The chief executive of the consortium that is building the pipeline is former German Chancellor Gerhard Schröder. Gazprom has a 51 per cent stake in the project, German enterprises Wintershall and EON Ruhrgas each a 20 per cent share, while the Dutch company Gasunie participates with 9 per cent.

decades from a traditionally reliable partner through a new route that eliminates transit-related risks (Rulska 2006). Other Member States, like Britain and Sweden, have also expressed the interest to be connected to the new pipeline (Larsson 2006b, 2007a). No agreement has, however, been signed as yet.

Gazprom and the Italian company ENI have established a strategic partnership,[17] the cornerstone of which is the 2007 agreement to build together the South Stream pipeline (CIEP 2007: 35). All potential recipient countries have welcomed the project as a significant additional route that will enhance the EU energy security. This includes a number of states that depend heavily on Russian gas (such as Bulgaria, Greece, Slovenia and Hungary). It is important to note that Hungary, an East European Member, made an impressive turn in its policy and backed South Stream in order to ensure supplies from Gazprom, although it initially fully supported the alternative Nabucco pipeline. Even the European Commission, which is sceptical regarding Russia's role and intentions in the EU gas market, welcomed the project. It appreciates that the EU needs Russian gas, while transit through countries as Ukraine and Belarus has created significant problems in the EU–Russia gas trade; direct pipelines are hence highly preferable (Papadopoulos 2008: 20–21).

Besides building new Russia–Europe gas infrastructure, bilateral trade follows increasing trends. While the EU got around 140 bcm of Russian gas in 2004, it bought more than 155 bcm in 2008. Russia has renewed its contracts with a number of customers[18] and is in negotiations for the extension of its contracts with a number of others (such as Greece). Two more developments are crucial here. Firstly, Gazprom has made inroads to new markets as the Dutch and the Danish ones and gradually establishes its presence there. Secondly, it has significantly boosted its share in the large, fully liberalized British market and has set the goal to further increase it in the following years. This holds significant potential since spot markets present larger margins for profits (CIEP 2007, Stern 2002). In sum, EU–Russia interdependence in the gas sector seems to be consolidated.

Diversification Policies

This line of action is not shared by East European Member States who act as drivers of diversification. The European Commission also disapproves of increasing dependence on Russian gas and advises that a more prudent policy should consist in more suppliers holding smaller shares in the EU market (European Commission 2006, 2009, 2010). Only this way, Commission officials claim, can competition actually work.

Starting with individual Member States' initiatives, Poland has since the 1990s been speculating the construction of an LNG terminal in its Baltic coast, as well

---

17   This includes the acquisition of assets in the upstream Russian sector by ENI. In exchange, Gazprom is awarded privileged distribution rights in the Italian market.

18   The contracts provided for increased gas quantities and extended their lifespan to 2030 for Wintershall and 2035 for EON Ruhrgas.

as a pipeline that will connect it to Denmark and supply it with Norwegian gas. The Czech Republic has signed a contract with Norway for the supply of gas quantities. It should be noted here that these two countries, together with Hungary, Slovakia and the three Baltic states, have joined forces in their attempt to lead an EU-wide energy strategy with the aim to marginalize excessive reliance on Russian gas (Cameron 2009). Poland has reached as far as suggesting that a new energy treaty within the EU should contain a NATO-style article 5, which would oblige all Members to come to the assistance of any one partner in case its energy security is threatened by external suppliers (Geden, Marcelis and Maurer 2006: 2, 24). Poland also obstructed for months EU–Russian talks on the renegotiation of their Partnership and Cooperation Agreement that was due for 2007 unless the EU adopted a dynamic common stance against Russian domineering energy diplomacy and actively promoted critical diversification projects (Barysch 2007: 3). These efforts have eventually led to provisions, albeit rather vague, on energy solidarity being incorporated in the Lisbon treaty. Core EU Member States, however, are afraid of giving 'wrong incentives for national energy policies ... a Member State partly insulated from supply risks by the solidarity clause may adopt a more risky energy policy, leaving other Member States to bear some responsibility for the consequences of those actions'. They have hence been cautious not to commit themselves to undertaking specific obligations (Egenhofer and Behrens 2008: 3, FECER 2009).

The EU has promoted a number of diversification plans in order to disentangle from overt dependence on Russian gas. First of all, it has wholeheartedly endorsed and benefited from US promotion of new pipelines that would bring Azeri resources to the West. Together with the construction of the Baku–Tbilisi–Ceyhan oil pipeline (see Chapter 3), an almost parallel gas line has been built from Baku to Erzerum. The South Caucasus gas pipeline, as it is called, feeds into ITGI, a pipeline connecting Turkey to Italy via Greece (Map 5.4). This pipeline has a capacity of 12 bcm per year (with a goal to reach 22 bcm within the next years). The leg linking Greece and Turkey is already on stream, while the second linking Greece with Italy is currently under construction. This pipeline is a genuine diversification project since it brings to the EU market Azeri gas and adds a new route of supply for the EU (Socor 2007b, Ypery 2007).

The cornerstone of the EU's diversification policy, however, is the Nabucco pipeline (Map 5.5). This is also designed to start from Turkey and supply Bulgaria, Romania, Hungary and Austria. As we saw above, it is seen as competitive to the Russian-sponsored South Stream project, since it aims at the same market. Although this pipeline has been on the news for many years, little has been actually achieved. The consortium has been formed, but the project remains at the stage of the feasibility study. The main problem is that there are not enough gas quantities to fill the pipeline. Azerbaijan can contribute but little gas at this stage; Iran is out of the picture due to its geopolitical stance and friction with the Western world. North African and Middle Eastern states, despite their significant potential (see Chapter 6) do not have the ability to offer any important gas quantities in

Map 5.4   Interconnector Turkey–Greece–Italy
Source: Author's map

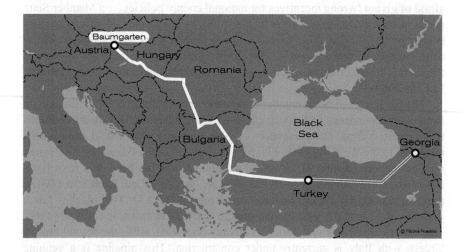

Map 5.5   Nabucco
Source: Author's map

the short-term (Giulio 2008: 4–6, Rowley 2009, Norling 2008). In this light, it seems that Nabucco could come on stream only with Russia's contribution. This prospect is not well taken by the EU, since it would allow Russia to meddle with its diversification policy. True diversification for the EU means non-Russian gas coming through non-Russian-controlled pipelines. In the absence of non-Russian resources that can guarantee the viability and profitability of the pipeline, nonetheless, it is difficult for Nabucco to come on stream any time soon (Locatelli 2010: 6–9, Finon 2009).

The Transadriatic pipeline (TAP) is projected to connect to ITGI and link Greece and Albania with Italy under the Adriatic Sea (Map 5.6). It is estimated

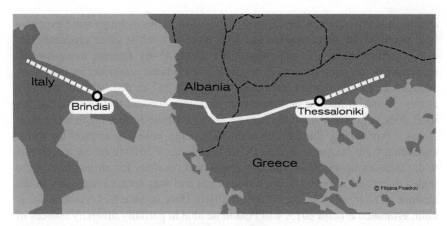

Map 5.6   The Transadriatic pipeline (TAP)
Source: Author's map

Table 5.3   Main diversification projects

Pipeline	(Estimated) Annual capacity (in bcm)
ITGI	12–22
Nabucco	33
TAP	10
AGRI	7
Total	**62–72**

to come on stream after 2015 with a projected throughput capacity that will not exceed 10 bcm per year. This pipeline faces the same problems with Nabucco. While the consortium[19] that aims to build the pipeline initially contracted gas quantities from Iran, the adverse political climate dashed early hopes for gas from new sources. It now looks at Azerbaijan to ensure gas quantities with which it will be able to supply the Italian market. In the absence of available alternative (non-Russian) gas quantities, TAP seems more to add competition to Nabucco than diversify sources of supply. It will, however, add a new route thus contributing to diversification of routes (*The Economist* 2010b).

Diversification basically boils down to strengthening the market share of existing suppliers against this of Gazprom, as well as introducing new exporters to the market. As we are going to see in Chapter 6, however, this is not feasible in the short-term. There is not a lot of potential for Norway to substantially increase its gas production the following years. Algeria's production is set to rise and thus more Algerian gas is estimated to come into the EU in the next years, through

---

19   The Swiss EGL and Norwegian Statoil each have 42.5 per cent, while German EON Ruhrgas has got a 15 per cent share in the project.

existing and possibly new pipelines. Neighbouring states as Libya and Egypt also hold potential for supplying the EU with more gas, while other producers can also contribute some gas quantities (CIEP 2008: 45–6). Despite this potential, nevertheless, the numbers are not so great. Even if these producers increase their supplies to the EU market, the actual aim of the EU to diversify substantially against Russia is hard to be met if one takes into account that demand for gas itself does not remain static but is expected to increase further (Jaffe and Soligo 2006). Even Poland, the pioneer of an EU energy policy to counter the threat emanating from Gazprom, agreed in the beginning of 2010 to renew its contract with Gazprom up to 2037. The agreement also provides for an increase in the traded quantities to cover Polish needs in gas and was deemed necessary in the absence of alternative sources (Cienski 2010). Only in case its LNG terminal is built, estimated around 2015, will Poland be able to partially diversify sources of gas supply (Stratfor 2010).

Due to the unavailability of non-Russian gas, EU Member States have turned to alternative sources of energy production. The Russo–Ukrainian crises of 2006 and 2009 made a number of Members' governments seriously contemplate a decisive shift towards nuclear energy. Britain and France have recently announced their intention to build a number of new nuclear power reactors (Wintour 2008). A number of other Member States, nevertheless, most prominently among them Germany, decline this option and refuse to become significantly dependent on nuclear power in fear of any dreadful nuclear leakages. Germany's powerful gas industry has ensured that the government's position remains rigid, since any deviation and subsequent increase of nuclear power would compete with gas and endanger its high profits (Sander 2007: 23). The destructive nuclear accident in Japan is certain to spread waves of scepticism with regard to the use of nuclear power and will at least serve to raise the costs for ensuring advanced safety standards in the future. Under this light, it is hard to imagine that its share in energy generation will increase in the near future. The EU is also encouraging the extensive use of renewable resources and their share in the EU energy mix is set to increase. Nonetheless, no impressive results can be anticipated for the near future. As already mentioned, even the Commission's goal for a 20 per cent share of renewables in the EU energy mix by 2020 is now considered rather ambitious.

The rationale of diversification is not confined to minimizing potential economic and technical risks that could lead to supply shortages and/or hiked prices. First of all, Russia's energy strategy has political underpinnings. Former Soviet satellites have suffered from politically motivated cut-offs. This is an unacceptable risk and should be tackled with. Secondly, energy dependence meddles with the capacity of the dependent to follow an independent foreign policy path; dependence on Russia thus carries the danger of political concessions and submission. The EU seems impotent to balance between its identity politics and material interests and oscillates between values and practice, actual deeds and rhetoric. Enforced interdependence adds to Member States' assuaging stance towards Russia's posture in the international system, as well as towards concrete Russian policies

(Larsson 2007b). Russia has evolved into a managed, not liberal, democracy with a substandard record on compliance with the rule of law and human rights. The elections are free but not fair and the freedom of NGOs to operate in Russia is significantly curtailed (Austin 2004: 11–14, Hale and Taagepera 2002: 1101–2, Trenin 2005: 100–107, Lucas 2008: 73–112). These, critics argue, are reasons why the EU should distance itself from Russia, not cultivate further economic ties in such a strategic sector as is the energy domain. Moreover, such dependence decreases the EU's leverage in going against Russia. The EU's mild reaction to the Russian military campaigns in Chechnya, as well as to the Russo–Georgian war in 2008, can be partially attributed to its high dependence on Russian gas (Larsson 2006a, Götz 2006).

Liberalization

The ECT (see Chapter 3) was a Dutch initiative to impose the rules of open markets to the whole Eurasian region. In case it was implemented, the gas industry of all Eurasian producers would be liberalized ensuring that the EU would enjoy supplies from a number of exporters through multiple routes (de Jong 2007: 60–61). Moreover, the EU has applied concerted pressure on Gazprom to unbundle into two distinct companies, one specializing in gas production and the other in gas transportation and distribution. It has also asked from Gazprom to break up its export monopoly, as well as its domestic pipeline monopoly, in order to create incentives for new entrants to produce and distribute gas in both Russia and Europe. Gazprom has declined all these proposals, not least to avoid the creation of gas-to-gas competition between Russian companies. Concentration in one giant, vertically integrated company that could manage the whole gas sector, in accordance with wider Russian foreign policy interests, suits Russian interests best (Finon and Locatelli 2007: 10).

Failing all these initiatives, the EU cannot forego the reality that when it comes to its energy security in the gas sector it only has three major suppliers. The Commission can do little about the inflow of non-EU gas to the EU market. The focus then is on the liberalization of its own market, meaning the operation of these suppliers in a single, unified economic space with no impediments to new entrants and with interconnections between the national markets. Liberalization cannot influence the external dimension of security of supplies but indirectly, through legislation of the rules by which these companies should abide when operating in the EU market (Morozov 2005: 6). This is not to downplay the significance of the Commission's initiatives and of the ongoing liberalization project, but only to illustrate their limits in relations with third countries and attribute to them the proper weight.

Nevertheless, liberalization brings changes in the EU–Russia gas trade and threatens the traditional role of Gazprom in the EU gas market. The rationale behind both North European Members' decision to liberalize their national gas sectors, as well as the Commission's directives for an EU-wide, single, unified and open gas market, was that it serves as a shield against monopolistic practices and players. The single most important aspect of open markets is that with the entrance of new players into the market and the development of competition, (quasi-)monopolies are no more able to decide on quantities and prices themselves. The prerequisite for a functional EU-wide market is the existence of interconnections between Member States (Cameron 2009: 25). As we saw in the previous chapter, there are two interconnectors linking continental Europe with Britain. This is crucial since it allows Russian and Norwegian gas (that makes up around 70 per cent of EU gas imports) to be directed further north or south (Futyan 2006). Moreover, a series of small pipelines linking Central European states are put in place. Those are strikingly absent, however, where they are most needed, in the eastern part of the EU (Helm 2009: 147). In the words of Nadejda and David Victor (2006: 157), for countries exposed to Russian aggressive policies 'the key to keeping Russia in line is the potential for alternative supplies through interconnections with the West rather than the actual contracting of those supplies'. Once EU-wide interconnections are established, in accordance with the EU's investment plans up to 2014, they will serve to marginalize the repercussions of growing dependence on Russia.

It should be noted here that the Commission engaged itself in a dispute with Gazprom on this particular issue. Each contract Gazprom signed with a gas distributor had destination clauses attached. These forbade distributors to sell the contracted gas to any other than their national market. In case destination clauses were not thwarted, the EU gas market would consist of fragmented national markets where the supplier would enjoy ample leverage. Such clauses, however, went contrary to the essence and spirit of free competition and would retain a disjointed EU market. Hence, the Commission initiated their annulment. Gazprom, albeit initially hesitant, was forced to accept the Commission's position earning in exchange the right to sell directly to the European customers (European Commission 2003: 1–3, 2004: 7, 2005, Soligo and Jaffe 2004: 11).

Moreover, the Commission revoked the import limitations attached to the EU–Russia gas trade. In the midst of the Cold War the EU Members agreed, under US pressure, not to be dependent on any one country for more than 30 per cent of their overall energy consumption. At that point of time this created no problem since no single EU Member depended significantly on Russian (oil or) gas. In the early 2000s, however, with the prospect of the ex-communist European states, which rely excessively on Russian gas, entering the EU, Russia became concerned that EU regulations would hamper its traditional energy links with Eastern Europe. The Commission acknowledged not only that those regulations were outdated, but that they also contravened market principles and thus rescinded them (European Commission 2002: 11, 2004: 9).

While these steps adhere to and further liberalization, some reverse steps have also been taken. These not only cast doubt on the commitment of the EU to pursue full liberalization, but also make one contemplate whether liberalization is the optimal strategy for energy security in the gas sector under all circumstances (Wright 2006). First of all, fixed long-term contracts go against the fundamentals of an open market since they obstruct flexibility. For this reason, the Commission endeavoured to eliminate them and to only allow gas trade in spot markets and through short-term contracts. Gazprom reacted fervently to these proposals arguing that long-term contracts guarantee security in gas markets. Unless suppliers have guarantees that their gas will be sold, they are hesitant to invest huge sums of money to exploration and transportation schemes. Eradicating the long-standing contractual basis of gas trade, Gazprom warned, could be counter-productive since it would provoke less investment and, as a result, fewer gas supplies for Europe in the mid-term. The Commission, under pressure from a handful of Member States and energy companies, accepted these arguments and acknowledged that the eclipse of long-term contracts might jeopardize, rather than enhance, the EU's energy security. Subsequently, a compromise was reached. Long-term contracts would continue to exist, albeit with reduced duration. At the same time, they should not capture all the gas quantities traded. At least a small portion of the gas supplied should be traded freely on spot markets (European Commission 2007, Finon and Locatelli 2002: 3, 10, Buchan 2002: 108–9).

Secondly, the Commission's unbundling initiatives (see Chapter 4) cannot be confined to domestic companies, but necessarily extend to foreign players (Checchi, Behrens and Egenhofer 2009: 22, McGowan 2008: 94, Cameron 2009, Goldirova 2007). This significantly complicates EU gas relations with foreign suppliers, predominantly Gazprom that controls the pipeline network linking Russia with Europe. According to the EU legislation, Gazprom has to surrender its control to an independent operator, which will have to allow throughput capacity for other, smaller suppliers as well. This will deprive Gazprom from the privilege it enjoys to fill the Russia–Europe pipelines with its own gas. Companies can ask for exceptions from TPA obligations, but those have to be approved by the Commission. Needless to say, these reforms are severely opposed by Gazprom that makes it explicit that it will not succumb to EU pressures (Milov 2006, Paillard 2007). These new regulations may even endanger the construction of Nord and South Stream in case a mutually agreed solution is not found.

The Commission's legislative plans imperil relations with the dominant supplier and ask a bold question: what will the EU do in case Russia chooses not to conform to the EU's legislation? Evidently, the EU does not want to find itself in a situation where it has a well regulated gas market that is short of gas. This is the most important reason why the Commission is likely to interpret leniently its new provisions and allow the smooth flow of Russian gas into the network. At the same time, the strong ties between European utilities and Gazprom operate as levers of pressure to reach a compromise. These companies stand to lose a lot in case Gazprom's traditional role as supplier is endangered and thus lobby Member States' governments and the European Commission to thwart such a possibility (Sander 2007). Thirdly, core EU Members do not want to strain relations with Russia and are likely to attempt to mediate a mutually acceptable and beneficial solution (Cameron 2009, Stratfor 2010). For the time being, a medium solution seems to have been found. No EU-wide rules are imposed and it depends on the

Member States themselves to decide whether they will allow foreign enterprises that have not proceeded to unbundling to operate into their markets. This allows room for zealous partners of Gazprom, as Germany and Italy, to maintain close relations with it, while at the same time permits more sceptical Members, as Poland and Lithuania, to adopt a more protectionist stance (Belyi 2009, Goldirova 2008).

These issues are illustrative of the dilemmas troubling the EU with regard to the liberalization project on the one hand and the need to deal with such a mighty energy company and indispensable partner as Gazprom on the other (Egenhofer and Behrens 2008). For the time being and the near future, however, the EU cannot escape the fact that it cannot be energy secure without Russian gas. A compromise hence seems requisite. Moreover, EU's deliberations and manoeuvres depict that energy security is at times at odds with, not furthered by, liberalization. An implicit acknowledgment that the supply of natural gas is a public good and thus may, under certain circumstances, deviate from market regulations seems to be at play (Spanjer 2008: 217–9).

Protectionism

As already stressed in Chapter 4, the fierce resistance the EU faces in its attempts to impose the liberalization project on external suppliers has led some scholars, a handful of Member States and the European Commission to contemplate a radical change of course and to suggest a reversion to protectionism as the only strategy that can maximize EU energy security (Percival 2008). While Russia 'is a traditional power, deploys diplomacy backed by force to reassert its influence in its "near abroad" and is determined to use its energy resources to exert geopolitical influence' (Finon and Locatelli 2007: 7), the EU passively endures Gazprom's aggressiveness short of any realistic plan to force Gazprom's retreat.

The paradox of the liberalization project is that it presents opportunities for the further penetration of quasi-monopolistic companies into the EU gas market. The unbundling of European ex-monopoly corporations gives Gazprom the chance to bid successfully and acquire shares in other companies in the downstream sector or to buy them out altogether. It is for this reason that the European Commission worked on the formulation of plans to protect the EU market from what it perceives as the looming Russian threat. As we saw in the previous chapter, Gazprom will be forbidden, according to these plans, from expanding its asset portfolio in the EU gas market, unless Russia accepts the penetration of EU companies into its upstream gas sector. The cornerstone of this protectionist policy, then, would be the application of the reciprocity clause. Russian and EU investments would have to follow symmetrical trajectories, if they are not to be frozen (McGowan 2008: 101, Goldirova 2007). The European Commission attempts thus to let Gazprom take the blame for the curtailment of their energy cooperation or the credit for an increase in bilateral deals.

The Commission's strong card is Russia's dependence on the EU market. However, taking into account that there are viable alternative outlets for Russian gas, Gazprom would in all probability speed up its diversification policies and pave its way out of a hostile, protectionist EU market within the span of a few years. This would severely undermine the EU's energy security in the gas sector. At a tactical level, then, it would most probably bring about the worst case scenario, rather than facilitate energy security. It seems that the EU cannot afford to take such a risk.

At the normative level, such a policy would undermine the EU's international stance. Although these measures may seem understandable amid Gazprom's offensive and uncompromising stance, they are totally out of line with the EU's liberal mindset. In case they prevail, the EU's credibility will stand to lose much internationally as it will be seen as a broacher of its own dogma of open markets, interdependence and cooperation which it has spread successfully by means of internal enlargement and external relations. At the same time, the EU's strength lies in setting the example for others to follow, as an integrative rather than divisive power. A shift towards realistic lines of policy-making that can breed conflict and away from interdependence that cultivates the dynamics of stability, cooperation and security, would signal an important retreat from six decades of European integration. It would also signal the abandonment of the endeavour to set its own rules of the game and the succumbing to those set by other actors (Larsson 2007b: 59).

It seems rather implausible for the EU to adopt such a stand vis-à-vis Gazprom, not least due to the reluctance of many Member States even to seriously contemplate such suggestions. Nevertheless, this protectionist package highlights European ambivalence and the fact that the EU becomes an increasingly reluctant and difficult partner for Gazprom. Hence, from a Russian perspective, it may be preferable for Gazprom to significantly diversify its gas trade away from Europe. This does not bode well with overall EU efforts to ensure security of supplies.

Conclusion

To conclude, Russia's energy strategy in Europe revolves around bilateral rather than multilateral deals and follows different approaches vis-à-vis 'old' and 'new' Europe. It has succeeded to sustain security of demand for Russian gas, as well as to retain Russian leverage in the eastern part of the EU. A number of new pipelines currently under construction, as well as Gazprom's penetration into the EU downstream sector and renewal and expansion of contracts with European customers, all guarantee Russia's dominant role in the EU gas market for the near future.

The EU's response, on the other hand, remains fragmented, uncoordinated and weak. Instead of forming a common stance, internal controversies remain unresolved. The EU strategy oscillates between interdependence and diversification policies, retains a dangerously polemic rhetoric vis-à-vis Gazprom and contemplates both protectionist measures and provisions of a liberal kind to keep Gazprom out. In the next chapter, we examine the EU's relations with the other suppliers, as well as their potential to substantially increase their share in the EU gas market and decrease EU reliance on Russian gas.

Chapter 6
Relations with the Other Producers

There are a number of differences between the EU–Russia energy approach and EU's relations with the other energy suppliers. These can be summarized as follows:

- The EU is not so dependent on any other gas supplier as it is on Russia. This also means that only Gazprom can apply decisive upward pressures for the price of gas, while the other producers enjoy significantly less market power.
- Russia's energy policy in 'new' Europe is frequently provocative and aggressive. This creates perceptions of threat to a number of Member States. Neither Algeria nor Norway or any of the other suppliers with limited shares in the EU gas market appear threatening to any of the EU Members. This is also due to Russia's overall political posture and ambitions as a great power. Neither Norway nor Algeria has similar status or goals.
- Russia and the EU do not share a normative background and disagree on the regulatory framework of gas trade. Although the changes in the rules of the game in the EU gas market do shape a diversified field for the other suppliers as well, they do not create so much friction in the absence of the first two factors.

For these reasons, the EU energy partnership with Algeria and Norway is much smoother and the following analysis focuses more on their pipeline networks, contracts with EU customers and projections of future supplies, rather than on controversies with the EU and policy dilemmas. We firstly examine Norway since it is the most important supplier after Gazprom. In the second sub-chapter we examine Algeria's strategy and place in the EU gas market. In this we also include the role other African states play as EU gas suppliers. The third sub-chapter studies the relations of the EU with regions that may become important suppliers, namely the Middle East and the Caspian. Lastly, we briefly examine more distant players' contribution to the EU's security of gas supplies and the potential for their increasing role in the EU gas market.

Norway

Norway has declined twice to enter the EU family. This is basically because it is a sparsely populated, rich state, not least due to its excessive mineral resources. In case it entered the EU, it would be a net donor to the EU budget and would have to surrender part of its sovereignty to supranational institutions. These losses seem to surpass perceived gains stemming from integration. Moreover, Norway faces no external political and military threats, against which integration into the EU would serve as a shield of protection. There is hence little point from a Norwegian perspective to accede to the EU. Nevertheless, Norway fully endorses the EU's *acquis communautaire* and political and economic mindset. It is long an established democracy, follows the orthodoxy of open markets and is a member of the EU free trade area. Those form a favourite background for extensive cooperation in the gas sector and explain why imports from Norway are considered supplies within the EU, rather than imports from an external supplier. In the words of the European Commission President Manuel Barroso (quoted in Offerdal 2010: 39), 'if all external suppliers were as sure and reliable as Norway, energy security would be much less of an issue within the EU today'.

EU gas trade with Norway dates back to the 1970s, when Norway first discovered significant gas deposits in the North Sea. Norway initially constructed two pipelines to bring gas to Europe. This pipeline network has been significantly enhanced, expanded and supplemented throughout these four decades (Map 6.1). The main pipelines linking Norway with the EU are:

- The Norpipe that connects Norwegian fields with Germany's Erden
- The Vesterled pipeline that connects Norway with Britain's St. Fergus
- The Zeepipe that brings gas to Belgium's Zeebrugge
- The Franpipe that links Norway with France's Dunkirk
- The growing demand for natural gas in the German market pushed Norway to build another two pipelines, Europipe I and II, to Germany
- The Langeled gas pipeline has added another route to supply the British market with Norwegian gas
- Norway has also created another small pipeline (of 8 bcm per year) to link to the main British gas grid (CIEP 2008: 38–41, 44–6).

The total capacity of this pipeline network approaches 130 bcm. Norway plans to further expand it with the construction of another two pipelines, the Europipe III which is designed to supply continental Europe with more than 23 bcm per year and a small pipeline to cater for the Scandinavian region (Denmark and Sweden). This latter pipeline, albeit estimated not to surpass a capacity of 12 bcm per year, may prove crucial for 'new' Europe's energy security, since it can supply Poland through the Danish transmission system (CIEP 2008: 38–41, 44–6).

Norway enjoys a share that marginally surpasses one fourth of imports in the EU market with more than 80 bcm per year. Estimations for the future production capacity deviate significantly. While the Norwegian Petroleum Directorate expects production to reach 140 bcm by 2030, IEA forecasts 127 bcm and Söderbergh, Jakobsson and Aleklett (2009) estimate maximum 115 bcm. The latter even view a scenario where gas production falls below 100 bcm as not unrealistic, thus expressing fears about Norway's dwindling gas output.

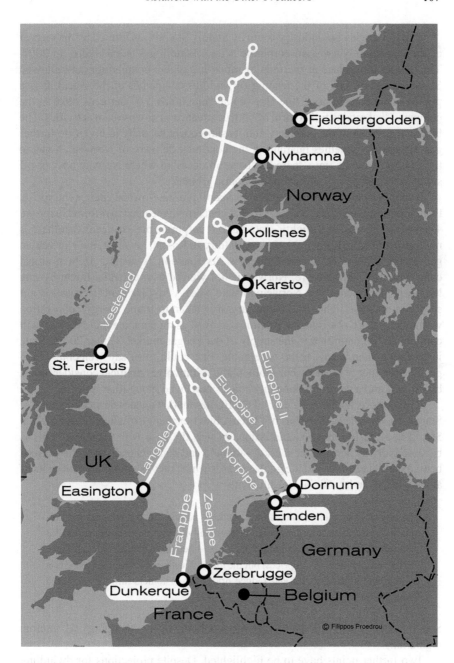

Map 6.1   Norway–Europe pipeline network
Source: Author's map

The Norwegian gas industry is run by Statoil. Statoil was formed by the merger of the two main Norwegian corporate actors, Statoil and NorskHydro, in 2007. The merger took place at the face of mounting global competition and allowed Statoil to remain one of the leading oil and gas companies of the world. It is a public-managed enterprise (the Norwegian state holds a 67 per cent stake in the company) that retains full control of both upstream and downstream activities. The financial strength of the company and its subsequent capacity to invest on further gas exploration schemes guarantees the continual delivery of Norwegian gas to the EU. At the same time, there has been no occasion where Norway has cut-off supplies to Europe on political or economic grounds.

It should be noted here that although Statoil is a state-owned energy enterprise, there has been no discourse similar to that concerning the need to reform Gazprom. The operation of such a mighty, state-backed corporate player means that there is no upstream competition in Norway. Contrary to Russia, however, the Norwegian gas sector adheres to liberal principles. Its function is distinct from political considerations. Furthermore, Norway is not viewed as a potential threat by any Member State. Hence, the Norwegian state's heavy involvement in Statoil is not seen in a negative light. To the contrary, it is taken to frame energy cooperation within cordial EU–Norwegian relations, as well as a guarantee that Norway will continue to be committed to the supply of the EU gas market (Ghiles 2009). State intervention then seems to be acceptable, one could even say welcome, when positive for energy security, but problematic if it involves political considerations, blackmails and a confrontational agenda, as perceived in the Russian case.

Furthermore, the liberalization of the EU gas market creates new challenges for Statoil. Nevertheless, there has not been a bitter exchange of allegations between Statoil and the European Commission, as was the case with Gazprom. This is because Norway accepts the market rationale and comprehends both the reasons behind the EU reforms and the goals towards which they are directed. Statoil itself acknowledges in its official website that:

> the objective of these changes is to increase competition in national markets and integrate them into regional and, eventually, a single EU-wide market for natural gas. It is difficult to predict the effect liberalization measures will have on the development of gas prices, but the main objective of the single gas market is to create greater choice and reduce prices for customers through increased competition.

Statoil hence seems willing to adjust its policies to the changing EU internal regulations.

Two further points have to be highlighted. Despite projections for dwindling gas production in the coming decades, Norway's High North is a rather promising region. Geological parameters, the need for compliance with the stricter environmental standards in such an ecologically sensitive region, sophisticated technical expertise and high investments needed, all pinpoint towards a mid-term horizon for gas to start flowing from this region. Nevertheless, it seems that Norway is set to remain an essential gas producer for decades (Offerdal 2010).

Moreover, the case of the Norwegian Arctic region becomes all the more important under the light of the daunting global climate change, the rise of global temperature and the subsequent melting of ice. These make it likely that the Arctic region will become explorable in a much narrower time-frame than previously estimated. Norway is one of the five countries (together with the US, Canada, Russia and Denmark) that can claim rights in the subsoil wealth of the region. In case no abrupt off-set of global climate change takes place, Norway's gas production is likely to be further boosted in the mid-term (Borgerson 2008).

North Africa

North Africa's gas reserves are estimated at around 7 tcm (Jaffe and Soligo 2006). The region thus holds the potential to become a significant supplier of the EU market. For the time being, Algeria is by far the region's most prominent EU producer, exporting more than 50 bcm per year and accounting for a bit less than one fifth of overall EU gas imports (IFP Energies Nouvelles 2006). Libya and Egypt also contribute small quantities, while there is potential for the linkage of Nigeria to the North African–European pipeline system (Maps 6.2 and 6.3). The existing and potential main corridors of this wide transmission network are as follows:

- The Transmed pipeline was constructed in the 1980s to bring Algerian gas to Sicily via Tunisia. The capacity of the pipeline has been extended to 33.5 bcm.
- The Maghreb pipeline starts from Algeria, transits Morocco and supplies Spain. The capacity of this pipeline has also been expanded from 12 bcm to 39 bcm per year.
- In 2009 the operation of the Medgaz pipeline from Algeria to Spain was inaugurated. The pipeline is quite small in throughput capacity, only 8 bcm annually, but reaches Spain's Almeria directly, without transit via Morocco.
- It should be noted here that Algeria was the first country to export LNG in the 1960s. It is thus an established LNG supplier, shipping LNG to Italy, Spain, France, Portugal, Belgium and Greece. There are also plans for the construction of more LNG terminals that will maximize exports in the coming years.
- There are also plans for the construction of the GALSI pipeline, which is, as we saw in Chapter 4, supported by the EU's investment package as well. This pipeline is designed to link Algeria to Sardinia and further east to Livorno in Toscana. The capacity of the pipeline will not exceed 10 bcm per year.
- Apart from Algeria, Libya has recently also begun to supply the EU gas market. With the construction of Greenstream to Sicily, Libya contributes 8 bcm per year to the EU. The projection is that the capacity of the pipeline will

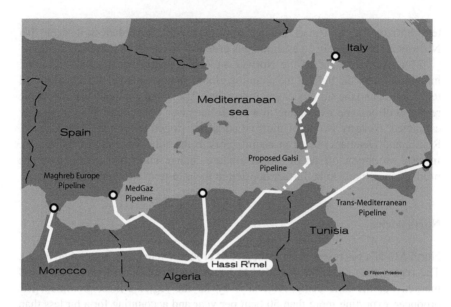

Map 6.2   Algeria–Europe pipeline network
Source: Author's map

be upgraded to reach 11 bcm annually. Libya also exports small quantities of
LNG and plans to expand its LNG infrastructure and export potential.

• There is also the possibility that Egypt will become a pipeline supplier to
the EU market. In case the Nabucco pipeline is built, the existing Arab Gas
Pipeline (AGP) that connects Egypt, Jordan, Syria, Turkey and Iraq could
link in Turkey to Nabucco and bring Egyptian gas to the EU market. For
the time being, however, Egypt exports only LNG. These exports are less
than 20 bcm per year. In the face of persistent delays to construct Nabucco,
Egypt contemplates to expand gasification facilities and increase its LNG
exports (Alami 2006).

• A significant expansion that will add a new source to the EU gas market,
if implemented, is the Nigeria–Algeria pipeline. This project remains at
the phase of speculation for the time being. In case it comes on stream
– this cannot realistically be expected before 2015 – Nigerian gas would
use the Algerian infrastructure to reach Europe. The NIGAL (Nigeria–
Algeria) pipeline, also known as the Trans-Saharan pipeline, would carry
18–25 bcm annually to the EU market. Nigeria is also a new LNG exporter,
equally suited for both the EU and US markets (CIEP 2008: 38–41, 44–6).

Algeria is considered a rentier state with allegations for corruption and
mismanagement abounding. Crucially, the wealth stemming from energy exports
is mainly captured by the elites, not devolved to the public. The Algerian economy
therefore remains profoundly problematic and dependent on energy-born revenues.

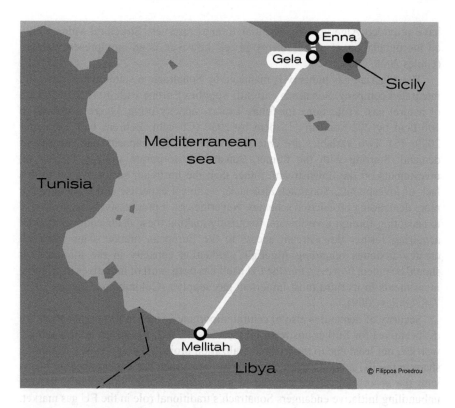

Map 6.3   Libya–Sicily pipeline
Source: Author's map

Table 6.1   North Africa–Europe pipeline network

Pipeline	(Estimated) Annual Capacity (in bcm)
Transmed (Algeria–Tunisia–Sicily)	33.5
Maghreb (Algeria–Morocco–Spain)	39
Medgaz (Algeria–Spain)	8
Greenstream (Libya–Sicily)	8
GALSI (Algeria–Sardinia–Livorno)	10
Total	**98.5**

Hydrocarbons account for 97 per cent of Algeria's export revenues, 60 per cent of its fiscal receipts and 40 per cent of its GDP. The natural gas sector is dominant, since it surpasses the size of the country's oil industry (Deutsche Bank 2008). No other industries are significantly developed, unemployment rates are high and living standards remain low. The challenge for Algeria is to build upon its rich subsoil and create a healthy, diversified economy. High energy prices since 2003 have provided Algeria with essential foreign reserves. Structural vulnerability on the fluctuation of global energy prices, however, is an omnipresent liability (Ghiles 2008, 2009).

The Algerian gas industry is managed by Sonatrach, a state-owned vertically integrated company. Sonatrach currently supplies Europe with more than 50 bcm of natural gas. Projections for future export capacity bring Algeria's exports to 100 bcm by 2020 and to 115 bcm by 2030 (Checchi, Behrens and Egenhofer 2009: 15). Two variables are crucial here, production capacity and security of demand. Starting with the former, Sonatrach's corporate strategy focuses on investments on the downstream, rather than the upstream sector. Added to this lack of investments, Sonatrach also lacks technical expertise and know-how for more demanding production schemes. Nevertheless, it progressively seems averse to accepting foreign investments, frequently making these deals contingent upon acquiring further downstream access to the European market. This approach creates anxieties regarding Algeria's production capacity in the mid-term. It should be noted, however, that the EU itself has been short of initiatives to promote investments in its third most important gas supplier (Colombo and Lesser 2010: 7–8, Ghiles 2009).

Security of demand is also of central importance, since in its absence there are disincentives for further upstream investments. In fact, Sonatrach is increasingly worried, not least due to the EU's liberalization project, that it may see its market share in the EU market decline. First of all, Sonatrach has experienced problems with the absorption of the contracted gas in Spain. More importantly, the EU unbundling initiative endangers Sonatrach's traditional role in the EU gas market. Under the new regime, it will be obliged to grant partial access to the pipelines it controls to third parties or negotiate exemptions with the European Commission. The new rules of the game thus remove the pre-existing certainties of gas trade and jeopardize its significant market share. At the same time, the liberalization project has led to the significant reduction of the duration of long-term contracts and enhanced the emergence of spot markets. The flooding of Europe with gas since 2008, as we saw in Chapter 3, created a great differential in spot gas prices vis-à-vis oil-linked long-term contracts prices leading to losses of revenues for Sonatrach. Lastly, the EU's rhetoric on the increased use of renewables and nuclear power creates additional worries to Sonatrach with regard to future demand for gas within the EU, albeit these fears seem far-fetched (Darbouche 2010: 79–80).

In order to tackle these dangers, Sonatrach is following multifaceted energy diplomacy. First of all, it exploits the opportunities that liberalization creates by penetrating South Europe's downstream sector. It has already established such a presence in the Italian, French, Spanish and British markets. These attempts, however, have met with the resistance of France, Spain and Italy and their national champions (Britain, to the contrary, welcomes new market players), causing frustration in the Algerian side (Ghiles 2009). Secondly, Sonatrach has signed a framework agreement with Gazprom. This provides for the formation of joint ventures and a wider cooperation agenda on gas issues. This partnership has augmented European fears for Sonatrach's tactics and goals in the EU market. These fears were furthered by Sonatrach's attempts within the GECF to restore oil parity in spot gas prices, since such manipulative efforts to control gas prices are evidently averse to the EU's economic liberal mindset and energy security (Darbouche 2010: 80). Last but not least, the liberalization of the EU gas market pushes Sonatrach to contemplate the expansion of its gasification terminals. This is a prudent diversification strategy for Algeria in order to disentangle from overt dependence on the EU gas market and allows it a strong negotiating stance in potential disagreements with the European Commission and/or individual Member States. Due to its geographical position, Algeria can supply more distant markets as well. Such hints should sound as alarm bells. In an open, globalizing gas market the EU cannot take any supplier for granted; to the contrary, it has to court them and bind them in a web of close interdependence to ensure supplies.

Broader political developments are not encouraging either. Since the early 1990s the EU has endeavoured to further bonds with peripheral states, Algeria included. The Euro-Mediterranean Partnership (EMP) was seen as a first attempt to facilitate convergence between the EU and its periphery. At that point there was also hesitant talk about the eventual possibility of the EU's periphery being integrated into EU structures (Bilgic 2010). This partnership, nevertheless, failed to yield tangible results (Schneider 2011). EU's disillusionment with successive rounds of enlargement and the 'enlargement fatigue' have gradually led to a significant reversal of the enlargement rhetoric. Burdened by a series of problems and dysfunctions since the early 2000s and the enlargement of 2004, the EU seems impotent to remain an open institution to every country fulfilling the basic criteria. This has led to the formation of the ENP, a curtailed alternative to accession that promises 'all but institutions' to the peripheral states of the EU. Interestingly enough, only Russia and Algeria declined to participate in these structures stressing the inappropriateness of this working framework and their deep embitterment with the EU mindset. Since 2008, the Union for the Mediterranean (UfM) has succeeded the ENP framework for the Maghreb and Mashreq countries (Esther-Barbe 2008). While within these new structures the EU works bilaterally with the Mediterranean states on the basis of individual action plans, it is astonishing how little work has been done in EU–Algerian relations. As Darbouche (2010) notes, the main deficiency is the weak institutionalization of their relations, which comes in stark contrast to their complementary interests in the energy sector. The EU does not consult Algeria regarding its liberalization reforms and does not take into account how they negatively affect Sonatrach's security of demand and how this can feed into its future production capabilities. From an Algerian point of view, the EU approach is

prosaically narrow and obsessed with rules and regulations, whereas its [Algeria's] expectation is of a cooperation model that is explicitly more strategic. The EU's proposed energy cooperation framework adds little value to the existing bilateral deals that Member States have been prepared to conclude [with Algeria] on the basis of more strategic dividends for Algeria (Darbouche 2010: 81).

Even worse, when in the beginning of the 2000s Algeria made an effort to reform its gas industry, the EU did not actively support it. This led to the collapse of the reforms in the face of fervent domestic opposition (Darbouche 2010: 74, 81). The recent upsurge of revolutions in North Africa and the Middle East attests to the EU's inadequate and defective diplomacy that, although preaching reforms, does not itself promote and is too hesitant to fully sanction (*The Economist* 2010e, 2011). In case the EU proactively supported the democratization of the region, which in most cases also leads to the endorsement of market economies, it would stand to greatly benefit in terms of fortifying its energy security.

These developments notwithstanding, the EU holds by and large amiable relations with North African states that hold significant export potential. Importantly, energy trade has not been politicized and does not seem to run this danger. This is conducive to further gas trade. Geographical proximity is another essential facilitator, since it reduces transaction costs and creates mutual gains for both sides. Although LNG gives the opportunity to reach distant markets, costs have not declined to such an extent that proximity becomes irrelevant. Moreover, North Africa is well-endowed with gas at the same time that it needs foreign investments to further explore its gas potential. Money and economic entrepreneurship, on the other hand, despite the currently difficult economic circumstances, form the strengths of the EU. The interests of both sides are thus complementary and not conflictive and could form the basis for an ever more solid energy partnership. The same holds true for the Middle Eastern region that will be examined below, although Iran presents a separate case (Belkin 2008: 17–19).

The Caspian and the Middle East

We lump together these two regions for two reasons: first of all, their actual contribution to EU energy security in the gas sector is currently minimal. Secondly, they are both well-endowed with mineral resources and can in the mid-term become important sources of diversification for the EU.

Before starting with the Caspian region, a quick look at Ukraine seems compulsory. Ukraine has a wide resource base – estimations are that it holds 2 tcm of natural gas – but a disproportionately feeble gas industry (Shapovalova 2010: 5). Its structurally distorted economy, ruled by the interests of a few conglomerates well connected with the political elites, forms a critical obstacle to further research and exploration of domestic resources (Economic Forum 2007). As a result, Ukraine is renowned for overt dependence on imports of Russian gas, not least due to its dreadful energy efficiency record. A reform of the Ukrainian economy, with an emphasis on a more transparent and positive investment climate, would lead to a significant inflow of foreign investments to the country and would allow it to switch from an importer to an exporter status (van der Linde and de Jong 2009,

Williams 2011: 3, Pirani 2007). The EU, however, has as yet taken no initiative towards this direction despite the obvious benefits at play.[1]

Going to the Caspian region we have to make clear that we refer to the gas potential of Azerbaijan, Turkmenistan, Kazakhstan (the other two Caspian states are Russia and Iran, which is included in the analysis for the Middle East) and Uzbekistan (although not bordering with the Caspian, but belonging to the wider Central Asian region). These four countries have overall gas reserves of around 8 tcm. The disintegration of the Soviet Union and the break-up of its mineral wealth to a number of states created high hopes within the EU for ample availability of gas from multiple suppliers and through a number of energy corridors. Reality, however, turned out to be quite different.

First of all, as we saw in Chapter 5, geography plays a decisive role in determining the flow of energy. Azerbaijan is a Caspian state, but the only (together with Iran) that is located westwards of the Great Lake. Contrary to Turkmenistan, Kazakhstan and Uzbekistan that can deliver gas either via a to-be built trans-Caspian pipeline or through the existing Russian pipeline system, Azeri gas only has to cross Georgian and Turkish territory. Hence, via the South Caucasus pipeline (see Chapter 5) and its linkage to ITGI, Azerbaijan has become a supplier of the EU gas market. This is the only pipeline linking the Caspian with the EU territory for the time being.

Azerbaijan concentrated early European hopes for a diversified gas imports portfolio. Nevertheless, these hopes were quickly dashed. Despite the country's ample gas reserves – estimated to 1 tcm – production levels are rather low. Production only begun in 2006 and in 2009 Azerbaijan produced around 16 bcm, exporting only six of them. Production basically comes from the Shah Deniz field, which swiftly attracted the attention of a number of multinationals that together with the state company SOCAR formed AIOC,[2] the joint venture that exploits the field, in what was named the contract of the century. While Azerbaijan has become and is set to remain a supplier of the EU market (Süleymanov 2008), its contribution in the mid-term cannot be groundbreaking.

We have to add here the persistent controversies that plague the region and jeopardize further energy streams. Azerbaijan is still embroiled in a frozen conflict with neighbouring Armenia over the enclave of Nagorno-Karabakh. From time to time bilateral rhetoric deteriorates dangerously making the outbreak of a conflict likely. The two sides seem to be nowhere close to a mutually acceptable solution, which further aggravates fears for the eventual eruption of a crisis (Kruger 2009, Paul 2010). Azerbaijan is also on hostile terms with Iran and retains territorial differences with Georgia, although this issue is not so pronounced and the potential for conflict significantly lesser compared to the Azeri–Armenian case

---

1   At the same time, Ukraine's storage capacity hosts more than 40 bcm of natural gas. As weird as it might sound it is unknown who owns these quantities. Moreover, there are no TPA arrangements in place for the transit of this gas (Pirani, Stern and Yafimava 2010: 31).

2   BP, Statoil and SOCAR are the most important shareholders in the venture.

(EIA 2010a). The fact that Georgia and Azerbaijan are energy partners serves to fortify amiable rather than polemical relations.

Secondly, legal issues are of paramount importance. As we saw in Chapter 5, the status of the Caspian Sea remains unresolved. Caspian states do not agree on a legal definition of the Caspian and thus disagreements on how its natural resources should be divided prevail. While there have been bilateral deals between some of the Caspian states, a clear demarcation of exploration rights is still missing. While Iran maintains that the sea has to be allocated to the five littoral states equally, Azerbaijan has begun exploration in disputed waters considering them its own territorial zone. Azerbaijan is also engaged in talks with Turkmenistan on allocating contested fields in the middle of the Caspian (EIA 2010a). This undefined status creates hurdles for the construction of a trans-Caspian pipeline that is essential if Russian territory is to be by-passed and the Caspian gas to get direct access to the West (Sheikhmohammady, Kilgour and Hipel 2010, Akiner 2004, Dekmejian and Hovann 2001).

Thirdly, energy diplomacy is detrimental. Russia, as we saw in Chapter 5, has put its thrust upon the Caspian states and formed a gas alliance with Turkmenistan, Kazakhstan and Uzbekistan. It has thus managed to lock up most of the region's gas production until around 2030. Nevertheless, Turkmenistan's pledge for higher prices for the gas it sells to Gazprom and subsequent disagreements paved the way for other states like China and Iran to get some quantities of Turkmen gas (Pirani, Stern and Yafimava 2010: 23). Despite the Memorandum of Understanding that the EU and Turkmenistan signed on a strategic energy partnership in April 2008 and Turkmenistan's alleged willingness to reserve 10 bcm for the EU in the near future, the EU is yet to be supplied by Turkmenistan. The main impediment remains the absence of an energy corridor (Boonstra 2010: 2–3, Cornell 2008). This applies equally to Kazakhstan. Its position between Russia and China, however, easily ensures security of demand for its gas, thus rendering it difficult and of disputable value to turn to the EU market (Larsson 2008, Yesdauletov 2009, Yenikeyeff 2008, Tsereteli 2008). Russia, on the other hand, besides its gas alliance with Central Asian states, has also agreed for the purchase of some Azeri gas. This will decrease overall supplies for the EU by its most promising alternative supplier.

The only way to marginalize Russian predominance would be to construct a trans-Caspian pipeline and bring Caspian gas to Azerbaijan and then to Europe. This, however, is quite expensive, will provoke the fierce resistance of Russia which can play the legal card (the unresolved status of the Caspian) and the environmental card (a sub-sea pipeline under the Great Lake carries many environmental hazards), as well as enforce geopolitical threats and countermeasures. Investors are thus sceptical to proceed not least out of fear for Russia's potentially destabilizing role. The US administration appears reluctant to push for the project taking into account Russian sensitivities in the region. The EU itself lacks efficient energy diplomacy. Although it sponsors the Nabucco project, it remains impotent to push for a trans-Caspian pipeline that, if implemented, would link to Nabucco and ensure its profitability. Hence, the Caspian states have concluded deals to sell most of their gas to Russia. In case no alternative energy corridors are created in the future, Caspian gas will continue to be a supplementary to Gazprom's export potential (as well as cater for other non-EU markets), rather than become an alternative source of supply for the EU (Socor 2007a).

It should be noted that among the reasons, albeit not the most essential, behind this failure is the EU's reluctance to develop partnerships with countries that fail to embrace democratic principles and open markets rules and to respect human rights norms, as well as its failure as yet to form a more holistic policy framework that will incorporate fully political considerations. This brings us to the trade-offs between energy security and normative commitments and constraints. In case the EU did form strategic partnerships with states as Uzbekistan and Turkmenistan, it would be as if it acquiesced to their non-democratic regimes. Even worse, it would be seen to support diplomatically and strengthen financially their dictatorial rule over their people. This would show the EU to go against its values and principles in order to ensure its material interests (Boonstra 2011). While all these hold true, the corollary is that Russia has ensured for itself most of the Caspian gas production and can fortify its role as the predominant supplier of the EU gas market. The dominant Russian position in the region can only be threatened by China, another country that has whatsoever no reservations to sign profitable energy deals with non-democratic states (Socor 2007a). It is for these reasons that the EU belatedly turns to approach these regimes. Energy security and normative commitments, however, seem to be at odds.

Coming to the Middle East, although the region is also excessively gas-rich, its gas industry is quite underdeveloped as it remains in the shadow of the core oil industry. Nevertheless, Qatar and the United Arab Emirates (UAE) (ranking third and fourth in worldwide gas reserves) have already reached important production levels and have established themselves as significant LNG exporters.

Starting with Qatar, the greatest LNG exporter in the world, its geographical position allows it to supply all three lucrative regional gas markets, namely the Asian, the US and the European one. While production was initially earmarked for the US and the EU markets, the higher prices that Asian importers offered re-oriented much of the produced gas to the East rather than the West. Small quantities, nevertheless, have reached the EU market as well. Qatar follows a diversified export portfolio with supply contracts to the EU (Belgium, Spain and Italy), as well as to the US and Asian markets (Japan, Taiwan, India and South Korea). There are reservations, however, pertaining to the continued supply of gas from Qatar. First of all, despite the ample gas reserves (Qatar has the largest single gas field in the world) and the fact that multinational energy companies (predominantly ExxonMobil) are engaged in exploration schemes, the state company Qatar Petroleum has acquired a controlling stake in the joint ventures that exploit gas reserves in the country. This critical role of the state means that the rate of production may fluctuate according to the government's preferences. This is also important as an example-setter for the rest of the Middle East gas-rich countries that gradually start to build up their gas industries. Secondly, the rising gas demand in the region makes it necessary to withhold part of the production for domestic and regional use. Thirdly, the EU has to compete with other lucrative importers that may be willing to offer higher prices than European Members. Under this light, while Qatar has the wherewithal to become a significant EU supplier, its export potential is not problem-free (CIEP 2008b).

The UAE, on the other hand, have yet to make significant openings to the EU market. Although the French company Total operates wells in UAE and small quantities reach the EU market, the bulk of the gas produced supplies the US and Asian markets. While production from mature fields is ongoing, there are no further developmental plans within the Emirates. Hence, UAE's short- to mid-term potential as a source of diversification for the EU remains marginal (CIEP 2008b: 40, Butt 2001: 240–44).

Iraq has started talks with the EU on joint gas exploration schemes and on the construction of a pipeline network for the transmission of gas. Political hardships in Iraq have delayed the whole process, but the potential is there since Iraq retains significant reserves of gas, estimated to surpass 3 tcm (CIEP 2008a: 47–8, 51). The Iraqi government has recently initiated a round of auctions for a number of its oil and gas fields. Royal Dutch Shell has earned the first contract and other multinational companies are expected to follow suit in the framework of overall governmental efforts to rejuvenate the Iraqi economy and restore normality and welfare to the country (EIA 2010b). The construction of the Nabucco pipeline could provide a great incentive for Iraq, as well as for all other Middle East (and Caspian) producers, to develop their gas industry. Nevertheless, the pipeline is not being built exactly in the absence of these states' commitment to produce the necessary quantities that would guarantee the viability of the pipeline. This vicious circle illustrates the difficult starting point for diversified supplies for the EU (CIEP 2008: 40–41).

Special reference should be made here to Iran that comes second in total gas reserves only behind Russia holding 14 per cent of the global gas wealth. The enduring friction between the West and Iran has led the former to impose extensive sanctions on the latter. These sanctions have inflicted significant damage on the Iranian economy; as a result, the energy industry has also suffered. Severe restrictions on trade and impediments for Western enterprises to do business in Iran have maintained Iran's underdevelopment. Nevertheless, if the EU is honestly seeking diversification from the Russian threat, then Iran presents the ideal partner in both economic and geographical terms. Iran can supply the EU market both through pipelines and by LNG. It can thus add more energy corridors and flexibility to gas supplies (Chappell 2010: 7–9). In its 20-year plan (2005–2025), Iran envisions that by 2025 its exports will have surpassed 150 bcm (Tehran Times 2008) and is contemplating the construction of a pipeline with a capacity of 37 bcm from its Southern Pars gas field to Europe. In 2007, the Swiss company EGL concluded a deal with Iran that provided for the purchase of 5 bcm per year for a 25-year period. This gas would supply the TAP that is designed to bring gas to the Italian market. This breakthrough, however, is indeterminately postponed due to political conditions in Iran and hostility with the West. The construction of TAP is set to go on, but its initial source of supply will be, as we saw in Chapter 5, Azerbaijan, not Iran (Offshore Energy Today 2010). Iran's significance is not restricted to its huge reserves but also to its potential role as a transit state for Caspian gas. As long as the deadlock in the Caspian continues and no trans-Caspian pipeline is built, Iran will remain the sole option for the transportation of Kazakh and Turkmen gas to Europe via a land pipeline (Cornell 2008: 151–2).

Iran's theocratic, fundamentalist regime, its political ambitions as a regional power in the wider Middle East and its established intention to build nuclear power plants render Iran a rather intricate partner. It would be weird if the EU, in its attempt to diversify from what it perceives as a Russian threat, substitutes it with that of Iran. Still, the mid-term evolution of the EU–Iran gas trade cannot be ruled out. Proximity, large gas reserves, high demand for gas and the feasibility of a pipeline system to link the two entities are the main factors that advocate an EU–Iranian energy partnership. From the Iranian perspective, the EU forms a lucrative market that can offer security of demand for Iranian gas as well as high profits. Even more importantly, it presents an excellent opportunity for Iran to escape isolation from the world community, penetrate more into the global economy and acquire a significant share of the market which can also translate into political leverage. It is true that the US sanctions, the EU's reluctance to stand up against US policies and the threat Iran is believed to pose as an emerging nuclear power, all render close energy relations between the EU and Iran a remote possibility. If one takes a closer look at transatlantic relations, however, it is clear that EU policies deviate from these of the US. The EU renounces military power and follows a much milder diplomacy. It sees economic cooperation as a potential driver of interdependence that can lead to improvements in hostile international relations and paves the way for a more peaceful international environment (Keukeleire and MacNaughtan 2008). It is also important here to draw a comparison with European states' decision in the 1960s and 1970s to conclude oil and gas contracts with the Soviet Union in the midst of the Cold War (Stern 1999: 151, Klinghoffer 1977: 180–96). Despite US indignation, EU–Russia energy trade evolved significantly and up to these days remains by and large smooth.

The Middle Eastern energy wealth is associated with the Arab world. As weird as it may sound, however, recent developments may make Israel a significant energy exporter in the region. Israel discovered two important gas fields, the Tamara field in 2009 and the much bigger Leviathan deposit in 2010 off the Israeli coast. Their combined reserves amount to 700 bcm. The first is estimated to yield gas from 2012 on, while the second around 2015. This creates the potential for Israel not only to cover its own domestic needs, but also to convert itself from a net importer to a net exporter. Proximity and close relations with Greece are conducive to bilateral gas trade, which may convert Greece into a regional gas hub for the South European gas market (where demand for gas is increasing) in the near future. Nevertheless, a number of obstacles have to be surpassed. First of all, Lebanon protests that (part of) the finds lie in Lebanese soil and warns Israel not to undertake any unilateral drilling activities against Lebanese sovereignty. The two sides are technically still at war, a factor that undermines the potential for a mutually agreed solution and heightens the risk for renewed conflict on the newly found subsoil wealth. There are augmenting fears that Hezbollah, a Lebanese paramilitary organization financed by Iran, will do everything in its power to impede production and destroy upstream facilities with an eye to strip Israel from energy-born revenues and wider geopolitical advantages (The Economist 2010d, Bronner 2010). An agreement with Cyprus over the same issue, on the other hand, has been swiftly concluded (Qatar Tribune 2010). The discovery of ample gas reserves in the Mediterranean offshore Israel has created high hopes for further discoveries not only in Israel, but also in Cyprus and Lebanon. To this aim, the two countries are expected to launch research offshore their coasts in quest for (oil and) gas. A chain of research activities thus seems to have been opened up that may add to overall availability of gas resources for the EU. These, however, are only speculations for the time being.

These developments not only aggravate Turkey's geopolitical environment (after harshly deteriorating relations with Israel and perpetual conflict with Cyprus), but also encumber its energy aspirations. Turkey's role as an indispensable transit country has been crucial, albeit frequently obstructionist (Nies 2008: 85–94). The consortium designing TAP has still signed no regulatory transit agreements with Turkey (CSIS 2010: 6). Due to its favourable geographical position, Turkey is eager to become a hub for North African, Caspian and Middle East gas destined for Europe. Therefore, it prefers to buy the gas itself and re-sell it at a profit, rather than simply allow transit of this gas westwards. This pledge had led to time-consuming negotiations for the transit of Azeri gas through ITGI and remains on the agenda for future supplies (Winrow 2009, Özdemir 2008). Current developments in the Southeast Mediterranean, however, may significantly lessen Turkey's role and subsequently its space for negotiating manoeuvres in the gas sector.

Turkey's policy goes against the will of the EU to avoid transit-dependency risks as well as transit-induced higher prices and has propelled plans to build a new, small pipeline in order to bypass Turkey. The Azerbaijan–Georgia–Romania Interconnector (AGRI) will use the trans-Caucasus pipeline up to Georgia and then tankers across the Black Sea to Romania to carry around 7 bcm annually either in LNG or CNG form. This network will connect to the newly inaugurated pipeline that links Romania with Hungary, a traditional European gas hub. AGRI's significance then is twofold; to add to the EU's route diversification goal, as well as to soften Turkey's ambitions for a pivotal role in the EU's gas supply (The Economist 2010).

The Other Suppliers

The EU is committed to expand its energy infrastructure in order to host more LNG in the near future (Jensen 2004, Vaszi, Varga and Svab 2010: 130–31).

Spain, Italy and Britain are leading the way due to their favourable geographical positions. Croatia, a Member-State-to-be, plans to construct the Krk LNG terminal as well as a pipeline to connect it with the Hungarian gas hub (CSIS 2010: 5). Once more, however, the problem is not so much infrastructure, but the supply side. Only a few distant producers contribute for the time being to the import portfolio of the EU providing together less than 20 bcm of LNG annually (CIEP 2008a: 51–2). One could argue that since the gas market gets globalized with the advent of LNG trade, the EU could link to more distant suppliers, decrease its reliance on Russian gas and render its gas market more flexible. Indeed, this can be the case with states as Qatar. With a significant gas production base and estimations for higher productivity, Qatar can increase gas deliveries to the EU, not least since its geographical position is favourable to this cause. Nevertheless, what will determine flows of energy in the global LNG market is competition for gas, geopolitical considerations as well as the height of prices importers are willing to pay. We have already established the EU's impotence and reluctance to become engaged in geopolitical games in order to ensure security of supplies. Intense competition also poses hurdles for the EU since the US, China and Japan are all pursuing more imports (van der Linde and de Jong 2009: 6). It is also questionable how much the EU is willing to pay for LNG from distant producers. Two further drawbacks have to be mentioned: firstly, LNG also carries its own risks of supply interruptions, for any technical, economic or political reasons. Secondly, LNG trade is rather capital-intensive (calling for de- and re-gasification terminals at both ends of the trade chain) and any terminal running idle involves high costs (Checchi, Behrens and Egenhofer 2009: 20–21). Therefore, the weaknesses of LNG trade and the EU's poor performance in energy diplomacy may lead it to re-consider the role of LNG in its market.

In general, the EU could increase its LNG supplies from some African and Middle East producers. It is much harder, nevertheless, to conclude significant deals with more distant suppliers. Long distance, which adds to final costs, is the first reason that makes such contracts less attractive. The second is the dynamics of regional markets. Producers in the Caribbean are embedded in intra-North American trade, while the East Asian regional market is well balanced providing security of demand for the producers. Japan has for decades formed a reliable and lucrative import market (it pays the highest prices for the gas it imports), while China presents a promising alternative. The economic logic then speaks against any EU supply from established exporters as Malaysia and Indonesia.

Conclusion

To conclude, the EU faces a significant supply deficit. Overt dependence on a handful of suppliers remains in the absence of a fourth corridor that will bring Caspian gas to the EU market. LNG will in all probability add to the EU's security of supply, but it is not expected to fundamentally bolster it. The EU's

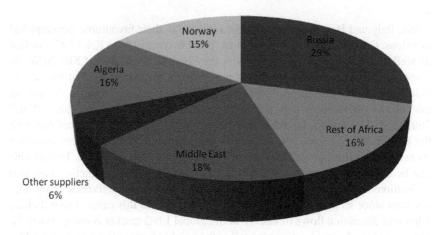

Figure 6.1   The EU's projected gas imports in 2030
Source: Ghiles 2009

import portfolio is likely to be more diversified in two decades than it is today, even though the three main suppliers (Russia, Norway and Algeria) seem set to retain their preponderant position in the EU gas market. Recent developments in Southeast Mediterranean are certainly important, but it is still premature to judge the size of a contribution they can make to EU's diversification policies.

Chapter 7
The Way Forward

A useful means for devising a prudent energy strategy is to identify current and potential threats and challenges that may endanger either one of the three core dimensions of energy security: security of supplies, economic efficiency and environmental sustainability. The EU pursues a state whereby it will face no energy shortages, will pay affordable prices for the energy it consumes so that they do not hold growth down and whereby its energy consumption will not compromise the welfare of future generations.

We also have to add here a fourth dimension: since the EU is not a nation-state but a hybrid, complex, *sui generis* international institution, we should be very cautious that energy issues do not create fertile ground for intense disagreements between its constituent Members that can threaten its existence. The debt crises that currently plague a handful of Member States and internal disagreement as to Members' and supranational organs' most appropriate stance, have cultivated a dangerous discourse on the very existence not only of the Eurozone but also of the EU itself. Under these circumstances, policy divergences and dilemmas pertaining to energy policy, as illustrated in the previous chapters, should not be left to add to current upheavals within the EU.

In this framework, we can discern four main concerns:

- Do energy politics severely undermine EU solidarity?
- How can excessive dependence on Gazprom be tackled with?
- Is growing consumption of gas prudent?
- Does the EU energy strategy meet the environmental goals set? Is it moving towards the establishment of a sustainable, green economy?

In what follows, we discuss how these risks can be successfully mitigated.

The EU's Energy Incoherence and the Need for Solidarity

Differing approaches between 'old' and 'new' Europe with regard to Russia's role in the gas market have created strong tensions within the EU. Besides the well-documented absence of a coherent EU energy policy, nevertheless, it is the case that certain initiatives of Member States, while serving their own energy security needs, at the same time threaten that of their partners. The case of Nord Stream is the most illustrative example. Poland has censured the Russo–German plan to build the Nord Stream as a new Molotov–Ribbentrop Pact, since it undermines its position as a transit country and exposes itself to Russian potential offensive energy policies. Not only were there no prior consultations within the EU with regard to Nord Stream, but once Poland and the other new European Members reacted ferociously to the agreement, Germany did not take their complaints and justified concerns very seriously (Smith 2009). At the same time, new European Members fail to understand that this agreement serves Germany's energy security interests and thus has a sound basis. In other words, both sides focus on the state of their own energy security, disregarding the notion of EU energy security (Larsson 2007b: 11). This is not a rhetorical problem, but a very practical one. European integration has bound together the fortunes of its Members. In case the new Member States' energy security deteriorates, EU partners will have to cater for the missing supplies in accordance with the most recent energy regulations; difficulties will not remain within their borders but will spread to the rest of the EU as well (as is amply manifested by the running debt crises that have spread havoc throughout the EU). Any political troubles of 'new' Europe with Russia or economic slowdown for this reason, will force European partners to come eventually to the help of the ailing Member States. It is for this reason that the German stand is myopic. Its policy is nurturing potential consequences, which it may be called upon to compensate for together with the rest of the EU partners.

Solidarity thus remains the missing link in EU energy policy. In any case, there are ways to accommodate the interests of all EU Members. The negotiation of provisions to expand the pipeline to Poland and other new Members would be preferable to the current bilateral Russo–German agreement. Alternatively, the establishment of interconnections with 'new' Europe, accompanied by guarantees by Germany for the provision of the region, would revoke the divisive character of the Nord Stream and facilitate the energy security of the eastern part of the EU as well. As long as the EU persists not to act in solidarity, however, Russia will be encouraged to continue its *divide et impera* policy in the EU (Smith 2010: 1).

This point opens up a much wider debate. The EU has developed impressively throughout the decades through what is called the Community method. Leaving aside the most difficult and potentially divisive issues, it focused on those sectors where cooperation was easier and could bring tangible results. This method was based upon an intergovernmental logic that was congruent with the constituent states' principal interests. With the enlargement to 27 Members, however, it is hard to reach consensus. This mode of policy-making seems to have exhausted its limits. At the same time, it is hard to postpone the solution of pressing issues any more, since their adverse consequences are all the more evident.

What then has to be re-conceptualized is the level of policy-making. Supranational institutions have fortified their stance vis-à-vis Member States within these six decades of European integration. Nevertheless, they still lack effective power in a number of areas. The persistence of national interests, however, is myopic and self-defeating in such an interdependent world. The formation of EU, rather than national, interests would serve EU-wide goals, rather than national ones. It is indeed an oxymoron that national policies remain preponderant in a progressively EU-wide, single and unified gas market. Since the energy challenges act on an international and not national level, energy problems should be dealt with at the supranational level (Butler 2009, Helm 2009: 142). The supranational institutions are the most appropriate structures to defend EU-wide interests and achieve EU-wide goals. A Deutsche Bank study endorses such a position underlining that 'piecemeal efforts at the national level have proved inadequate. Only a concerted European energy policy can generate hope for a sustainable future' (Auer 2007: 1). The European Commission would be much more suitable for dealing with foreign suppliers, in a fashion similar to the one it operates in the WTO representing its Member States under a close surveillance system, than Germany or Poland individually are. Power for the EU does not lie only in integration, but mostly in solidarity and unity. All the efforts put in coordinating EU energy policy will prove futile unless the political mindset itself does not change towards more collective forms of governance (Egenhofer and Behrens 2008: 7, 10).

The Fading of Gazprom's Threat?

The primary liability of the EU energy strategy is overt dependence on Russian gas. This issue has two dimensions. The first refers to the economic and political leverage Gazprom enjoys in the EU market and the subsequent threats of higher prices, supplies shortages and political concessions and blackmails. The second is exactly the opposite, namely how to retain strong energy ties with an indispensable partner, Gazprom. Russia's looming gas deficit, frustration with the EU liberalization and diversification rhetoric and approach, as well as its drive to progressively supply the Asian market, all raise the possibility that the EU may lose its traditional supplier and turn gas poor in the near future.

Before elaborating on the optimal strategy for the EU, a theoretical perspective must come in the discussion. The predominance of the realist theory has led scholars to focus on conflictive elements in international politics. We are accustomed to expecting the outburst of crises and then to explain them in terms of anarchical systemic effects and/or as the result of the greedy human nature and the incessant pursuit of power. International relations literature is full of such analyses and narratives (Baldwin 1993, Dunn and Schmidt 2007, Mearsheimer 2001, Gilpin 2001, Grieco 1990, Schweller 2003). Less focus has been placed on how cooperation is sustained and forms a steady characteristic of world politics. The realist explanation that periods of non-conflict are just intervals between two conflicts cannot sustain themselves as serious, academic and rigorous explanations, especially when they span decades. Since war and conflict are as central features of global politics as peace and cooperation, we have to search for the main causes that account for them. Going beyond the liberal utopianism of the early twentieth century, the neo-liberal school of thought has provided us with invaluable insights. The commonality of interests (Keohane and Axelrod 1993,

Axelrod 1997), solid institutional structures (Keohane 1984) and the notion of interdependence (Keohane and Nye 1972, Nye 2003) can form a sound basis for cooperation. Social constructivist scholars and critical theorists have concentrated their analytical emphasis on the existence of a common ideational and normative background as a framework conducive for cooperation (Risse 2010, Wendt 1999, Linklater 2007). The global system then is characterized not only by conflict, but by cooperation as well. Even more important, conflict is all the more seen as a rather costly, imprudent and inappropriate means to achieve one's goals. To the contrary, cooperation is progressively seen as *necessary* in this globalized and interdependent international system (Hill 2003: 135).

Accordingly, energy politics is at least as much about international cooperation as it is about conflict (Florini and Sovacool 2009, Goldthau and Witte 2009, 2010). No doubt there is competition for natural resources, 'great games' with regard to energy corridors and trade patterns following geopolitical alliances (Barnes and Jaffe 2006, Klare 2008, Orban 2008, Stulberg 2008, Zweig and Jianhai 2005). On the other hand, however, producers and consumers operate jointly in the market and share the interest of smooth trade that will yield security of supplies to the importers and high revenues to the exporters. There is a well-developed pipeline network serving trading states for decades and in most cases the inflow of energy is not held back even to hostile countries. The most prominent example is Western Europe's supply with Russian oil and gas since the 1960s. Amidst the height of the Cold War, the Soviet Union's need for hard currency and Western Europe's need to ensure diversified supplies (especially after the 1973 oil crisis) transcended geopolitical rivalries. The two entities have launched an energy partnership for almost half a century that has passed through rather turbulent times (the end of communism and the demise of the Soviet Union) and, despite ongoing disputes, has been significantly expanded during the 2000s.

In the same way that states face a security dilemma, they also face an energy security dilemma. In the same way, however, that the security dilemma does not need to lead to war in all occasions, the energy security dilemma does not need to lead to termination of cooperation either, but can be dealt with. It depends on how the actors perceive of each other and shape their approach to one another. It is here where the vital role of trust comes in. Mistrust can lead to actions that may cause total fallout. By means of open and transparent deliberations, institutional links and efficient collaboration, states can cooperate instead of conflict (Keohane 1984, Risse 2000).

Prescriptions for the Future

The challenge for the EU is how to overcome the points of divergence with Russia in order to construct more cordial relations with it and regulate their energy relations in a mutually beneficial way. The following policy prescriptions have the goal to illustrate how such a policy is feasible.

Enforce interdependence and promote cautious diversification schemes The core debate within the EU is whether diversification or interdependence with major producers is the optimal strategy. We depicted the dividing lines within the EU on this subject matter on Chapter 5. Starting with interdependence, there is a lot of substance and pragmatism in it. Contrary to flexible oil markets, gas markets are more rigid. Flexibility and diversification are difficult to achieve and security of gas supplies has traditionally been accomplished through the dynamics of interdependence. Liberalization regulations, LNG trade and the move towards a global gas market are changing these dynamics, albeit with indeterminate results. Moreover, this shift entails its own costs and risks. Therefore, it is still premature to judge whether these changes will add to or negatively impact upon security of supplies. In this context, deteriorating relations with traditional suppliers does not seem to be a prudent policy. Especially in the face of Asian markets seeking closer cooperation with Gazprom and challenging the EU's privileged position as Russia's principal market, it is important for the EU to contract large gas quantities from Gazprom, as well as modernize and update the pipeline system linking the two entities. Moreover, the argument that no supplier would leave a market if it is well embedded in a solid energy partnership is a powerful one. German arguments, hence, on courting Russia and securing supplies for the EU are valid.

Nevertheless, one cannot but see the limits to such an approach. It is wrong to put one's eggs into one basket, since Russia's looming gas deficit or an abrupt change of preferences in Russian export strategy may leave the EU in a dramatic situation. At the same time, the business sector pushes for further cooperation to suit its own interests. This is respectable, but should not come to the detriment of consumers. Alternative sources are important as means not only of diversification, but also of potentially lower prices. Sticking to cooperation with Russia may also provoke inertia and prevent energy companies from striking preferential deals with other suppliers, introducing more LNG from traditional as well as more distant sources and adding elasticity to the market. Diversification both of sources and routes is essential, since it adds flexibility and allows the market to withstand temporary shortages.

As we saw extensively in the previous chapter, however, there are no alternative gas sources for the time being that could justify (and replace) any significant reduction in the supply of Russian gas. Hence, substantial diversification can only (and should) be a pragmatic approach in the mid-term. The key issue, here, for the most fervent supporters of diversification, the East European Members, is that they de-politicize relations with Russia. Although Russia frequently provides indications for an aggressive energy policy in the region, these states should form an agenda of letting the past behind. Traumas stemming from past conquests and occupations cannot act as guiding principles for their contemporaneous foreign and energy policy. The twenty-first century presents many serious challenges to be tackled with and the ghosts of the past only serve as a distraction to their resolution. The utmost priority, instead, for these states is to embed close German–Russian energy ties into an EU-wide framework. At the same time, they have to advance the agenda of multiple interconnections that will allow the operation of a truly single market that can function as a shield of protection against Russian blackmailing policies.

In this light, a mix of these strategies is essential. Although this is not well taken in the eastern part of the EU, Russia is and will in all probability remain an indispensable energy partner for the future. This means that enforced interdependence can assure invaluable quantities from the most well-endowed gas country in the world. At the same time, overreliance on Gazprom is problematic in a number of ways and alternative gas has to come in to balance Gazprom's major role. These two policies then, interdependence and diversification, must not be seen in a contradictory, but in a supplementary light. The drawback is that the EU is not currently following consciously such a policy. Therefore, not only is it not well-coordinated, but it is also undermined by the adversary rhetoric of the EU's two camps.

The case of Nabucco offers a good starting point. The project is on the agenda for years, but lack of gas availability delays its construction. Russia's contribution seems to be the only way for the implementation of the project in the coming years. Unless Russia is allowed to participate, the most probable outcome is that Nabucco will remain in the contemplation phase for long or, if implemented, will only operate at partial capacity and thus profitability rate. The EU should consider whether it prefers some more billion cubic meters from alternative sources to flow into the EU market through a joint project with Russia or risk not having a fourth gas corridor built at all in the following years. In case the EU allowed Gazprom to become a partner, it would show good will to Gazprom and commitment to furthering EU–Russian interdependent relations, at the same time that it would proceed with mediocre diversification without upsetting its main supplier (Egenhofer and Behrens 2008: 12, Locatelli 2010: 6–9).

Escape the temptation of protectionism and embed suppliers in the liberalization project   Liberalization is essentially a strategy to maximize the interests of the consumers. While it also creates opportunities for the business sector and thus also for external suppliers, it imposes certain limitations to their operations. It is therefore important to understand the reaction and legitimate interests of the suppliers and in particular Gazprom. The EU has pressurized Gazprom to break up its export monopoly and allow other Russian enterprises to export gas to Europe. Although such reforms would enhance the overall effectiveness of the Russian gas sector, they would create gas-to-gas competition, yield lower final prices and accelerate the pace of eradication of Russian natural resources. Since gas-born revenues are essential for the Russian economy and gas is considered a strategic good to be reserved for future generations as well, it is debatable whether this would be a prudent strategy for Russia to follow (Helm 2009: 150, Fredholm 2005: 4, Gorst 2004: 8, Chufrin 2004: 18, CIEP 2004: 15–16).

Furthermore, suppliers follow a model of vertical integration to cut costs and increase profit margins and seek guarantees that their energy is going to be absorbed as a prerequisite to invest. Such organizational and contractual schemes evidently contravene and hinder competition. The EU's legislation that attempts to amend them, however, risks alienating Gazprom. The European Commission seems to prioritize meticulous regulation to substantial security of supplies. What would the EU reaction be in case foreign suppliers, first of all Gazprom, were unwilling to adhere to such regulations and did not invest on exploration and infrastructure projects exactly due to insecurity and uncertain gains (Checchi, Behrens and Egenhofer 2009: 22–4, Helm 2004)? The most possible reaction would then be Member States' intervention to give guarantees for security of demand and proceed to energy investments themselves, a state rather than a market response (Helm 2009: 142, Butler 2009: 134). This would constitute not only a drastic deterioration of the state of EU energy security, but also a blatant contradiction of the EU itself. This scenario should at all costs be averted.

The EU has failed to create a unified liberalized regulatory framework for the Eurasian region. Hence, we find open markets, unbundling regulation and competition together with monopolies and state-backed policies. The key challenge is how to deal with these foreign players that do not succumb to liberalization regulations. Protectionism may seem to be a solution. Especially the application of the reciprocity clause would force foreign suppliers either to restrict their activities in the EU gas market or open up theirs to European investments. However, such an approach undermines and reverses the decades-long liberalization process. Most importantly, it repeals the EU's traditional role as norm-setter (Larsson 2007: 59). At the same time, it creates friction and obstacles that may drive these suppliers away from the EU market. It should not be lost that such measures are enthusiastically supported by former Soviet satellites that retain a polemical mindset vis-à-vis Russia. It would be a mistake for the EU energy strategy to be misguided by such perceptions.

What is of crucial significance is that the suppliers' interests become incorporated in the EU energy strategy (Egenhofer and Behrens 2008: 11). The EU seems to retain the role of the regulator in principle, but not in effect. This does not add to its energy security. Once it accepts that dialogue and compromise can facilitate security of supplies, protectionist measures can be removed from the agenda and energy cooperation can be built on sounder grounds. To take an example, the foreign dimension of unbundling was certain to create friction with Gazprom (and Sonatrach). A preferable approach to simply presenting the Commission's decisions to Gazprom would be to comprehensively discuss the unbundling plan with Gazprom and co-decide on the detailed provisions of the new regulation. The compromise reached regarding the role of long-term contracts in the EU gas market reveals the potential for understanding and resolution of differences.

Harmonize action and rhetoric   The EU follows a mix of diversification and interdependence policies with its three major gas suppliers. Nevertheless, its rhetoric is quite one-sided. Gazprom is demonized, while diversification is heralded as the panacea to EU gas security (perceived as) threatened by Gazprom's preponderant role. Nevertheless, it is absurd for the EU to emphasize diversification as the building block of its energy security strategy in the gas sector when new developments are restricted to a small pipeline (ITGI) that brings very little gas to the EU. Even worse, Nabucco fails to qualify as the cornerstone of this policy, since the possibility of its construction in the near future remains contentious. With North African states unable to significantly boost their domestic production in the short-term and the Middle East gas industry at a premature level, there will hardly be any supplies to fill this pipeline. The incongruence between the EU's actions and rhetoric belittles its reliability and undermines its energy security since in its attempt to foster its own diversification, all it succeeds in is to drive Russia to endorse itself more enthusiastically a diversification agenda. The EU then has to bring its rhetoric in line with the actual policies it follows.

Illustrating a Possible Pathway

It would be useful here to portray what seems to be a quite plausible scenario for the EU–Russia gas trade in the near future. The possibilities are that it will evolve in a much less politicized and amiable direction. This is so for three main reasons:

- A number of initiatives are already working into the direction of enforced interdependence. Lucrative contracts, new pipelines and EU–Russian business networks further bonds between the two entities. The prospective curtailment of transit dependency will marginalize significant hotspots in EU–Russia energy relations and will guarantee sustained gas trade for the near future. Since an exit from this situation is disadvantageous for both sides, the EU–Russia energy partnership is solidly grounded.
- Secondly, diversification policies under way from both sides will progressively allow for more flexibility. The inflow of more non-Russian gas into EU territory, as well as the existence of parallel outlets for Russian gas, will offer to both entities alternative suppliers/markets. This will serve to release tensions and loosen the energy security dilemma EU and Russia face. It will thus enhance the further building of trust and allow the two sides to strengthen their energy partnership.
- Thirdly, two developments will in all probability lessen Russian leverage in the former communist world that has been incorporated into the EU, which remains the most problematic aspect of EU–Russia energy relations. Firstly, gradual diversification will reduce (albeit not eradicate) dependence on Russian gas. Secondly, the liberalization project involves a number of interconnections between national EU markets. Once these are put in place and with destination clauses gone for good, East European states will be able to get (Russian and non-Russian) gas from their EU partners in cases of supply shortages. This will diminish Russia's leverage to use energy for political causes.[1]

_____

1   For an elaborate analysis and substantiation of these predictions see Proedrou 2010.

The End of (Cheap) Gas

The third concern comprises two distinct, but highly interrelated issues. Firstly, gas consumption is growing at rapid levels, not least outside the EU with states as China aiming to substantially increase the usage of gas. This exacerbates the fears that in the not so distant future we are going to be talking about the end of gas in a way similar to the one the discussion about the end of oil is dominant today. True, gas reserves have a lifetime of a couple of more decades than do oil reserves and oil is set to remain the dominant fossil fuel (albeit their drift is shrinking) (Müller-Kraenner 2008: 7). Nevertheless, gas reserves are not inexhaustible. It is important to understand then that increased gas usage is a mid-term strategy to offset oil supplies' related problems, but fails to face the fundamental challenge of our time: how to retain high levels of growth and welfare at a diminishing availability of fossil fuels. We will return to this point below.

Secondly, it is quite possible that gas prices are going to become more expensive in the near future. Since gas prices have traditionally followed those of oil, which have increased manifold since the late 1990s, gas has ceased to be the cheap resource it was up to then. No wonder its price may go down again. Most analysts, however, make the point that the global population has to become used to live in a world of expensive oil and hence also gas (Butler 2009: 129–31).

The oil-based gas price, as we saw in Chapter 3, however, is a remnant of a previous era when natural gas was considered oil's little brother. This contractual formula is contrary to liberal economics and it seems plausible that gas prices will progressively be set by supply and demand determinants. Increased competition and LNG supplies have created the dynamics for this shift. The European gas market has started, albeit at a slow pace, to move away from oil-indexation (Stern 2007, 2009). This development means that geological parameters, the height of investments, technological know-how and distance that make up the costs of specific exploration and transportation projects will form the basis of the future gas price. Such a switch to independent gas pricing is likely to raise gas prices considerably, if one takes into account tougher geological conditions for exploration, as well as higher investments and sophisticated technological know-how needed. Although, as discussed in Chapter 2, there is currently a gas glut, this is probable to be bridged in the light of rising gas consumption and/ or inadequate investments in the context of economic stagnation. The potential declining ratio between natural gas reserves and consumption rates can only act as instigator of higher prices. If you add the concentration of most gas reserves in a few countries, the likely persistence of monopolistic structures and the increasing global competition for gas supplies, gas is probable to become more expensive in the near future (Gorst 2004, Monaghan and Montanaro-Jankovski 2006).

The question then inevitably arises: is the EU going to be in a position to pay for (significantly) higher gas prices in the future? Has this scenario been thought through? Is hence its policy of gas promotion prudent? What usually happens is that when a fossil fuel becomes inefficient economically, consumers switch to other sources of energy. This, however, is a slow process evolving high costs. One could well argue here that it is not to the interest of producers to raise gas prices to such an extent that their customer base will be threatened. While this holds true, intense global competition may allow producers to raise prices and still yield considerable profits. Such a possibility poses the question whether the EU should contemplate more radical solutions to deal with its dependency on gas. In case it does, high gas prices will, paradoxically, prove not to be a problem in itself, but rather what will facilitate the solution to the EU's overarching problem of energy security (Egenhofer and Behrens 2008: 6). It is this possibility that we now turn to examine.

A Green Energy Scene for the Twenty-first Century

Although the debate on environmental degradation has grown quite mature during the last years, the fact that changes occur rather slowly and follow fluctuations throughout the years has played its role in the creation of two distinct camps with regard to how best to pursue sustainable development: the first, the reformist, is not convinced that environmental degradation proceeds so quickly and thus considers gradual measures to reverse it to be sufficient; the second one, the radical, to the contrary, maintains that climate change is irreversible unless immediate action is taken to retract current trends. This reformist/radical dichotomy impedes agreement on how to deal with the problems posed by the increasing impact of human action on the environment. Although globalization propels debates on the need for global governance and progressively cements the conviction that the whole of humanity shares this common fundamental cause, we are still quite far from comprehensive collective governance on environmental issues. Varied national and regional needs, interests and preoccupations, linked with a number of correlated geopolitical issues, act as barriers to a universally beneficial common understanding (Müller-Kraenner 2008: 17). Climate change has as yet not succeeded in reformulating the main actors' – states and energy industries – strategies in favour of sustainable development. As a result, 'the existing global energy governance fails to address the major energy challenges in an integrated manner' (Cherp, Jewell and Goldthau 2011: 85).

We can discern three logics operating at three different levels. While the first, the reformist, is predominant, we argue that the other two logics must necessarily come into play. The second calls for more radical goals to reverse environmental damage, while the third calls us to contemplate how we can fundamentally reshape our societies. Creating a new societal context can prove the most innovative way to deal with the dual energy and environmental challenge.

The Inadequacy of the Reformist Agenda

Despite its enthusiastic pro-environmental rhetoric, the EU follows reformist rather than radical environmental policies. It envisions a future situation where its industry will be less energy-intensive and more energy-efficient, where reliance on external suppliers will decrease to a degree that security of supplies is not endangered by third countries and where alternative sources of supply will play an increasing role in the EU energy mix. One means to achieve that is the promotion of gas usage. This policy, however, while constructive in the short-term, bears negative long-term implications for sustainable development. Current investments on gas need at least two decades for sunk costs to be recovered. This means that established gas consumption will serve in the following years as a deterrent to and thus retard the more ground-breaking policy of substitution of hydrocarbons with renewables (Larsson 2007: 19). One could well raise objections with regard to the prudence of such policies that, although seemingly positive, create hurdles to a decisive switch away from hydrocarbons.

Furthermore, since 80 per cent of emissions of greenhouse gases stem from energy consumption, the projection is that, taking into consideration the estimated increase of energy consumption in the following years in the EU, they will have increased by 5 per cent by 2030. This is great news compared to the 55 per cent increase estimated for global emissions, but still remains very far from matching the 20 per cent decrease target set by the Commission (European Commission 2007b). In other words, current policies are far from accomplishing declared goals and thus inadequate.

The prominent counter-argument to such critiques is that a shift to alternative sources of energy is too expensive and thus unrealistic. Industries would suffer high costs and thus become less competitive globally, in case they switched to alternative sources of energy. This is why states and firms are reluctant to invest heavily on renewable resources. Nevertheless, one has to contemplate whether climate change itself does not involve high economic costs. To take an example, hurricanes and typhoons have become more destructive as a result of higher global temperatures. The devastation of New Orleans after the hurricane Katrina called for huge sums of money to rebuild the city. Nicholas Stern, former chief economist of the World Bank, has put the costs of climate change for the British government to 5–20 per cent of global economic output (British Government 2006). This does not include any further expenses that will be bred by potential wars and crises induced by resource competition and energy poverty (Müller-Kraenner 2008: 16). Hence, while substituting hydrocarbons with more environmentally-friendly sources of energy bears high costs, not taking this path will prove much more expensive in the mid-term.

The Need for a More Radical Agenda

Current planning of ways to deal with the environment are based upon a normative, ideational and values background of the industrial era. This era, however, seems to have approximated its limits. It is hard to conceive how growth can be maintained without a lethal deterioration of the global environment. Scholars increasingly agree that our global society is no more viable in its current form since with current rates and methods of consumption we are going to have exhausted most seafood, natural resources and photosynthesis capacity, as well as have brought the global temperature to such a point in which many species will be threatened with extinction or have become already extinct within a few decades (Diamond 2006; Rifkin 2010: 42–3, 476–511). Taking the radical pathway then seems to make much more sense. Surpassing the mediocre goals set by the European Commission, Sweden has set itself the task of running its economy on renewable sources of energy by 2020. Iceland fulfils its energy demands almost exclusively with local hydropower and geothermal energy, while it aims to replace its limited oil imports with liquid hydrogen produced from renewable sources (Müller-Kraenner 2008: 21). Those countries serve as proper examples for a much more ambitious agenda. The EU is not well-endowed with fossil fuels, but could exploit its potential in solar, wind and geo-thermal energy to further develop alternative sources of energy. The two former, in particular, have significantly increased during the last decades, while further investments, especially of a regional or interregional nature with adjusting regions as the Middle East or Africa, will serve to bring costs down and make these sources of energy more competitive. This is all the more important if one takes into account that solar energy can also be used in the transportation sector as well (Hoogwijk, Vries and Turkenburg 2004, EWEA 2007, Ummel and Wheeler 2008, Patt 2009). As Butler (2009: 136) points out the focus must be:

> away from the current dependence on hydrocarbons ... Over time the answer ... could be in building solar capacity in the Sahara and transporting that electricity through a new line into Europe ... the need now is to move from concepts and ideas to material propositions for technology which can actually be used in different countries around Europe.

A resolute passage to the hydrogen economy is also a critical option for a sustainable future (Rifkin 2003), while new technologies for storing solar and wind power pave the way for advanced energy efficiency.[2] Such moves carry the additional advantage that:

> every step in the development of new and alternative fuels, in the creation of new vehicles, powered by electricity, in the establishment of new infrastructure and in the pursuit of energy efficiency will bring both direct and indirect employment. Furthermore, innovation and the application of existing technology can bring new business opportunities. The potential exists not only to transform Europe's own economy but also to create companies which can be global leaders as the rest of world comes to terms with the need for radical changes in the way energy is produced and consumed (Butler 2009: 139).

---

2   Rechargeable devices are already in place, firstly used by the armed forces; the space for improving their capacity and extending their duration is promising for the future, see Slater 2011.

In fact, recent developments create fertile ground for the extensive penetration of renewables. The devastating nuclear accident in Japan has augmented the already pressing need for more energy born from alternative sources of energy. At the same time, the revolutionary upsurge in North Africa and Middle East becomes a critical factor for democratization. Both older regimes with staying power as well as the newly elected governments will have to be highly responsive to the people's needs. The democratization wave means that the EU will find it easier to interact with democratic governments and stands better chances for exporting its own political, economic, developmental and energy regulatory model there. This can also enhance the establishment of transmission lines that will link Africa with Europe and will supply the latter predominantly with solar energy (Ruchser 2011).

Kevin Featherstone (2009: 94–6) goes as far as to detect this policy area as the finest opportunity for the EU to exit its policy inertia. He suggests that the EU should 'develop an initiative that combines concerns on energy supply and climate change ... [that] link the new politics of the "green" agenda with matters of economic security'. He thus proposes the creation of a new independent body, the 'European Sustainable Development Agency' that would operate according to the European Central Bank model and ensure energy security and sustainable development for the EU.

Towards a New Societal Context

Radical measures that introduce alternative sources of energy can retain high energy consumption rates without further deteriorating the state of the environment. One can also, however, contemplate whether we need to consume so much energy in any form. For example, instead of searching for more energy-efficient ways to run our cars, we can think better whether we need to use our cars so much, whether we need to cover long distances to the same extent as is the case nowadays.

It is useful to remember that high energy consumption rates are not permanent features of human societies. To the contrary, they were historically determined by the advent of the Industrial Revolution since the late eighteenth century that introduced efficient techniques for mass production of commodities. Offer of labour in the factories attracted more people to the cities. The subsequent urbanization created massive markets for the rising conglomerates that in their turn provided further incentives for urbanization. A number of big cities were built up and expanded impressively up to our days. They are the ones that today have the worse traffic jams, the higher levels of air and water pollution and the higher disease rates (Diamond 2006).

Nevertheless, the digital revolution since the 1970s allows us to fundamentally reshape our societies. Digital and satellite technology allow the transcendence of borders. A significant part of global trade consists of services, not commodities and thus can be equally accomplished at long distances. Furthermore, an increasing number of jobs can be carried out from remote regions. As James and Patomaki (2008) underline:

dominant practices of production and exchange have transformed and with it the nature of work for many has changed ... [while] the "old industrial economy" was fundamentally organized around standardized mass production, the New Economy is organized around "flexible" production of goods and services including financial services ... is a knowledge and idea-based economy where the key to economic growth lies in innovative ideas and technology embedded in services and manufactured products ... The late twentieth century had seen the relaying and reframing of industrial capitalism by what might be called [electronic] techno-scientific capitalism.

The need for over-concentration is thus dwindling. Instead of reproducing the same societal structures, we now have the possibility to live in a much more decentralized way. This would be by far the most drastic way to bring energy consumption down. Beyond the reformist/radical debate, reshaping the contours of our societies is the most far-sighted strategy to sustain the high welfare level of the West, as well as accommodate the rising needs and ambitions of the developing world.[3]

Combining the two latter logics, allow me to conclude presenting the example of my home country, Greece, which has been at the centre of attention lately due to the boom of its public sector deficit. Greece has eleven million citizens, around half of which resides in the capital, Athens. The result is intense energy consumption, enormous traffic jams, decades-long pollution in Athens and, not least, a serious negligence and underdevelopment of the countryside. The enforcement of de-centralization would create more balanced development, would release much of the environmental burden of the capital and would create fertile ground and enabling conditions for entrepreneurship in the countryside (Kufidu and Mihail 1999, Papadopoulou et al. 2010). Furthermore, there is hardly any rationale for sunny Greek islands torn by strong winds not to be energy-autarkic. It is indeed rather absurd that they are currently supplied with energy by the centre. The richness of the country in renewable resources is not fully exploited, a rather imprudent strategy for a country deeply indebted.

To conclude, the EU's energy challenges operate at two levels. At the first, the EU ought to balance between its internal divisions and implement a coherent strategy guided by the principle of European solidarity. It has to efficiently tackle the dual threat Gazprom poses, namely both mitigate the political and economic leverage Gazprom enjoys due to its dominant market share, as well as retain ample inflows of Russian gas without which security of supplies will be severely

---

3   In this context, the EU's recent initiative to orchestrate environmental action more at the local rather than the supranational level is crucial. The EU encourages the devolution of authorities to the local governments and has established the Covenant of Mayors as an important coordinating and executive instrument. Nevertheless, these innovations will bring few tangible results if they only focus on the promotion of renewable sources of energy and are not driven by a decentralization rationale, see Núñez Ferrer, Alessi and Egenhofer 2010.

threatened. At the second level, the EU policies for sustainable development seem rather mediocre in the face of daunting environmental degradation. It has been argued that what is needed is a much bolder, radical agenda that will consist of two pillars. The first will be setting ambitious goals for energy-efficiency, energy savings and de-carbonization of the economy through extensive substitution of fossil fuels with renewable resources. The second refers to a careful re-planning of our societies to accommodate current needs. Decentralization, de-urbanization and flexibility are much more appropriate guiding principles for our global society.

Bibliography

Aalto, P. 2006. *European Union and the Making of a Wider Northern Europe.* London and New York: Routledge.

Akiner, S. (ed.) 2004. *The Caspian: Politics, Energy and Security.* New York: Routledge.

Alami, R. 2006. Egypt's domestic natural gas industry. *OIES NG 12* [Online]. Available at: http://www.oxfordenergy.org/order_new.php?buy=1 [accessed: 12 December 2009].

Alexander, J. 1998. *Neofunctionalism and After.* Oxford: Blackwell Publishers.

Andoura, S., Hancher, L. and van der Woude, M. 2010. Towards a European Energy Community: A policy proposal. *Notre Europe* [Online]. Available at: http://www.google.gr/#hl=el&pwst=1&sa=X&ei=uIL–TIf_G8Ku8gP–k6G MCw&ved=0CBYQevwUoAQ&q=a+common+energy+policy+for+Europe. pdf&spell=1&fp=d9aacd362822acee [accessed: 13 December 2010].

Auer, J. 2007. EU energy policy: High time for action! *Deutsche Bank Research, EU Monitor 44* [Online]. Available at: http://www.eesc.europa.eu/resources/ docs/deutsche_bank_eu_energy_policy.pdf [accessed: 12 December 2009].

Austin, G. 2004. Political change in Russia: Implications for Britain. *Foreign Policy Centre* [Online]. Available at: http://fpc.org.uk/fsblob/329.pdf [accessed: 24 June 2006].

Axelrod, R. 1997. *The Complexity of Cooperation.* Princeton: Princeton University Press.

Axelrod, R. and Keohane, R. 1993. Achieving cooperation under anarchy: Strategies and institutions, in *Neorealism and Neoliberalism: The Contemporary Debate*, edited by D. Baldwin. New York: Columbia University Press, 85–115.

Baghat, G. 2004. Russia's oil potential: Prospects and implications. *OPEC Review*, 133–47.

Baldwin, D. 1993. Neoliberalism, neorealism and world politics, in *Neorealism and Neoliberalism: The Contemporary Debate*, edited by D. Baldwin. New York: Columbia University Press, 3–28.

Bank of Finland 2005. Russian economy – The month in review. *BOFIT Yearbook* [Online]. Available at: http://www.suomenpankki.fi/bofit_en/seuranta/ venajatilastot/julkaisu/Documents/BRR2005.pdf [accessed: 12 November 2008].

Baran, Z. 2008. Developing a cohesive EU approach to energy security, in *Europe's Energy Security: Gazprom's Dominance and Caspian Supply Alternatives*, edited by S. Cornell and N. Nilsson. Washington: CACI and SRSP, 155–66.

Barnes, J. and Jaffe, A. 2006. The Persian Gulf and the geopolitics of oil. *Survival*, 48(1), 143–62.

Barton, B., Redgwell, C., Rønne, A. and Zilman, D. 2004. *Energy Security: Managing Risk in a Dynamic Legal and Regulatory Environment*. Oxford: Oxford University Press.

Barysch, K. 2007. Russia, realism and EU unity. *CER Policy Brief* [Online]. Available at: http://www.cer.org.uk/pdf/policybrief_russia_FINAL_20july07. pdf [accessed: 11 November 2009].

Belkin, P. 2008. The European Union's energy security challenges. *CRS Report for Congress* [Online]. Available at: http://www.fas.org/sgp/crs/row/RL33636. pdf [accessed: 23 February 2009].

Belyi, A. 2009. Reciprocity as a factor of the energy investment regimes in the EU– Russia energy relations. *Journal of World Energy Law and Business*, 2(2), 117–28.

Bilgic, A. 2010. Security through trust-building in the Euro-Mediterranean cooperation: Two perspectives for the partnership. *Journal of Southeast European and Black Sea Studies*, 10(4), 457–73.

Birol, F. 2009. World Energy Outlook for 2009 [Online: IEA]. Available at: http:// www.statoil.com/en/InvestorCentre/Presentations/Downloads/World%20Energy %20Outlook%202009%2017%20Nov%202009.pdf [accessed: 2 March 2010].

Bohi, D. and Toman, M. 1996. *The Economics of Energy Security*. New York: Springer.

Boonstra, J. 2010. The EU–Turkmenistan energy relationship: Difficulty or opportunity? *EDC 2020 Policy Brief 5* [Online]. Available at: http://www.edc2020. eu/fileadmin/publications/Pbrief_No_5_Oct_2010_The_EU_Turkmenistan_ energy_relationship_difficulty_or_opportunity.pdf [accessed: 4 March 2011].

Boonstra, J. 2011. The EU's interests in Central Asia: Integrating energy, security and values into coherent policy. *EDC 2020 Working Paper* [Online]. Available at: http://www.edc2020.eu/fileadmin/publications/EDC_2020_Working_paper _No_9_The_EU%E2%80%99s_Interests_in_Central_Asia_v2.pdf [accessed: 19 March 2011].

Bordoff, J., Dashpande, M. and Noel, P. 2010. Understanding the interaction between energy security and climate change policy, in *Energy Security: Economics, Politics, Strategies and Implications*, edited by C. Pascual and J. Elkind. Washington: The Brookings Institution, 209–48.

Borgerson, S. 2008. The arctic meltdown. *Foreign Affairs*, March/April, 63–77.

BP 2010. BP Statistical Review of World Energy [Online]. Available at: http:// www.bp.com/liveassets/bp_internet/globalbp/globalbp_uk_english/ reports_and_publications/statistical_energy_review_2008/STAGING/ local_assets/2010_downloads/statistical_review_of_world_energy_full_ report_2010.pdf [accessed: 31 January 2011].

BP 2011. BP Energy Outlook 2030 [Online]. Available at: http://www.bp.com/ liveassets/bp_internet/globalbp/globalbp_uk_english/reports_and_publication s/statistical_energy_review_2008/STAGING/local_assets/2010_download s/2030_energy_outlook_booklet.pdf [accessed: 31 January 2011].

Bradshaw, M. 2006. Russian and transnational energy companies: Conflict and cooperation in Pacific Russia, in *Russian Business Power: The Role of Russian*

Business in Foreign and Security Relations, edited by A. Wenger, R. Orttung and J. Perovic. London: Routledge, 133–54.

Braun, J. 2011. EU energy policy under the treaty of Lisbon rules: Between a new policy and business as usual. *EPIN Working Paper 31* [Online]. Available at: http://www.ceps.eu/system/files/book/2011/02/EPIN%20WP31%20Braun%20on%20EU%20Energy%20Policy%20under%20Lisbon.pdf [accessed: 26 March 2011].

British Government. 2006. *Stern Review: The Economics of Climate Change. Executive Summary.* London [Online]. Available at: http://webarchive.nationalarchives.gov.uk/+/http://www.hm-treasury.gov.uk/d/Executive_Summary.pdf [accessed: 12 January 2009].

Bronner, E. 2010. Natural gas deposits improve Israel's energy outlook. *The New York Times* [Online]. Available at: http://www.nytimes.com/2010/08/21/world/middleeast/21israel.html?_r=1 [accessed: 12 January 2011].

Bruce, C. 2005. Fraternal friction or fraternal fiction? The gas factor in Russian–Belarusian relations. *OIES NG 8* [Online]. Available at: http://www.chathamhouse.org.uk/files/3234_bp0501gas.pdf [accessed: 4 June 2008].

Buchan, D. 2002. The threat within: Deregulation and energy security. *Survival*, 44(3), 105–16.

Buchan, D. 2007. Europe's mid-summer blues. *Oxford Energy Comment* [Online]. Available at: http://www.oxfordenergy.org/wpcms/wp-content/uploads/2011/01/Aug2007-Europesmidsumme-blues-DavidBuchan.pdf [accessed: 28 May 2009].

Buckley, N. 2008. Gazprom signs fuel supply deal with Libya. *Business Standard* [Online]. Available at: http://www.business-standard.com/ft/storypage_ft.php?&autono=320567 [accessed: 19 May 2010].

Business Insider 2010. Foreign state-owned energy companies dominating Iraq's oil revolution. Leaving U.S. ambitions in the dust [Online]. Available at: http://www.businessinsider.com/sovereign-backed-oil-companies-creamed-the-multinationals-in-iraq-2010-2 [accessed: 10 January 2011].

Butler, N. 2009. Why we need a common European energy policy, in *The EU in a World in Transition: Fit for what Purpose?*, edited by L. Tsoukalis. London: Policy Network, 129–40.

Butt, G. 2001. Oil and gas in the UAE, in *United Arab Emirates: A New Perspective*, edited by I. Al Abed and P. Hellyer. London: Trident Press, 231–48.

Cable, V. 2010. *The Storm: The World Economic Crisis and What it Means.* London: Atlantic Books.

Calder, K. 2007. Sino-Japanese energy relations: Prospects for deepening strategic competition. Paper presented at the conference on Japan's contemporary challenges in honor of the memory of Asakawa Kan'ichi. New Haven Connecticut: Yale University [Online]. Available at: http://eastasianstudies.research.yale.edu/japanworld/calder.pdf [accessed: 11 June 2010].

Cameron, F. 2009. The politics of EU–Russia energy relations, in *EU–Russia Energy Relations: Legal and Political Issues*. Brussels: Euroconfidentiel and OGEL, 20–29.

Cameron, F. 2010. The European Union as a model for regional integration. *CEPS Working Paper* [Online]. Available at: http://www.cfr.org/eu/european-union-model-regional-integration/p22935 [accessed: 17 February 2011].

Campaner, N. 2007. The Eastern vector of Russian oil and gas exports: What impact on the EU energy security? *CGEMP, University of Dauphine* [Online]. Available at: www.iaee.org/en/publications/proceedingsabstractpdf.aspx?id=391 [accessed: 30 June 2009].

Chappell, M. 2010. Turkey, Russia and Iran: Common interests, common positions? *CIR Reports and Analyses* [Online]. Available at: http://csm.org.pl/fileadmin/files/Biblioteka_CSM/Raporty_i_analizy/2010/Reports%20and%20Analyses_Turkey_Russia_Iran.pdf [accessed: 14 March 2011].

Checchi, A, Behrens, A. and Egenhofer, C. 2009. Long-term energy security risks for Europe: A sector-specific approach. *CEPS Working Document 309* [Online]. Available at: http://aei.pitt.edu/10759/1/1785.pdf [accessed: 3 May 2010].

Cherp, A., Jewell, J. and Goldthau, A. 2011. Governing global energy: Systems, transitions, complexity. *Global Policy*, 2(1), 75–88.

Chufrin, G. 2004. Russia's Caspian energy policy and its impact on the US–Russian relationship. *The energy dimension in Russian global strategy, The James A. Baker III Institute for Public Policy of Rice University* [Online]. Available at: http://www.rice.edu/energy/publications/docs/PEC_chufrin_10_20041.pdf [accessed: 11 May 2006].

Chyong, C., Noël, P. and Reiner, D. 2010. The economics of the Nord Stream pipeline system. *CWPE 1051 and EPRG 1026* [Online]. Available at: http://www.econ.cam.ac.uk/dae/repec/cam/pdf/cwpe1051.pdf [accessed: 21 January 2011].

Cienski, J. 2010. Poland's PGNiG signs deal with Gazprom. *Financial Times* [Online]. Available at: http://www.ft.com/cms/s/0/a13af4a8–0c35–11df–8b81–00144feabdc0.html#axzz1JR1rrtoD [accessed: 12 April 2010].

CIEP 2004. *Natural Gas Supply for the EU in the Short to Medium Term* [Online: Clingedael International Energy Programme, The Hague]. Available at: http://www.clingendael.nl/publications/2004/20040300_ciep_paper.pdf [accessed: 27 May 2007].

CIEP 2008a. *The Gas Supply Outlook for Europe: The Roles of Pipeline Gas and LNG* [Online: Clingedael International Energy Programme, The Hague]. Available at: http://www.clingendael.nl/publications/2008/20080800_ciep_energy.pdf [accessed: 8 June 2009].

CIEP 2008b. *The Geopolitics of EU Gas Supply: The Role of LNG in the EU Gas Market* [Online: Clingedael International Energy Programme, The Hague]. Available at: http://ec.europa.eu/energy/gas_electricity/studies/doc/gas/2008_05_lng_facilities_part_2_task_a.pdf [accessed: 1 May 2010].

CIEP 2010. *Energy Company Strategies in the Dynamic EU Energy Market* [Online: Clingedael International Energy Programme, The Hague]. Available at: http://www.clingendael.nl/publications/2010/20100608_CIEP_Energy_Paper_Energy_Company_Strategies.pdf [accessed: 9 March 2011].

Clare, N. 2002. *Resource Wars: The New Landscape of Global Conflict.* New York: A Metropolitan/Owl Book.

Colombo, S. and Lesser, I. 2010. The Mediterranean energy scene: What now? What next? Summary Report. *IAI Documenti 10* [Online]. Available at: http://www.iai.it/pdf/DocIAI/iai1006.pdf [accessed: 11 May 2010].

Cornell, S. 2008. Trans-Caspian pipelines and Europe's energy security, in *Europe's Energy Security: Gazprom's Dominance and Caspian Supply Alternatives,* edited by S. Cornell and N. Nilsson. Washington: CACI and SRSP, 141–53.

Cornell, S., Tsereteli, M. and Socor, V. 2005. Geostrategic implications of the Baku–Tbilisi–Ceyhan pipeline, in *The Baku–Tbilisi–Ceyhan Pipeline: Oil Window to the West,* edited by F. Starr and S. Cornell. Washington: CACI and SRSP, 17–38.

Cottier, T., Matteotti-Berkutova, S. and Nartova, O. 2010. Third country relations in EU unbundling of natural gas markets: The 'Gazprom clause' of Directive 2009/73 EC and WTO law. *Swiss National Centre of Competence in Research, Working Paper 2010/06* [Online]. Available at: http://www.wti.org/fileadmin/user_upload/nccr-trade.ch/wp5/Access%20to%20gasgrids.pdf [accessed: 20 March 2011].

CSIS 2010. Re-linking the Western Balkans: The energy dimension. *CSIS–EKEM Policy Report 3* [Online]. Available at: http://www.ekemprogram.org/csis/images/stories/staff/energy.pdf [accessed: 8 December 2010].

Curlee, R. and Sale, M. 2003. Water and energy security. *UCWR* [Online]. Available at: http://ucowr.siu.edu/proc/T18C.pdf [accessed: 16 May 2007].

Dannreuther, R. 2007. *International Security: The Contemporary Agenda.* Cambridge: Polity Press.

Daojiong, Z. 2006. China's energy security: Domestic and international issues. *Survival*, 48(1), 179–90.

Darbouche, H. 2010. Energising EU–Algerian relations. *The International Spectator*, 45(3), 71–83.

De Jong, J. 2008. The energy story: A key common interest, in *The European Union and Russia: Perception and Interest in the Shaping of Relations,* edited by A. Gerrits. The Hague: CIEP, 37–63.

Deffeyes, K. 2001. *Hubbert's Peak.* Princeton: Princeton University Press.

Dekmejian, H. and Hovann, S. 2001. *Troubled Waters: The Geopolitics of the Caspian Region.* London: I.B. Tauris Publishers.

Dellecker, A. 2008. Caspian Pipeline Consortium, Bellwether of Russia's investment climate? *IFRI Russia/NIS Center, Russie.Nei.Visions 31* [Online]. Available at: http://www.ifri.org/files/Russie/ifri_RNV_Dellecker_CPC_ENG_juin2008.pdf [accessed: 5 May 2009].

Dempsey, J. 2006. Russian-owned gas company seeks to expand in U.K. *International Herald Tribune*, 16 May, 17.

Deutch, J. 2004. Future United States energy security concerns. *MIT Joint Program on the Science and Policy of Global Change, Report 115* [Online]. Available at: http://web.mit.edu/globalchange/www/MITJPSPGC_Rpt115.pdf [accessed: 14 May 2008].

Deutsche Bank 2008. Algeria: Mediterranean state with a wealth of natural resources. *Deutsche Bank Research, Talking Point* [Online]. Available at: http://www.dbresearch.de/PROD/DBR_INTERNET_DE-PROD/PROD 0000000000223102.pdf [accessed: 26 May 2010].

Deutsche Bank 2010. Gas glut reaches Europe: Major impact on prices, security and market structure. *Deutsche Bank Research* [Online]. Available at: http://www.dbresearch.com/PROD/DBR_INTERNET_EN-PROD/PROD 0000000000259898.pdf [accessed: 22 November 2010].

Diamond, J. 2006. *Collapse: How Societies Choose to Fail or Succeed.* New York: Penguin.

Downs, E. 2010. Who is afraid of China's oil companies?, in *Energy Security: Economics, Politics, Strategies and Implications*, edited by C. Pascual and J. Elkind. Washington: The Brookings Institution, 73–103.

Dunne, T. and Schmidt, B. 2007. Realism, in *The Globalization of World Politics: An Introduction.* 3rd Edition, edited by J. Baylis, S. Smith and P. Owens. Oxford: Oxford University Press, 90–106.

Echagüe, A. 2007. The European Union and the Gulf Cooperation Council. *FRIDE Working Paper 39*, Madrid [Online]. Available at: www.fride.org/.../ WP39_EU_Persian_Gulf_EN_may07.pdf [accessed: 1 May 2009].

Economic Forum 2007. *Foreign Policy of Ukraine* [Online]. Available at: http:// www.forum-ekonomiczne.pl/public/upload/ibrowser/raporty/U2007/05roz_ chapter_3.pdf [accessed: 13 January 2010].

Egenhofer, C. and Behrens, A. 2008. Two sides of the same coin? Securing European energy supplies with internal and external policies. *CEPS*, Brussels [Online]. Available at: http://sideurope.files.wordpress.com/2008/05/background-vijver berg-energy-ceps-20-05-20081.pdf [accessed: 24 May 2009].

EIA 2010a. *Country Analysis Briefs: Azerbaijan* [Online]. Available at: http:// www.eia.doe.gov/cabs/Azerbaijan/pdf.pdf [accessed: 12 January 2011].

EIA 2010b. *Country Analysis Briefs: Iraq* [Online]. Available at: http://www.eia. doe.gov/cabs/iraq/pdf.pdf [accessed: 12 January 2011].

EIA 2010c. US primary energy flow by source and sector, 2009. *Annual Energy Review* [Online]. Available at: http://www.eia.doe.gov/aer/pecss_diagram. html [accessed: 11 November 2010].

EIA 2010d. *China. Background* [Online]. Available at: http://www.eia.doe.gov/ emeu/cabs/China/Background.html [accessed: 12 December 2010].

EIA 2011. *Petroleum Navigator* [Online]. Available at: http://tonto.eia.doe.gov/ dnav/pet/hist/LeafHandler.ashx?n=PET&s=MTTIMUSVE1&f=M [accessed: 30 November 2010].

Energy Charter Official Website [Online]. Available at: http://www.encharter.org/ index.php?id=7 [accessed: 5 December 2010].

Eng, G. 2003. Energy security initiative: Some aspects of oil security. *APERC* [Online]. Available at: http://www.ieej.or.jp/aperc/pdf/project2002/security.pdf [accessed: 30 May 2005].

Esther-Barbe, E. 2008. The EU as a modest 'force for good': The European Neighborhood Policy. *International Affairs*, 84(1), 81–96.

EU Energy Commissioner 2006. *Global Energy Industry* [Online: Speech at Russian International Energy Week, Moscow]. Available at: http://europa.eu/rapid/pressReleasesAction.do?reference=SPEECH/06/646&format=HTML&aged=0&language=EN&guiLanguage=en [accessed: 13 March 2009].

Euractiv, *IEA Warns of High Oil Prices if Climate Pledges are Not Met* [Online]. Available at: http://www.euractiv.com/en/energy/iea-warns-high-oil-prices-if-climate-pledges-not-met-news-499588 [accessed: 11 January 2011].

European Commission 1995. *Green Paper: For a European Union Energy Policy, COM 659*. Brussels.

European Commission 1996. *1996/92/EC Electricity and Gas Directive* [Online]. Available at: http://eur-lex.europa.eu/LexUriServ/LexUriServ.do?uri=CELEX:31996L0092:EN:HTML [accessed: 11 November 2010].

European Commission 1998. *1998/30/EC Electricity and Gas Directive* [Online]. Available at: http://eur-lex.europa.eu/LexUriServ/LexUriServ.do?uri=CELEX:31998L0030:EN:HTML [accessed: 11 November 2010].

European Commission 2000. *Green Paper: Towards a European Strategy for the Security of Energy Supply, COM 769*. Brussels.

European Commission 2002. *Commission Staff Working Paper: Energy Dialogue – Update on Progress, SEC 1272*. Brussels.

European Commission 2003a. *2003/55/EC Electricity and Gas Directive* [Online]. Available at: http://eur-lex.europa.eu/LexUriServ/LexUriServ.do?uri=OJ:L:2003:176:0057:0057:EN:PDF [accessed: 11 November 2010].

European Commission 2003b. Commission reaches breakthrough with Gazprom and ENI on territorial restriction clauses, IP/03/1345. Brussels [Online]. Available at: http://europa.eu/rapid/pressReleasesAction.do?reference=IP/03/1345&format=HTML&aged=0&language=EN&guiLanguage=en [accessed: 23 June 2006].

European Commission 2004. *Communication from the Commission to the Council and the European Parliament: The Energy Dialogue between the European Union and the Russian Federation between 2000 and 2004, COM 777*. Brussels.

European Commission 2005a. Competition: Commission secures improvements to gas supply contracts between OMV and Gazprom. *Recent Press Releases and Speeches* [Online]. Available at: http://www.delrus.ec.europa.eu/en/news_682.htm [accessed: 12 May 2010].

European Commission 2005b. *Latest Report Underlines Progress in the EU–Russia Energy Dialogue, IP/05/1238* [Online]. Available at: http://europa.eu.int/rapid/pressReleasesAction.do?reference=IP/05/1238&format=HTML&aged=0&language=EN&guiLanguage=en [accessed: 13 December 2009].

European Commission 2006a. *Green Paper. Towards a European Strategy for the Security of Energy Supply, COM 105*. Brussels.

European Commission 2006b. An external policy to serve Europe's energy interests. *Paper from Commission/SG/HR for the European Council* [Online]. Available at: http://www.consilium.europa.eu/uedocs/cms_data/docs/pressda ta/en/reports/90082.pdf [accessed: 11 March 2011].

European Commission 2007a. *Communication from the Commission: An Energy Policy for Europe, 5282, COM 1*. Brussels.

European Commission 2007b. *EU Commission Proposes Integrated Energy and Climate Change Package to Cut Emissions for the 21st Century* [Online]. Available at: http://www.europa-eu-un.org/articles/en/article_6665_en.htm [accessed: 12 November 2010].

European Commission 2007c. *European Union – Russia Energy Dialogue* [Online]. Available at: http://ec.europa.eu/energy/russia/overview/index_ en.htm [accessed: 19 September 2010].

European Commission 2007d. *Communication from the Commission to the Council and the European Parliament. Black Sea Synergy – A New Regional Cooperation Initiative, COM 160*. Brussels.

European Commission 2008. Second Strategic Energy Review: An EU energy security and solidarity action plan. Europe's current and future energy position: Demand – resources – investments. *Commission Staff Working Document accompanying the Communication from the Commission to the European Parliament, the Council, the European Economic and Social Committee and the Committee of the Regions, COM 781*. Brussels.

European Commission 2009a. Directive 2009/73/EC of the European Parliament and of the Council of 13 July 2009 concerning common rules, for the internal market in natural gas and repealing Directive 2003/55/EC. *Official Journal of the European Union*, 94–136.

European Commission 2009b. *Energizing Europe – a Real Market with Secure Supply (Third Legislative Package). Gas and Electricity* [Online]. Available at: http://ec.europa.eu/energy/gas_electricity/third_legislative_package_en.htm [accessed: 7 January 2011].

European Commission 2010a. *Communication from the Commission: Europe 2020. A strategy for Smart, Sustainable and Inclusive Growth, COM 2020*. Brussels.

European Commission 2010b. Regulations: Regulation (EU) No 994/2010 of the European Parliament and of the Council of 20 October 2010 concerning measures to safeguard security of gas supply and repealing Council Directive 2004/67/EC (Text with EEA relevance). *Official Journal of the European Union, L 295/1*, 1–22.

European Commission 2010c. *Report from the Commission to the Council and the European Parliament on the Implementation of the European Energy Programme for Recovery, COM 191*. Brussels.

European Commission 2011a. *Energy Production and Imports* [Online]. Available at: http://epp.eurostat.ec.europa.eu/statistics_explained/index.php/Energy_pro duction_and_imports [accessed: 12 March 2011].

European Commission 2011b. *Security of Gas Supply in the EU* [Online]. Available at: http://ec.europa.eu/energy/security/gas/gas_en.htm [accessed: 26 March 2011].

European Commission 2011c. Energy priorities for Europe. *Presentation of J.M. Barroso, President of the European Commission, to the European Council of 4 February 2011* [Online]. Available at: http://ec.europa.eu/europe2020/pdf/energy_en.pdf [accessed: 1 April 2011].

European Commission 2011d. *Report from the Commission to the European Parliament and the Council under Article 7 of Decision 2006/500/EC (Energy Community Treaty), COM 105*. Brussels.

European Commission, DG Energy 2008. *EU Energy Security and Solidarity Action Plan: Second Strategic Energy Review*, MEMO/08/703 [Online]. Available at: http://europa.eu/rapid/pressReleasesAction.do?reference=MEM O/08/703&format=HTML&aged=0&language=en&guiLanguage=en [accessed: 5 May 2009].

European Commission, DG Energy 2010. *Denmark* [Online]. Available at: http://ec.europa.eu/energy/observatory/eu_27_info/doc/denmark_2010_d2008.pdf [accessed: 3 February 2011].

European Commission, DG Energy 2011. *Energy Infrastructure: Priorities for 2020 and Beyond – a Blueprint for an Integrated European Energy Network*. Luxembourg: Publications Office of the European Union, 1–41.

EWEA 2007. *European Market for Wind Turbines Grows 23 per cent in 2006* [Online: European Wind Energy Association, Brussels]. Available at: http://ec.europa.eu/energy/renewables/studies/doc/wind_energy/2007_statistics2006.pdf [accessed: 3 April 2010].

Featherstone, K. 2009. Legitimacy through output: The quest for leadership and a big new idea, in *Rescuing the European Project: EU Legitimacy, Governance and Security. An EU 'Fit for Purpose' in the Global Age*, edited by O. Cramme. London: Policy Network, 87–96.

FECER 2009. Shaping Europe's energy sector for the decade ahead. *Position Paper of FECER for the EU Legislative Period 2009–2014* [Online]. Available at: http://www.fecer.eu/positional-papers/shaping-europeper centE2per cent80per cent99s-energy-sector-for-the-decade-ahead/ [accessed: 13 January 2011].

Feklyunina, V. 2008. The 'great diversification game': Russia's vision of the European Union's energy projects in the shared neighbourhood. *Journal of Contemporary European Research*, 4(2), 130–48.

Ferdinand, P. 2007. Russia and China: Converging responses to globalization. *International Affairs*, 83(4), 655–80.

Ferguson, C. 2007. *Nuclear Energy: Balancing Benefits and Risks*. Washington: Council on Foreign Relations, CSR 28.

Finon, D. 2008. Why would oil-indexation in gas contracts survive in Europe? *EU Energy Policy Blog* [Online]. Available at: http://www.energypolicyblog. com/2008/06/29/why-would-oil-indexation-in-gas-contracts-survive-in-europe/ [accessed: 19 December 2010].

Finon, D. 2009. Lessons of Nabucco: The limits of EU direct intervention in transit pipeline development. *FEEM/EUI/CIEP Workshop*, Milan [Online]. Available at: http://www.feem.it/userfiles/attach/201011419255748.Finon_Lessons_of_Nabucco.pdf [accessed: 19 December 2010].

Finon, D. and Locatelli, C. 2002. The liberalization of the European gas market and its consequences for Russia. *RECEP Policy Paper* [Online]. Available at: http://hal.archives-ouvertes.fr/docs/00/17/78/28/PDF/CL_DF_GazRusse_02Engl.pdf [accessed: 17 May 2009].

Finon, D. and Locatelli, C. 2007. Russian and European gas interdependence. Can market forces balance out geopolitics? *CIRED Working Paper* [Online]. Available at: http://halshs.archives-ouvertes.fr/docs/00/12/96/18/PDF/Cahier 41bis.pdf [accessed: 20 April 2008].

Florini, A. and Sovacool, B. 2009. Who governs energy? The challenges facing global energy governance'. *Energy Policy*, 37(12), 5239–48.

Fredholm, M. 2005. The Russian energy strategy and energy policy: Pipeline diplomacy or mutual dependence. *Russian Series 05/41, CSRC, UK Defence Academy* [Online]. Available at: www.da.mod.uk/colleges/arag/document.../russian/05(41)-MF.pdf [accessed: 13 April 2006].

Frei, C. 2007. Dossier energy: Blueprint for a global energy authority. *Europe's World: Policy Dossier* [Online]. Available from: http://www.europesworld.org/NewEnglish/Home_old/Article/tabid/191/ArticleType/articleview/ArticleID/20747/language/en-US/Default [accessed: 12 December 2010].

Futyan, M. 2006. The Interconnector pipeline: A key link in Europe's gas network, *OIES* [Online]. Available at: http://www.oxfordenergy.org/wpcms/wp-content/uploads/2010/11/NG11-TheInterconnectorPipelineAKeyLinkInEuropesGasNetwork-MarkFutyan-2006.pdf [accessed: 7 June 2010].

Gaddy, C. and Ickes, B. 2008. Russia's slowing production: Policy failure or strategic decision?, in *Pipelines, Politics and Power. The Future of EU–Russia Energy Relations*, edited by K. Barysch. London: CER, 61–70.

Gallis, P. 2006. CRS Report for Congress: NATO and energy security. *Congressional Research Service* [Online]. Available at: https://transnet.act.nato.int/WISE/StrategicV/StrategicV0/NATOandEne/file/_WFS/032306CRS_NATO.pdf [accessed: 13 February 2007].

Gault, J. 2004. EU energy security and the periphery, in *European Union Foreign and Security Policy: Towards a Neighborhood Strategy*, edited by R. Dannreuther. London: Routledge, 170–85.

Gault, J. 2007. European energy security: Balancing priorities. *FRIDE Comment*, Madrid [Online]. Available at: http://www.fride.org/publication/213/european-energy-security:-balancing-priorities [accessed: 14 February 2009].

Geden, O., Marcelis, C. and Maurer, A. 2006. Perspectives for the European Union's external energy policy: Discourse, ideas and interests in Germany, UK, Poland and France. *SWP Working Paper FG1*, Berlin [Online]. Available at: http://www.swp-berlin.org/fileadmin/contents/products/arbeitspapiere/External_KS_Energy_Policy__Dez_OG_.pdf [accessed: 29 May 2007].

Geny, F. 2010. Can unconventional gas be a game changer in European gas markets? *OIES NG 46* [Online]. Available at: http://www.sbc.slb.com/About_SBC/~/media/Files/Point%20of%20View%20Docs/Can%20Unconventional%20Gas%20be%20a%20Game%20Changer%20in%20European%20Gas%20Markets.ashx [accessed: 28 January 2011].

Ghiles, F. 2009. Algeria: A strategic gas partner for Europe. *Journal of Energy Security* [Online]. Available at: http://www.ensec.org/index.php?option=com_content&view=article&id=176:algeria-a-strategic-gas-partner-for-europe&cat id=92:issuecontent&Itemid=341 [accessed: 20 December 2010].

Ghiles, F. 2010. At long last, a change at the Algerian ministry of Energy. *CIDOB* [Online]. Available at: http://www.cidob.org/en/publications/opinion/seguridad_y_politica_mundial/at_long_last_a_change_at_the_algerian_ministry_of_energy [accessed: 20 December 2010].

Gilpin, R. 2001. *Global Political Economy: Understanding the International Economic Order*. Princeton: Princeton University Press.

Giulio, M. 2008. Nabucco pipeline and the Turkmenistan conundrum. *Caucasian Review of International Affairs*, 2(3), 1–9.

Goldirova, R. 2007. Non-EU firms face energy market shutout. *BusinessWeek* [Online]. Available at: http://www.businessweek.com/globalbiz/content/aug2007/gb20070831_554679.htm?link_position=link20 [accessed: 24 November 2010].

Goldirova, R. 2008. EU weakens 'Gazprom clause' on foreign energy investors. *Euobserver.com* [Online]. Available at: http://euobserver.com/9/26914 [accessed: 8 December 2010].

Goldthau, A. and Witte, J. 2009. Back to the future or forward to the past? Strengthening markets and rules for effective global energy governance. *International Affairs*, 85(2), 373–90.

Goldthau, A. and Witte, J. 2010. *Global Energy Governance: The New Rules of the Game*. Washington, DC: Brookings Institution Press.

Gorst, I. 2004. Russian pipeline strategies: Business versus politics. *The energy dimension in Russian global strategy, The James A. Baker III Institute for Public Policy of Rice University* [Online]. Available at: http://www.rice.edu/energy/publications/docs/PEC_Gorst_10_2004.pdf [accessed: 2 October 2006].

Götz, R. 2005a. The North European pipeline: Increasing energy security or political pressure? *SWP Comments 42* [Online]. Available at: http://www.swp-berlin.org/en/nc/products/swp-comments-en/browse/17.html [accessed: on 11 March 2007].

Götz, R. 2005b. Russia and the energy supply of Europe: The Russian energy strategy to 2020. *SWP Working Paper FG5* [Online]. Available at: http://www.swp-berlin.org/fileadmin/contents/products/arbeitspapiere/FG5_2005_06_gtz_ks.pdf [accessed: 13 May 2009].

Götz, R. 2006. Russian gas and alternatives for Europe. *SWE FG 5* [Online]. Available at: http://www.swp-berlin.org/fileadmin/contents/products/arbeits papiere/EuroFutureGas_ks.pdf [accessed: 9 May 2007].

Grieco, J. 1990. *Cooperation among Nations: Europe, America and Non-Tariff Barriers to Trade*. Ithaca: Cornell University Press.

Grigoriadis, I. 2008. Natural gas corridors in Southeastern Europe and European energy security. *ELIAMEP Thesis 2* [Online]. Available at: http://www.eliamep.gr/en/wp-content/uploads/2008/09/eliamep_thesis_no_2.pdf [accessed: 18 December 2009].

Grigoriev, L. 2010. The global recession and energy markets. *CASE Network E-Briefs 01* [Online]. Available at: http://www.case.com.pl/upload/publikacja_plik/28014496_E-Brief_Grigoriev+.pdf [accessed: 17 May 2011].

Gros, D. and Egenhofer, C. 2010. Decision time for Europe on climate change. Keep the head buried in the sand or get tough? *CEPS Commentary*, Brussels [Online]. Available at: http://www.ceps.eu/book/decision-time-europe-climate-change-keep-head-buried-sand-or-get-tough [accessed: 10 May 2011].

Haas, E. 1958. *The Uniting of Europe: Political, Social and Economic Forces, 1950–1957*. Stanford: Stanford University Press.

Haase, N. 2008. European gas market liberalization. Are regulatory regimes moving towards convergence? *OIES NG 24* [Online]. Available at: http://doc.utwente.nl/67281/1/Haase08european.pdf [accessed: 7 May 2009].

Haghighi, S. 2007. *Energy Security: The External Legal Relations of the European Union with Major Oil- and Gas-Supplying Countries*. Portland: Hart Publishing.

Hale, H. and Taagepera, R. 2002. Russia: Consolidation or collapse? *Europe–Asia Studies*, 54(7), 1101–25.

Hallouche, H. 2006. The gas exporting countries forum: Is it really a gas OPEC in the making? *OIES NG 13* [Online]. Available at: http://www.oxfordenergy.org/wpcms/wp-content/uploads/2010/11/NG13-TheGasExportingCountriesForumIsItReallyAGasOpecInTheMaking-HadiHallouche-2006.pdf [accessed: 5 April 2008].

Hayes, M. 2006. The Transmed and Maghreb projects: Gas to Europe from North Africa, in *Natural Gas and Geopolitics: From 1970 to 2040*, edited by D. Victor, A. Jaffe and M. Hayes. Cambridge: Cambridge University Press, 49–90.

Hayes, M. and Victor, D. 2006. Politics, markets and the shift to gas: Insights from the seven historical case studies, in *Natural Gas and Geopolitics: From 1970 to 2040*, edited by D. Victor, A. Jaffe and M. Hayes. Cambridge: Cambridge University Press, 319–53.

Heather, P. 2010. The evolution and functioning of the traded gas market in Britain. *OIES NG 44* [Online]. Available at: http://www.oxfordenergy.org/wpcms/wp-content/uploads/2010/11/NG44-TheEvolutionandFunctioningOfTheTradedGasMarketInBritain-PatrickHeather-2010.pdf [accessed: 29 April 2011].

Helm, D. 2004. Reinventing energy policy, in *Energy, the State and the Market: British Energy Policy since 1979*, edited by D. Helm. Oxford: New College, 412–25.

Helm, D. 2007. *The Russian Dimension and Europe's External Energy Policy*. Oxford: University of Oxford.

Helm, D. 2009. Energy and environmental policy: Options for the future, in *The EU in a World in Transition: Fit for What Purpose?*, edited by L. Tsoukalis. London: Policy Network, 141–52.

Henderson, J. 2010. *Non Gazprom Gas Producers in Russia*. Oxford: OIES.

Hill, C. 2003. *The Changing Politics of Foreign Policy*. Basingstoke: Palgrave Macmillan.

Hill, F. 2005. Beyond co-dependency: European reliance on Russian energy. *The Brookings Institution U.S.–Europe Analysis Series* [Online]. Available at: http://www.brookings.edu/~/media/Files/rc/papers/2005/07russia_hill/hill 20050727.pdf [accessed: 12 November 2006].

Hinnebusch, R. 2007. The American invasion of Iraq: Causes and consequences. *Perceptions* [Online]. Available at: http://www.sam.gov.tr/perceptions/vol ume12/Spring07_raymond.pdf [accessed: 21 November 2010].

Hirman, K. 2001. The position of the Visegrad countries in energy relations between Russia and the EU. *Slovak Foreign Policy Affairs*, 2(1), 82–96.

Hix, S. and Høyland, B. 2011. *The Political System of the European Union*. 3rd Edition. London: Palgrave Macmillan.

Hoffmann, S. 2000. Towards a common foreign and security policy. *Journal of Common Market Studies*, 38(2), 189–98.

Holz, F., von Hirschhausen, C. and Kemfert, C. 2008. Perspectives of the European natural gas markets until 2025. *Discussion Papers 823*, DIW Berlin [Online]. Available at: http://ideas.repec.org/p/diw/diwwpp/dp823.html [accessed: 4 September 2009].

Hoogwijk, M., Vries, B. and Turkenburg, W. 2004. Assessment of the global and regional geographical, technical and economic potential of onshore wind energy. *Energy Economics*, 26(5), 889–919.

Houser, T. and Levy, R. 2008. Energy security and China's diplomacy. *China Security*, 4(3), 63–73.

IEA 2000. *Regulatory Reform in European Gas: Energy Market Reform*. Paris: OECD/IEA.

IEA 2004. *Security of Gas Supply in Open Oil Market*. Paris: OECD/IEA.

IEA 2008a. *Energy in the Western Balkans: The Path to Reform and Reconstruction*. Paris: OECD/ IEA.

IEA 2008b. *The European Union: IEA Energy Policies Review*. Paris: OECD/IEA.

IEA 2009. *World Energy Outlook 2009: Executive Summary*. Paris: OECD/IEA [Online]. Available at: http://www.worldenergyoutlook.org/docs/weo2009/ WEO2010_es_english.pdf [accessed: 16 January 2010].

IEA 2010. *World Energy Outlook 2010: Executive Summary*. Paris: OECD/ IEA [Online]. Available at: http://www.worldenergyoutlook.org/docs/weo2010/ WEO2010_es_english.pdf [accessed: 23 March 2011].

IEA Energy Statistics. *China* [Online]. Available at: http://www.iea.org/country/n_ country.asp?COUNTRY_CODE=CN&Submit=Submit [accessed: 12 March 2011].

IEA Energy Statistics. *United States* [Online]. Available at: http://www.iea.org/
country/m_country.asp?COUNTRY_CODE=US [accessed: 12 March 2011].

IFP Energies Nouvelles 2006. *The Strategy of Players on the European Gas
Market* [Online: Panorama]. Available at: http://www.ifpenergiesnouvelles.
com/information-publications/notes-de-synthese-panorama/panorama-2006/
la-strategie-des-acteurs-du-marche-gazier-europeen [accessed: 11 July 2010].

Istock Analyst 2010. *China's Natural Gas Consumption in Energy Mix to Double
during 2011–2015* [Online]. Available at: http://www.istockanalyst.com/
article/viewiStockNews/articleid/4278326 [accessed: 3 January 2011].

Jacobs, M. 2010. Is it all over for climate change policy in the United States? *Current
Affairs and Culture* [Online]. Available at: http://inside.org.au/is-it-all-over-for-
climate-change-policy-in-the-united-states [accessed: 3 December 2010].

Jaffe, A. and Soligo, R. 2006. Market structure in the new gas economy: Is
cartelization possible?, in *Natural Gas and Geopolitics: From 1970 to 2040*,
edited by D. Victor, A. Jaffe and M. Hayes. Cambridge: Cambridge University
Press, 439–64.

Jaffe, A., Hayes, M. and Victor, D. 2006. Conclusions, in *Natural Gas and
Geopolitics: From 1970 to 2040*, edited by D. Victor, A. Jaffe and M. Hayes.
Cambridge: Cambridge University Press, 467–83.

James, P. and Patomaki, H. 2008. Globalization and finance capitalism: Beyond
all-or-nothing arguments. *Arena Journal 29/30*, 101–30.

Jensen, J. 2004. *The Development of a Global LNG Market: Is it Likely? If So
When?* Oxford: OIES.

Jesse, J. and van der Linde, C. 2008. Oil turbulence in the next decade: An
essay on high oil prices in a supply constrained world [Online: Clingedael
International Energy Programme, The Hague]. Available at: http://www.
clingendael.nl/publications/2008/20080700_ciep_energy_jesse.pdf [accessed:
15 April 2009].

Jupille, J. 1999. The European Union and international outcomes. *International
Organization*, 53(2), 409–25.

Kalicki, J. and Goldwyn, D. 2005. Introduction: The need to integrate energy and
foreign policy, in *Energy and Security: Toward a New Foreign Policy Strategy*,
edited by J. Kalicki and D. Goldwyn. Washington: Woodrow Wilson Center,
1–15.

Kang, S. 2008. *Korea's Pursuit of Energy Security*. Paper prepared for the 2008
Northeast Asia Energy Outlook Seminar, Korea Economic Institute Policy
Forum. Washington DC.

Karaganov, S. 1997. Russia and the Slav vicinity, in *Russia and Europe: The
Emerging Security Agenda*, edited by V. Baranovsky. Oxford: Oxford
University Press, 289–303.

Keohane, R. 1984. *After Hegemony: Cooperation and Discord in the World
Political Economy*. Princeton: Princeton University Press.

Keohane, R. and Nye, J. 2001. *Power and Interdependence*. 3rd Edition. New
York: Longman.

Keukeleire, S. and MacNaughtan, J. 2008. *The Foreign Policy of the European Union.* New York: Palgrave MacMillan.

Khandker, S., Barnes, D. and Samad, H. 2010. Energy poverty in rural and urban India: Are the energy poor also income poor? *IDEAS* [Online]. Available at: http://ideas.repec.org/p/wbk/wbrwps/5463.html [accessed: 3 January 2011].

Kirton, J. 2006. The G8 and global energy governance: Past performance, St Petersburg's opportunities. *Paper presented at a conference on the World Dimension of Russia's Energy Security* [Online]. Available at: http://www.g8.utoronto.ca/scholar/kirton2006/kirton_energy_060623.pdf [accessed: 11 January 2009].

Klare, M. 2008. *Rising Powers, Shrinking Planet: The New Geopolitics of Energy.* New York: Metropolitan Books.

Klinghoffer, A. 1977. *The Soviet Union and International Oil Politics.* New York: Columbia University Press.

Kong, B. 2009. *China's International Petroleum Policy.* Santa Barbara, California: Praeger.

Kramer, A. 2006. News Analysis: Moscow bites the hand of an ally: Belarus feels lash of Gazprom's reach. *International Herald Tribune*, 29 December, 14.

Kramer, F. and Lyman, J. 2009. Transatlantic cooperation for sustainable energy security. Report of the global dialogue between the European Union and the United States. *CSIS* [Online]. Available at: http://www.acus.org/files/publication_pdfs/523/EnergySecurityReport.pdf [accessed: 24 May 2010].

Kruger, H. 2009. *The Nagorno–Karabakh Conflict: A Legal Analysis.* Berlin: Springer.

Kufidu, S. and Mihail, D. 1999. Decentralization and flexibility in Greek industrial relations. *Employee Relations*, 21(5), 485–99.

Kupchinsky, R. 2009. Russian gas flaring: A political or technical problem? *Eurasia Daily Monitor* [Online], 6(211). Available at: http://www.jamestown.org/single/?no_cache=1&tx_ttnews%5Btt_news%5D=35735 [accessed: 6 July 2010].

Larsson, R. 2006a. *Russia's Energy Policy: Security Dimensions and Russia's Reliability as an Energy Supplier.* Stockholm: FOI.

Larsson, R. 2006b. *Sweden and the NEPG: A Pilot Study of the North European Gas Pipeline and Sweden's Dependence on Russian Energy.* Stockholm: FOI.

Larsson, R. 2007a. *Nord Stream, Sweden and Baltic Sea Security.* Stockholm: FOI.

Larsson, R. 2007b. *Tackling Dependency: The EU and its Energy Security Challenges.* Stockholm: FOI.

Larsson, R. 2008. Europe and Caspian energy: Dodging Russia, tackling China and engaging the US, in *Europe's Energy Security: Gazprom's Dominance and Caspian Supply Alternatives*, edited by S. Cornell and N. Nilsson. Washington: CACI and SRSP, 19–40.

Leonard, M. and Popescu, N. 2007. A power audit of EU–Russia relations. *European Council on Foreign Affairs Policy Paper* [Online]. Available at:

http://ecfr.eu/page/-/documents/ECFR-EU-Russia-power-audit.pdf [accessed: 18 June 2008].

Lesage, D., van de Graaf, T. and Westphal, K. 2009. G8+5 collaboration on energy efficiency and IPEEC: Shortcut to a sustainable future? *Energy Policy*, 38(11), 6419–27.

Lesser, I., Larrabee S., Zanini, M. and Vlachos-Dengler K. 2001. *Greece's New Geopolitics*. Pittsburgh: Rand.

LeVine, S. 2011. The oily subtext of South Sudanese independence. *Foreign Policy* [Online]. Available at: http://oilandglory.foreignpolicy.com/posts/2011/01/11/the_oily_subtext_of_south_sudanese_independence [accessed: 3 February 2011].

Lewis, S. 2004. Energy security: Implications for US–China–Middle East relations. The James A. Baker III Institute for Public Policy of Rice University, Energy Security in Northeast Asia: The Potential for Cooperation Among the Major Energy Consuming Economies of China, Japan and the United States [Online]. Available at: http://www.rice.edu/energy/publications/docs/SIIS_SWLEWIS_chinajapanUScooperation_071805.pdf [accessed: 6 April 2006].

Linklater, A. 2007. *Critical Theory and World Politics: Citizenship, Sovereignty and World Politics*. London: Routledge.

Liu, X. 2006. China's energy security and its grand strategy. *Policy Analysis Brief, The Stanley Foundation* [Online]. Available at: http://www.stanleyfoundation. org/publications/pab/pab06chinasenergy.pdf [accessed: 9 July 2009].

Locatelli, C. 2008. EU gas liberalization as a driver of Gazprom's strategies? *IFRI Russia/NIS Center, Russie.Nei.Visions 26* [Online]. Available at: www.ifri.org/downloads/Ifri_RNV_locatelli_gazprom_ANG_janv2007.pdf [accessed: 2 May 2010].

Locatelli, C. 2010. Europe's gas supplies: Diversification with Caspian gas and the 'Russian risk'. *LEPII, Cahier de recherché 29* [Online]. Available at: http://halshs.archives-ouvertes.fr/docs/00/45/92/02/PDF/CL_CR29_2010.pdf [accessed: 13 January 2011].

Lohmann, H. 2006. *The German Path to Natural Gas Liberalization: Is it a Special Case?* Oxford: OIES.

Loskot-Strachota, A. and Antas, L. 2010. Nord Stream on the liberalizing EU gas market. *CES Policy Briefs* [Online]. Available at: http://www.osw.waw.pl/sites/default/files/punkt_widzenia_22.pdf [accessed: 25 April 2011].

Losoncz, M. 2006. Analysis: Energy dependence and supply in Central and Eastern Europe. *Euractiv* [Online]. Available at: http://www.euractiv.com/en/energy/analysis-energy-dependence-supply-central-eastern-europe/article-155274 [accessed: 12 October 2008].

Lucas, E. 2008. *The New Cold War: How the Kremlin Menaces both Russia and the West*. London: Bloomsbury.

Mares, D. 2010. Resource nationalism and energy security in Latin America: Implications for the global oil supplies. *Working Paper, James A. Baker III Institute for Public Policy, Rice University* [Online]. Available at: http://www.

bakerinstitute.org/publications/EF-pub-MaresResourceNationalismWorkPap
er-012010.pdf [accessed: 4 January 2011].

McFaul, M. 2006. The gas war. *The Hoover Digest* [Online]. Available at: http://
www.hoover.org/publications/digest/2912226.html [accessed: 18 February
2008].

McGowan, F. 2008. Can the European Union's market liberalism ensure energy
security in a time of 'Economic Nationalism'? *Journal of Contemporary
European Research*, 4(2), 90–106.

Mearsheimer, J. 2001. *The Tragedy of Great Power Politics*. New York: Norton.

Meunier, S. 2000. What single voice? European institutions and EU–US trade
negotiations. *International Organization*, 54(1), 103–35.

Milov, V. 2006. The EU–Russia energy dialogue: Competition vs. monopolies.
IFRI Russia/NIS Center, Russie.Nei.Visions 13 [Online]. Available at: www.
ifri.org/downloads/ifrimilovenergiesept2006eng.pdf [accessed: 12 May 2008].

Mitchell, J. 2002. Renewing energy security. *The Royal Institute of International
Affairs* [Online]. Available at: www.se2.isn.ch/.../3038_renewing_energy_
security_mitchell_july_2002%5B1%5D.pdf [accessed: 26 October 2006].

Mitchell, J. and Lahn, G. 2007. Oil for Asia. *EEDP BP 07/01. Chatham House
Briefing Paper* [Online]. Available at: http://www.chathamhouse.org.uk/
files/6350_bp0307anoc.pdf [accessed: 14 June 2009].

Monaghan, A. and Montanaro-Jankovski, L. 2006. EU–Russia energy relations:
The need for active engagement. *EPC Issue Paper 45* [Online]. Available at:
www.se2.isn.ch/serviceengine/Files/.../EPC_Issue_Paper_45.pdf [accessed:
19 April 2007].

Moravcsik, A. 1999. *The Choice for Europe: Social Purpose and State Power
from Messina to Maastricht*. London: UCL Press.

Morozov, V. 2005. *Russia's role in a new Europe: The Russian–EU energy
dialogue. Paper presented at the conference Post-Soviet In/Securities: Theory
and Practice organized by the Mershon Centre, Ohio State CSRC, Russian
Series 05/41, UK Defense Academy* [Online]. Available at: https://kb.osu.edu/
dspace/bitstream/1811/30222/6/MorozovPaper.pdf [accessed: 29 May 2006].

Müller-Kraenner, S. 2008. *Energy Security*. 3rd Edition. London: Earthscan.

Nies, S. 2008. *Oil and Gas Delivery to Europe: An Overview of Existing and
Planned Infrastructures*. Paris: IFRI.

Nincic, D. 2009. Troubled waters: Energy security as maritime security, in *Energy
Security Challenges for the 21st Century: A Reference Handbook*, edited by G.
Luft and A. Korin. Santa Barbara, California: Praeger, 31–43.

Nitzov, B. 2011. Eurasian energy: Hot and cold. *Dinu Patriciu Eurasia Center,
Atlantic Council* [Online]. Available at: http://www.acus.org/files/publication_
pdfs/403/011211_ACUS_Nitzov_EurasiaEnergy.PDF [accessed: 16 May
2011].

Nivola, P. and Carter, E. 2010. Making sense of 'energy independence', in *Energy
Security: Economics, Politics, Strategies and Implications*, edited by C.
Pascual and J. Elkind. Washington: The Brookings Institution, 105–18.

Nonneman, G. 2007. EU–GCC relations: Dynamics, patterns and perspectives. *Journal of Social Affairs*, 23(92), 13–33.

Norling, N. 2008. The Nabucco pipeline: Reemerging momentum in Europe's front yard, in *Europe's Energy Security: Gazprom's Dominance and Caspian Supply Alternatives*, edited by S. Cornell and N. Nilsson. Washington: CACI and SRSP, 127–40.

Nugent, N. 2010. *The Government and Politics of the European Union.* 7th Edition. London: Palgrave MacMillan.

Núñez Ferrer, J., Alessi, M. and Egenhofer, C. 2010. Greening EU cities: The emerging EU strategy to address climate change. *CEPS Task Force Report* [Online]. Available at: http://www.ceps.eu/book/greening-eu-cities-emerging-eu-strategy-address-climate-change [accessed: 29 March 2011].

Nye, J. 2003. *Understanding International Conflicts: An Introduction to Theory and History*. 4th Edition. New York: Longman.

Ocheje, P. 2006. The Extractive Industries Transparency Initiative (EITI): Voluntary codes of conduct, poverty and accountability in Africa. *Journal of Sustainable Development in Africa*, 8(3), 222–39.

Odell, P. 2004. *Why Carbon Fuels Will Dominate the 21st Century's Global Energy Economy*. Brentwood, Essex: Multi-Science Publishing.

OECD 2004. Russia's gas sector: The endless wait for reform? *OECD Economics Department Work Papers* 402 [Online]. Available at: http://www.oecd-ilibrary. org/docserver/download/fulltext/5lgsjhvj75zv.pdf?expires=1306097696&id= id&accname=guest&checksum=507FCC869BBF86F5CA0291C1B76F2D7E [accessed: 18 April 2006].

Offerdal, K. 2010. Arctic energy in EU policy: Arbitrary interest in the Norwegian High North. *Arctic*, 63(1), 30–42.

Offshore Energy Today. *Transadriatic Pipeline Reconfirms Shah Deniz II (Azerbaijan) as the Initial Gas Source for the Pipeline* [Online]. Available at: http://www.offshoreenergytoday.com/trans-adriatic-pipeline-reconfirms-shah-deniz-ii-azerbaijan-as-the-initial-gas-source-for-the-pipeline/ [accessed: 24 November 2010].

Olcott, M. 2004. Vladimir Putin and the geopolitics of oil. *The energy dimension in Russian global strategy, The James A. Baker III Institute for Public Policy of Rice University* [Online]. Available at: http://www.rice.edu/energy/ publications/docs/PEC_Olcott_10_2004.pdf [accessed: 7 April 2006].

OPEC 2002. *Oil and Energy Outlook to 2020* [Online]. Available at: http:// www.opec.org/opec_web/static_files_project/media/downloads/publications/ AR002002.pdf [accessed: 11 June 2005].

Orban, A. 2008. *Power, Energy and the New Russian Imperialism*. Westport, CT: Praeger.

Orttung, R. 2006. The role of business in Russian foreign policy and security dimensions, in *Russian Business Power: The Role of Russian Business in Foreign and Security Relations*, edited by A. Wenger, R. Orttung and J. Perovic. London: Routledge, 22–44.

Ottinger, R. 2010. Introduction: Copenhagen climate change conference—Success or failure? *Pace Environmental Law Review*, 27(2), 411–19.

Özdemir, V. 2008. Turkey's role in European energy security, in *Europe's Energy Security: Gazprom's Dominance and Caspian Supply Alternatives*, edited by S. Cornell and N. Nilsson. Washington: CACI and SRSP, 99–114.

Paillard, C. 2007. Gazprom, the fastest way to energy suicide. *IFRI Russia/NIS Center, Russie.Nei.Visions 17* [Online]. Available at: http://www.lsa.umich.edu/UMICH/ceseuc/Home/ACADEMICS/Research%20Projects/Energy%20Security%20in%20Europe%20and%20Eurasia/Gazprom%20the%20Fastest%20Way%20to%20Energy%20Suicide.pdf [accessed: 16 September 2009].

Papadopoulos, C. 2008. Greek–Turkish economic cooperation: Guarantor of détente or hostage to politics? *Occasional Paper 08/08, St Antony's College, University of Oxford* [Online]. Available at: http://www.sant.ox.ac.uk/seesox/pdf/G-TEconomicCooperationMar08.pdf [accessed: 30 May 2009].

Papadopoulou, E., Papalexiou C., Hasanagas, N. and Ventouri, E. 2010. Rural development policy delivery and governance in Greece. *Paper prepared for presentation at the 118th seminar of the EAAE 'Rural Development: Governance, Policy Design and Delivery', Ljubljana, Slovenia* [Online]. Available at: http://ideas.repec.org/p/ags/eaa118/94616.html [accessed: 22 May 2011].

Parsons, C. and Brown, J. 2003. The 'Asian Premium' and dependency on Gulf oil. *CITS Working Papers* [Online]. Available at: http://www.econ.ynu.ac.jp/cits/publications/pdf/CITSWP2003-02.pdf [accessed: 6 September 2005].

Pascual, C. and Zambetakis, E. 2010. The geopolitics of energy: From security to survival, in *Energy Security: Economics, Politics, Strategies and Implications*, edited by C. Pascual and J. Elkind. Washington: The Brookings Institution, 9–36.

Patt, A. 2009. Effective regional energy governance – not global environmental governance – is what we need right now for climate change. *Journal of Global Environmental Change*, 728, 1–3.

Paul, A. 2010. Nagorno–Karabakh – A ticking time bomb. *EPC Commentary* [Online]. Available at: http://epceu.accounts.combell.net/documents/uploads/pub_1148_nagorno-karabakh.pdf [accessed: 1 February 2011].

Percebois, J. 2008. The supply of natural gas in the European Union – strategic issues. *OPEC Energy Review*, 32(1), 33–53.

Percival, B. 2008. The risk of energy securitization on the Eurasian continent. *CIEP Briefing Paper* [Online]. Available at: http://www.clingendael.nl/publications/2008/20080700_ciep_briefing_paper_percival.pdf [accessed: 15 March 2010].

Peterson, J. and Sjursen, H. 1998. Conclusion: The myth of the CFSP, in *A Common Foreign Policy for Europe? Competing Visions of the CFSP*, edited by J. Peterson and H. Sjursen. London and New York: Routledge, 167–92.

Pike, W. 2010. Challenges and solutions for 2011 and beyond. *World Oil*, December Issue, 29–30.

Pirani, S. 2007. *Ukraine's Gas Sector*. Oxford: OIES.

Pirani, S. (ed.) 2009. *Russian and CIS Gas Markets and their Impact on Europe.* Oxford: OIES.

Pirani, S., Stern, J. and Yafimava, K. 2010. The April 2010 Russo-Ukrainian gas agreement and its implication for Europe. *OIES NG 42* [Online]. Available at: http://www.oxfordenergy.org/wpcms/wp-content/uploads/2011/05/NG_42. pdf [accessed: 4 April 2011].

Pleines, H. 2006. Russian energy companies and the enlarged European Union, in *Russian Business Power: The Role of Russian Business in Foreign and Security Relations*, edited by A. Wenger, R. Orttung and J. Perovic. London: Routledge, 47–66.

Pollitt, M. 2008. The arguments for and against ownership unbundling of energy transmission networks. *Energy Policy*, 36(2), 704–13.

Poussenkova, N. 2004. From rigs to riches: Oilmen vs. financiers in the Russian oil sector. *The energy dimension in Russian global strategy, The James A. Baker III Institute for Public Policy of Rice University* [Online]. Available at: http://www.rice.edu/energy/publications/docs/PEC_Poussenkova_10_2004. pdf [accessed: 6 September 2005].

Powers, J. 2010. Oil addiction: Fueling our enemies. *Truman National Security Project* [Online]. Available at: http://www.trumanproject.org/files/papers/Oil_ Addiction_-_Fueling_Our_Enemies_FINAL.pdf [accessed: 3 January 2011].

Proedrou, F. 2010. Sensitivity and vulnerability shifts and the new energy pattern in EU–Russia gas trade. Prospects for the near future. *Studia Diplomatica – The Brussels Journal of International Relations*, 63(1), 85–104.

Qatar Tribune 2010. *Cyprus Israel Sign Maritime Border Demarcation Deal* [Online]. Available at: http://www.qatar-tribune.com/data/20101219/content. asp?section=europe1_2 [accessed: 12 January 2011].

Qingyi, W. 2006. Energy conservation as security. *China Security*, Summer Volume, 89–105.

Reuters 2007. *EU's Eastern Newcomers to Plot Common Energy Policy* [Online]. Available at: http://uk.reuters.com/article/oilRpt/idUKL148701220071214 [accessed: 14 April 2010].

Ria Novosti 2011a. *Russia's Gazprom to Expand Underground Gas Storage to 6.5 Bcm by 2016 – CEO* [Online]. Available at: http://en.rian.ru/ russia/20100625/159571853.html [accessed: 14 January 2011].

Ria Novosti 2011b. Russia's Putin Wants Independent Gas Producers to Get Access to Pipelines [Online]. Available at: http://en.rian.ru/ business/20110209/162522210.html [accessed: 12 March 2011].

Richardson, J. (ed.) 2001. *European Union: Power and Policy-Making.* 2nd Edition. London: Routledge.

Rifkin, J. 2003. *The Hydrogen Economy: The Creation of the Worldwide Energy Web and the Redistribution of Power on Earth.* New York: Penguin.

Rifkin, J. 2010. *The Empathic Civilization: The Race to Global Consciousness in a World in Crisis.* Cambridge: Polity Press.

Risse, T. 2000. Let's argue: Communicative action in world politics. *International Organization*, 54(1): 1–39.

Röller, L., Delgado, J. and Friederiszick, H. 2007. *Energy: Choices for Europe.* Brussels: Bruegel Blueprint Series.

Rosamond, B. 2000. *Theories of European Integration.* Basingstoke and New York: Macmillan and St. Martin's Press.

Rousseau, R. 2010. How oil price hikes force the Russian economy to urgently modernize. *Europe's World* [Online]. Available at: http://www.europesworld. org/NewEnglish/Home_old/CommunityPosts/tabid/809/PostID/1854/ HowOilPriceHikesForcetheRussiaEconomytoUrgentlyModernize.aspx [accessed: 12 November 2010].

Rowley, M. 2009. The Nabucco pipeline project: Gas bridge to Europe? *Pipeline and Gas Journal*, 236(9), 72–3.

Ruchser, M. 2011. The current column: Fukushima and the liberation movements in North Africa: What future for Desertec and 'Electricity from the Desert'? *German Development Institute* [Online]. Available at: http://www.europesworld. org/NewEnglish/Home_old/PartnerPosts/tabid/671/PostID/2397/The CurrentColumnFukushimaandtheliberationmovementsinNorthAfricaWhat futureforDesertecandelectricityfromthedesert.aspx [accessed: 8 April 2011].

Rulska, A. 2006. *The European Union Energy Policy: An Initiative in Progress* [Online]. Available at: www.ceeisaconf.ut.ee/orb.aw/class=file/action.../id.../ rulska_energy.doc [accessed: 12 May 2010].

Sander, M. 2007. A 'strategic relationship'? The German policy of energy security within the EU and the importance of Russia, in *Dealing with Dependency. The European Union's Quest for a Common Energy Foreign Policy*, edited by M. Overhaus, H. Maull and S. Harnisch. *Foreign Policy in Dialogue* [Online], 8(20). Available at: http://theseus.uni-koeln.de/fileadmin/Files/Presentations/ Umbach/Energy_Foreign_Policy_2007.pdf [accessed: 19 June 2008].

Schmidt, V. 1995. The new world order, incorporated: The rise of business and the decline of the nation state. *Daedalus* [Online], 124(2). Available at: http:// www.mtholyoke.edu/acad/intrel/schmidt.htm [accessed: 24 February 2009].

Schmidt-Felzmann, A. 2008. Editorial: The European Union's external energy policy. *Journal of Contemporary European Research*, 4(2), 67–70.

Schneider, M. 2011. The crumbling facade of Europe's bulwark of stability: Tunisia's Jasmine revolution unmasks the EU's misguided policy approach in the Southern backyard. *Europe's World* [Online]. Available at: http:// www.europesworld.org/NewEnglish/Home_old/CommunityPosts/tabid/809/ language/en-US/Default.aspx?PostID=2207&CurrentPage=0&filter=4 [accessed: 21 January 2011].

Schwartz, M. 2008. *War Without End: The Iraqi War in Context.* Chicago: Haymarket Books.

Schweller, R. 2003. The progressiveness of neoclassical realism, in *Progress in International Relations Theory: Appraising the Field*, edited by C. Elman and M. Elman. Cambridge, MA: MIT Press, 311–48.

Seliverstov, S. 2009. Energy security of Russia and the EU: Current legal problems. *IFRI* [Online]. Available at: http://www.ifri.org/files/Energie/Seliverstov.pdf [accessed: 2 September 2010].

Shapovalova, N. 2010. The battle for Ukraine's energy allegiance. *FRIDE Policy Brief 55* [Online]. Available at: www.fride.org/descarga/PB55_Ukraine_allegiance_ENG_sep10.pdf [accessed: 17 January 2011].

Sheikhmohammady, M., Kilgour, D. and Hipel, K. 2010. Modeling the Caspian Sea negotiations. *Group Decision and Negotiation*, 19(2), 149–68.

Shelley, L. 2003. International dimensions of corruption: The Russian case. Princeton [Online]. Available at: http://www.princeton.edu/~lisd/publications/wp_russiaseries_shelley.pdf [accessed: 12 December 2009].

Sjursen, H. 1998. Missed opportunity or eternal fantasy? The idea of a European Security and Defense Policy, in *A Common Foreign Policy for Europe? Competing Visions of the CFSP*, edited by J. Peterson and H. Sjursen. London and New York: Routledge, 95–112.

Slater, J. 2011. Storing power: The wind, the sun and the future of energy storage. *Europe's World* [Online]. Available at: http://www.europesworld.org/NewEnglish/Home_old/CommunityPosts/tabid/809/language/en-US/Default.aspx?PostID=2205&CurrentPage=0&filter=4 [accessed: 22 January 2011].

Smith, K. 2009. Russian energy dependency and the conflicting interests of old and new Europe. *CSIS* [Online]. Available at: http://csis.org/files/publication/20090512_RussiaEnergy.pdf [accessed: 11 April 2010].

Smith, K. 2010. Russia–Europe energy relations. Implications for U.S. policy. *CSIS* [Online]. Available at: http://csis.org/files/publication/100218_Smith_RussiaEuropeEnergy_Web.pdf [accessed: 21 February 2011].

Socor, V. 2007a. Central Asia–Europe energy projects: Itemizing what went wrong. *Eurasia Daily Monitor* [Online], 4(106). Available at: http://jamestown.org/edm/article.php?article_id=2372200 [accessed: 14 November 2009].

Socor, V. 2007b. Shah–Deniz gas buttressing Georgia, Azerbaijan economically and politically. *Eurasia Daily Monitor* [Online], 4(12). Available at: http://www.jamestown.org/single/?no_cache=1&tx_ttnews[tt_news]=32396 [accessed: 26 June 2009].

Socor, V. 2008. A Russian-led 'OPEC for gas'? Design, implications, countermeasures. *Lithuanian Foreign Policy Review*, 20, 112–19.

Söderbergh, B., Jakobsson, K. and Aleklett, K. 2009. European energy security: The future of Norwegian natural gas production. *Energy Policy*, 37(12), 5037–55.

Soligo, R. and Jaffe, A. 2004. Market structure in the new gas economy: Is cartelization possible? *The James A. Baker III Institute for Public Policy of Rice University, Program on Energy and Sustainable Development* [Online]. Available at: http://iis-db.stanford.edu/pubs/20705/Gas_OPEC_final.pdf [accessed: 16 April 2007].

Spanjer, A. 2008. *Structural and Regulatory Reform of the European Natural Gas Market: Does the Current Approach Secure the Public Service*

Obligations? Leiden [Online]. Available at: https://openaccess.leidenuniv.nl/bitstream/1887/13356/1/Manuscript+definitief%2C+09-10-08.pdf [accessed: 12 May 2009].

Srivastava, L. and Mathur, R. 2007. Global energy security: India's energy security. *Dialogue on Globalization, FES Briefing Paper 14* [Online]. Available at: http://library.fes.de/pdf-files/iez/global/04809.pdf [accessed: 27 September 2009].

Staab, A. 2008. *The European Union Explained: Institutions, Actors, Global Impact*. Indiana: Indiana University Press.

Statoil Official Website. *The EU Gas Directive* [Online]. Available at: http://www.statoil.com/annualreport2009/en/ouroperations/regulation/pages/gasdirectiveoftheeuropeanunion.aspx [accessed: 1 April 2011].

Steenblik, R. 2010. Subsidies in the traditional energy sector, in *Global Challenges at the Intersection of Trade, Energy and the Environment*, edited by J. Pauwely. Geneva: CEPR, 183–92.

Stern, J. 1999. Soviet and Russian gas: The origins and evolution of Gazprom's export strategy, in *Gas to Europe: The Strategies of Four Main Suppliers*, edited by R. Mabro and I. Wybrew-Bond. Oxford: Oxford University Press, 135–200.

Stern, J. 2002. Security of European natural gas supplies: The impact of import dependence and liberalization. *The Royal Institute of International Affairs* [Online]. Available at: http://www.chathamhouse.org.uk/files/3035_sec_of_euro_gas_jul02.pdf [accessed: 6 September 2006].

Stern, J. 2005. *The Future of Russian Gas and Gazprom*. Oxford: Oxford University Press.

Stern, J. 2007. Is there a rationale for the continuing link to oil product prices in continental European long-term gas contracts? *OIES NG 19* [Online]. Available at: http://www.oxfordenergy.org/wpcms/wp-content/uploads/2010/11/NG19-IsThereARationaleFortheContinuingLinkToOilProductPricesinContinentalEuropeanLongTermGasContracts-JonathanStern-2007.pdf [accessed: 11 April 2009].

Stern, J. 2009a. Continental European long-term gas contracts: Is a transition away from oil product-linked pricing inevitable and imminent? *OIES NG 34* [Online]. Available at: http://www.oxfordenergy.org/wpcms/wp-content/uploads/2010/11/NG34-ContinentalEuropeanLongTermGasContractsIsATransitionAwayFromOilProductLinkedPricingInevitableandImminent-JonathanStern-2009.pdf [accessed: 3 September 2010].

Stern, J. 2009b. Future gas production in Russia: Is the concern about lack of investment justified? *OIES NG 35* [Online]. Available at: http://www.oxfordenergy.org/wpcms/wp-content/uploads/2010/11/NG35-FutureGasProductioninRussiaIsTheConcernAboutLackofInvestmentJustified-JonathanStern-2009.pdf [accessed: 26 August 2010].

Stern, J. and Honore, A. 2004. Large scale investments in liberalized gas markets: The case of the UK. *OIES* [Online]. Available at: http://www.oxfordenergy.org/wpcms/wp-content/uploads/2011/02/Presentation17-LargeScaleInvestme ntsinLiberalisedGasMarketsTheUKCase-JSternAHonore-2004.pdf [accessed: 4 May 2011].

Stokes, D. and Raphael, S. 2010. *Global Energy Security and American Hegemony (Themes in Global Social Change)*. Baltimore: The John Hopkins University Press.

Strange, S. 1996. *The Retreat of the State: The Diffusion of Power in the World Economy*. Cambridge: Cambridge University Press.

Stratfor 2010. *The EU Threatens Gazprom Monopoly* [Online]. Available at: http://www.stratfor.com/memberships/173729/geopolitical_diary/20101014_eu_threatens_gazproms_monopoly_europe [accessed: 8 December 2010].

Stulberg, A. 2008. *Well-Oiled Diplomacy: Strategic Manipulation and Russia's Energy Statecraft in Eurasia*. New York: State University of New York Press.

Süleymanov, E. 2008. Azerbaijan – A partner for Europe in energy security, in *Europe's Energy Security: Gazprom's Dominance and Caspian Supply Alternatives*, edited by S. Cornell and N. Nilsson. Washington: CACI and SRSP, 115–24.

Tehran Times 2008. Iran, *Russia Eying European Energy Market: FM* [Online]. Available at: http://www.tehrantimes.com/index_View.asp?code=161873 [accessed: 12 December 2009].

The Economist 2009. *The Next Oil Giant? Brazil's Oil Industry Has Big Hurdles to Clear* [Online]. Available at: http://www.economist.com/node/13348824 [accessed: 6 January 2011].

The Economist 2010a. The abominable gas man: How technological change and new pipelines improve energy security. *Europe's Gas Pipelines* [Online]. Available at: http://www.economist.com/node/17260657 [accessed: 31 October 2010].

The Economist 2010b. *Constellation's Cancellation: America's Nuclear Renaissance is Mightily Slow in Coming* [Online]. Available at: http://www.economist.com/node/17254442 [accessed: 14 November 2010].

The Economist 2010c. *New Movement on Old Pipes* [Online]. Available at: http://www.economist.com/blogs/easternapproaches/2010/07/pipeline_tangles [accessed: 11 December 2010].

The Economist 2010d. *What a Gas! Israel's New Gas Finds May Affect its Strategic Friendships Too* [Online]. Available at: http://www.economist.com/node/17468208 [accessed: 12 January 2011].

The Economist 2010e. *After Three Decades of Economic Progress but Political Paralysis, Change Is in the Air, Says Max Rodenbeck* [Online]. Available at: http://www.economist.com/node/16564206?story_id=16564206 [accessed: 31 January 2011].

The Economist 2011. *The Test for Ashton and Europe* [Online]. Available at: http://www.economist.com/blogs/charlemagne/2011/02/eus_foreign_policy [accessed: 5 February 2011].

The Economist Intelligence Unit. *Europe Gas: Cyprus Gears up for Offshore Gas Exploration* [Online]. Available at: http://www.eiu.com/index.

asp?layout=ib3Article&article_id=227838607&country_id=1030000303 &pubtypeid=1142462499&industry_id=740001074&category_id=&rf=0 [accessed: 24 February 2011].

Tindale, S. 2011. EU 'Energy Summit'. *EU Business* [Online]. Available at: http:// www.eubusiness.com/Members/climateanswers/energy-summit.11 [accessed: 11 March 2011].

Tonnensson, S. and Kolas, A. 2006. *Energy Security in Asia: China, India, Oil and Peace*. Report to the Norwegian Ministry of Foreign Affairs. Oslo: PRIO.

Toyin, F. and Genova, A. 2005. *The Politics of the Global Oil Industry.* London: Praeger.

Trenin, D. 2005. Russia and anti-terrorism, in *What Russia Sees*, edited by D. Lynch. Paris: Chaillot Papers 74.

Trenin, D. and Malashenko, A. 2004. *Russia's Restless Frontier: The Chechnya Factor in Post-Soviet Russia.* Washington: Carnegie Endowment for International Peace.

Trofimenko, H. 1999. *Russian National Interests and the Current Crisis in Russia.* Sydney: Ashgate.

Tsakiris, T. 2011. Europe finalizes major gas security regulation to prepare for next crises. *EKEM European Energy Policy Observatory* [Online]. Available at: http://www.ekemeuroenergy.org/en/index.php?option=com_content&view =article&id=91:europe%E2%80%93finalizes%E2%80%93major%E2%80% 93gas%E2%80%93security%E2%80%93regulation%E2%80%93to%E2%80 %93prepare%E2%80%93for%E2%80%93next%E2%80%93crises&catid=49 :eu%E2%80%93policies%E2%80%93&Itemid=66 [accessed: 1 April 2011].

Tsereteli, M. 2008. The Black Sea/Caspian region in Europe's economic and energy security, in *Europe's Energy Security: Gazprom's Dominance and Caspian Supply Alternatives*, edited by S. Cornell and N. Nilsson. Washington: CACI and SRSP, 41–56.

Twining D. 2006. Putin's power politics. *The Weekly Standard* [Online], 11(17). Available at: http://www.gmfus.org/news_analysis/news_article_ view?newsarticle.id=828 [accessed: 21 June 2008].

Ummel, K. and Wheeler, D. 2008. Desert power: The economics of solar thermal electricity for Europe, North Africa and the Middle East. *Working Paper 156, Center for Global Development.* Washington, DC [Online]. Available at: http:// ideas.repec.org/p/cgd/wpaper/156.html [accessed: 12 September 2009].

Utility Week 2009. *Gas Interconnectors in Eastern Europe will Spur Competition* [Online]. Available at: http://www.utilityweek.co.uk/news/news_story.asp?id =55027&title=Gas+interconnectors+in+eastern+Europe+will+spur+competiti on [accessed: 13 March 2011].

Vahtra, P. and K. Liuhto. 2004. Expansion or exodus: Foreign operations of Russia's largest corporations. *Turku School of Economics and Business Administration* [Online]. Available at: http://www.tse.fi/FI/yksikot/erillislaitokset/pei/ Documents/Julkaisut/Vahtra_Liuhto_82004.pdf [accessed: 10 September 2009].

Valasek, T. 2005. New EU members in EU's security policy. *Cambridge Review of International Affairs*, 18(2), 217–28.

Van Damme, E. 2004. Pragmatic privatisation: The Netherlands 1982–2002. *TILEC Discussion Paper 2004–007, Tilburg University* [Online]. Available at: http://papers.ssrn.com/sol3/papers.cfm?abstract_id=870257 [accessed: 10 October 2009].

Van der Linde, C. and de Jong, J. 2009. *Upping the Stakes: Some Lessons for the EU from the Recent Russia–Ukraine Gas Crisis* [Online: Clingedael International Energy Programme, The Hague]. Available at: http://www.clingendael.nl/publications/2009/20090200_ciep_briefing_paper_russia_ukraine.pdf [accessed: 8 June 2010].

Vaszi, Z., Varga, A. and Svab, J. 2010. The new ways of natural gas transport and their effect for Slovakia. *Acta Metallurgica Slovaca*, 16(2), 127–32.

Vaughan, A. 2010. Cancun climate agreements at a glance. *The Guardian* [Online]. Available at: http://www.guardian.co.uk/environment/2010/dec/13/cancun-climate-agreement [accessed: 28 December 2010].

Verrastro, F. and Ladislaw, S. 2007. Providing energy security in an interdependent world. *The Washington Quarterly*, 30(4), 95–104.

Victor, N. 2008. Gazprom: Gas giant under strain. *Program on Energy and Sustainable Development Working Paper 71*, Stanford [Online]. Available at: http://iis-db.stanford.edu/pubs/22090/WP71,_Nadja_Victor,_Gazprom,_13Jan08.pdf [accessed: 11 June 2009].

Victor, N. and Victor, D. 2006. Bypassing Ukraine: Exporting Russian gas to Poland and Germany, in *Natural Gas and Geopolitics: From 1970 to 2040*, edited by D. Victor, A. Jaffe and M. Hayes. Cambridge: Cambridge University Press, 122–68.

Wallace, H. and Wallace, W. (eds) 2000. *Policy-Making in the European Union*. 4th Edition. Oxford: Oxford University Press.

Watson, J. 2007. Can new nuclear power strengthen energy security? *Sussex Energy Group Policy Briefing 2* [Online]. Available at: http://www.sussex.ac.uk/sussexenergygroup/documents/security_brief_webonly.pdf [accessed: 10 October 2008].

Wendt, A. 1999. *Social Theory of International Politics*. Cambridge: Cambridge University Press.

Weyman-Jones, T. 1997. Energy policy in the European Community, in *New Challenges to the European Union: Policies and Policy-Making*, edited by S. Stavridis, E. Mossialos, R. Morgan and H. Machin. Aldershot: Dartmouth, 545–69.

Williams, V. 2001. Playing with power: The US role in Europe–Russia natural gas politics. *European Focus 13* [Online]. Available at: http://www.pasos.org/www-pasosmembers-org/publications/playing-with-power-the-us-role-in-europe-russia-natural-gas-politics [accessed: 9 May 2009].

Winrow, G. 2009. Problems and prospects for the 'fourth corridor': The positions and role of Turkey in gas transit to Europe. *OIES NG 30* [Online]. Available at:

http://www.oxfordenergy.org/wpcms/wp-content/uploads/2010/11/NG30-Pro
blemsandProspectsForTheFourthCorridorThePositionandRoleofTurkeyinGas
TransitToEurope-GarethWinrow2009.pdf [accessed: 6 February 2010].

Winstone, R., Bolton, P. and Gore D. 2007. Energy security. *House of Common
Library, Research Paper 07/42* [Online]. Available at: http://www.parliament.
uk/documents/commons/lib/research/rp2007/rp07-042.pdf [accessed: 22 July
2009].

Wintour, P. 2008. Britain and France to take nuclear power to the world: Brown and
Sarkozy agree joint measures on energy and illegal immigration. *The Guardian*
[Online]. Available at: http://www.guardian.co.uk/environment/2008/mar/22/
nuclearpower.energy1 [accessed: 14 December 2010].

World Oil 2011. *Israel Could Become Net Gas Exporter* [Online]. Available
at: http://www.worldoil.com/Israel_could_become_net_gas_exporter.html
[accessed: 6 January 2011].

Wright, P. 2006. *Gas Prices in the UK: Markets and Insecurity of Supply*. Oxford:
OIES.

Wybrew-Bond, I. 1999. Setting the scene, in *Gas to Europe: The Strategies of
Four Main Suppliers*, edited by R. Mabro and I. Wybrew-Bond. Oxford:
Oxford University Press, 5–32.

Wyciszkiewicz, E. 2008. EU external energy policy: Between market and strategic
interests. *PISM Strategic Files* [Online]. Available at: http://www.isn.ethz.ch/
isn/Digital-Library/Publications/Detail/?ots591=0c54e3b3-1e9c-be1e-2c24-
a6a8c7060233&lng=en&id=93296 [accessed: 14 January 2010].

Xuetang, G. 2006. The energy security in Central Eurasia: The geopolitical
implications to China's energy strategy. *China and Eurasia Forum Quarterly*,
4(4), 117–37.

Yafimava, K. 2010. The June 2010 Russian–Belarusian gas transit dispute: A
surprise that was to be expected. *OIES NG 43* [Online]. Available at: http://
www.oxfordenergy.org/wpcms/wp-content/uploads/2010/11/NG43-TheJune
2010RussianBelarusianGasTransitDisputeASurpriseThatWasToBeExpected-
KatjaYafimava-2010.pdf [accessed: 8 April 2011].

Yenikeyeff, S. 2008. Kazakhstan's gas: Export markets and export routes. *OIES
NG 25* [Online]. Available at: http://www.oxfordenergy.org/wpcms/wp-
content/uploads/2010/11/NG25-KazakhstansgasExportMarketsandExportRou
tes-ShamilYenikeyeff-2008.pdf [accessed: 18 September 2009].

Yergin, D. 2006. Ensuring energy security. *Foreign Affairs*, 85(2), 69–82.

Yesdauletov, A. 2009. Kazakhstan's energy policy: Its evolution and tendencies.
Journal of US–China Public Administration, 6(4), 31–9.

Young, J. and Kent, J. 2004. *International Relations since 1945: A Global History*.
Oxford: Oxford University Press.

Youngs, R. 2007. Europe's external energy policy: Between geopolitics and the
market. *CEPS Working Paper* 278 [Online]. Available at: www.sites.google.
com/site/newcompetitiveness/EuropeanESecurity.pdf   [accessed: 3   April
2009].

Youngs, R. 2009. *Energy Security: Europe's New Foreign Policy Challenge*. New
    York: Routledge.
Ypery, E. 2007. The EU's energy security and Turkey's energy strategy. *Turkish
    Review of Eurasian Studies*, 5–26.
Yueh, L. 2010. An international approach to energy security. *Global Policy*, 1(2),
    1–2.
Zaiko, L. 2006. Russia and Belarus: Between wishing and reality. *Russia in Global
    Affairs*, 4(1), 108–16.
Zweig, D. and Jianhai, B. 2005. China's global hunt for energy. *Foreign Affairs*,
    84(5), 25–38.

Index

accountability 62
acquis (communautaire) 70, 72, 106
Africa 7–8, 34–5, 37, 70–71, 105, 134–5
    North Africa 41, 45, 49, 54, 71, 90, 95,
        109, 111, 114, 120–21, 130, 135
Algeria 4, 21, 43, 50, 57–8, 67, 89, 97,
        105, 109–14, 122
Angola 13, 35
Arab 7–8, 35, 44, 110, 119,
Arctic 6, 86, 109
Austria 67, 78–80, 84–5, 92, 95
Azerbaijan 46, 71, 89, 95, 97, 115–16, 119,
        120

Baku Initiative 71
Balkan 67–8, 72
Baltic states 49, 62, 67, 77, 95
    Baltic sea 81
Belarus 77–8, 82–4, 87, 91, 94
Belgium 67–8, 79, 106, 109, 117
bio-fuels 1–2, 23, 29
Black Sea 71, 84, 120
    Black Sea Synergy 71
Bolivia 5, 27
Bosnia-Herzegovina 70, 84
Bosporus Straits 46
Brazil 15, 52, 70
Britain 14, 45, 55–6, 61, 92, 94, 98, 100,
        106, 112, 121
Brussels 66
Bulgaria 67, 68, 71, 77, 79, 84, 94–5

Canada 6, 25, 28, 30, 54, 109
capitalism 34, 136
Caribbean 28, 54, 121
cartel 7, 9, 13, 64, 90
Caspian 8, 15, 24–5, 34, 43, 45, 47, 58, 67,
        71–2, 89, 105, 114–21
Central Asia 8, 21, 34, 37, 43, 71, 89, 115,
        116

Central Europe 66–8, 93, 100
Chechnya 13, 99
ChevronTexaco 26
China 5, 6, 8, 12–15, 17–18, 20, 23, 25–8,
        31–9, 43–4, 52, 70, 90–91, 116–17,
        121, 131
climate change 3, 30–31, 33, 43, 45, 54,
        109, 132–3, 135
CNG 54, 120
coal 1, 5, 11, 16, 20, 23, 25–6, 29, 31–3,
        37–8, 41, 45, 47, 53
    clean coal 29, 32, 38, 47
coherence 21, 49, 123, 136
Cold War 43, 77, 100, 119, 126
Commonwealth of Independent States
        (CIS) 80, 86
communism 46, 126
competition 14–15, 17–18, 23–4, 28, 34,
        37, 42, 46–7, 51–2, 55, 58, 60–64,
        71–2, 74, 87, 89, 93–4, 97, 99–100,
        108, 121, 126, 128–9, 131–3
conflict 4, 12, 14, 33, 35–6, 53, 63, 103,
        114–15, 120, 125–6
cooperation 8, 12, 14, 17–18, 21, 31, 34–6,
        39, 43, 47, 67, 70, 74, 77–8, 80,
        83, 89, 92–3, 95, 102–3, 106, 108,
        112–13, 119, 124–7, 129
Croatia 70, 84, 121
Cyprus 49, 56, 67, 120
Czech Republic 67, 79, 95
    Czechoslovakia 77

demand 4, 6, 9, 10–12, 15–16, 18–19,
        23–8, 34–9, 42–4, 53, 55, 60–61,
        64, 67, 69, 73, 77, 80, 83–4, 86, 91,
        98, 103, 106, 112–13, 116, 118–19,
        121, 129, 131, 134
    demand destruction 9, 28
democracy 34, 62, 73, 99, 106
Denmark 56, 61, 67–8, 95, 106, 109

dependence 11, 15, 27, 28–30, 34–5, 37,
     39, 54, 57, 62, 77–8, 86, 90–92,
     94–5, 98, 99–100, 102, 113–14,
     121, 123, 125, 130, 134
deregulation 60, 63–4, 74
development 1, 3–4, 7–8, 11, 15–16, 20,
     25, 28–9, 33, 38–9, 42, 44, 47, 51,
     53, 56, 58–60, 62, 64–5, 70 ,72–5,
     87, 89, 94, 100, 108, 113–14,
     118–20, 122, 130–37
diversification 4, 6, 17, 21, 29–30, 37, 45,
     47, 54–5, 58, 68, 74, 77–8, 89–98,
     103, 113–14, 118, 120, 122, 125,
     127–30

Eastern Europe 77, 100
economic crisis 23, 57, 66
Egypt 57, 98, 109
electricity 2, 4, 30–31, 37, 47, 49, 51, 61,
     63, 67, 134
emissions 11, 29, 31–2, 37–8, 44–5, 47,
     53–4, 133
Energy Charter Treaty 46
Energy Community Treaty 70–71, 75
energy companies 6, 8–9, 13, 43, 49, 50,
     60, 62, 64–5, 72, 92–3, 101, 117,
     127; see also energy enterprises;
     energy industry
energy conservation 6, 20, 30, 38, 53, 70
energy diplomacy 3, 21, 33, 34, 43, 49, 73,
     81, 95, 112, 116, 121
energy efficiency 11–12, 20, 24–5, 30,
     38–9, 48, 53, 70, 87, 114, 134, 137
energy enterprises 34, 49–50, 52, 62
energy industry 13–14, 16, 19, 48–50, 52,
     58, 118
energy poverty 3, 16–17, 24, 71, 133
energy savings 20, 137
energy security dilemma 15, 78, 126, 130
ENI 50, 84, 94
enlargement 91, 103, 113, 124
environment 1, 3–4, 11–12, 15–20, 24–33,
     37–9, 41, 44–5, 47–8, 50–53, 58,
     70–71, 73, 77, 86–7, 89, 108, 116,
     119–20, 123, 132–3, 135–7
EON Ruhrgas 93
     operator 63, 65, 101

European Commission 44–5, 47–52, 58,
     60–64, 68–70, 74, 87, 94, 101–2,
     106, 108, 112–13 , 125, 129, 134
20–20–20 Policy Initiative 11, 47
European Energy Recovery Program
     (EERP) 66
Third Energy Package 60, 63
European Neighborhood Policy (ENP) 71,
     113
Extractives Industry Transparency
     Initiative (EITI) 71
ExxonMobil 26, 117

Finland 79, 92
     energy crisis 4–5, 8, 15, 17
     first energy crisis 27, 30
     second energy crisis 43
flexibility 14, 47, 54–5, 61, 74, 101–18,
     127, 130, 137
fossil fuels 1, 5, 15–16, 24, 41, 44, 47, 79,
     131, 134, 137
France 45, 49, 63, 67–8, 77, 79, 92, 98,
     106, 109, 112

gas deficit 20, 56, 86, 125, 127
gas directive 47, 63
Gas Exporting Countries Forum (GECF)
     90, 113
gas glut 25, 131
gas prices 10–11, 25, 44, 54, 56, 62, 64, 74,
     83, 88, 108, 112–13, 131–2
Gazprom 50–52, 56, 62, 64–5, 77, 79–90,
     92–4, 97–103, 105, 108, 112,
     116–17, 123, 125, 127–9, 136
geopolitics 73
Georgia 46, 99, 115–16, 120
geothermal energy 1, 2, 48, 134
Germany 11, 50, 56, 61, 63, 67–8, 78–81,
     84, 92–3, 98, 102, 106, 124–5
global economy 18, 119; see also world
     economy
global energy market 1, 16, 18, 20, 23–4,
     38, 39, 41–2, 50
global energy mix 1, 2, 20, 23–4; see also
     global fuel mix
global fuel mix 23
global warming 6, 16
globalization 17–18, 90, 132

Greece 67–8, 77–80, 84–5, 92, 94–6, 109, 119, 136
green agenda 44, 52, 58, 135
green economy 1, 44, 123
growth 1–3, 18, 25, 32, 38, 41, 44, 61, 79, 86, 90, 123, 131, 133, 136
Gulf Cooperation Council (GCC) 34–5, 72

human rights 34, 43, 73, 99, 117
Hungary 67–8, 77, 79, 84, 94–5, 120
hydrogen 134
hydropower 23, 31, 38, 134

IEA 15, 17–18, 23–4, 32–3, 38, 54, 57, 68, 70, 106
independence 13, 16, 19, 35, 83, 89
independent producers (Russia) 87
India 5–6, 14–15, 17–18, 25, 28, 36, 43, 52, 70, 117
Indonesia 8, 28, 36–7, 54–5, 90, 121
integration 17, 21, 59, 67, 71–2, 74, 103, 106, 115, 124–5, 128
interconnections 55, 59–60, 66, 68, 71, 90, 99–100, 124–8, 130
interdependence 9, 18, 19, 21, 28, 34, 39, 45, 78, 92–4, 98, 103, 113, 119, 126–30
international institutions 18, 73
investments 5–6, 12, 18–19, 23–5, 35, 46, 62–3, 74, 86, 88, 93, 102, 108, 112, 114, 129, 131, 133–4
Iran 6–8, 16, 25, 27, 29, 34, 36, 42, 55–6, 83, 86, 90, 95, 97, 114, 115, 116, 118–20
Iraq 12–13, 16, 27, 29, 42, 110, 118
Israel 7, 15, 35, 119–20
Italy 50, 61, 67–8, 79–80, 84, 93, 95–6, 102, 109, 112, 117, 121

James Baker Institute World Gas Trade Model 6, 53, 57
Japan 13–15, 23, 29, 35–6, 38, 52, 54, 90–91, 98, 117, 121, 135

Kazakhstan 36–7, 46, 115–16
Kremlin 80, 82, 88, 91
Kyoto Protocol 30, 45, 47

Latin America 7–8, 17, 24, 27, 34–5, 37
Latvia 67, 79, 81
Lebanon 119–20
liberalization 10, 20, 46–7, 49, 51, 58–66, 68, 72–4, 84–5, 93, 99–100, 102, 108, 112–13, 125, 127–30
Libya 42, 57, 98, 109–11
Lithuania 49, 65, 67, 79, 81, 102
LNG 4, 28, 33–4, 36–7, 54–5, 63, 67, 89–90, 92, 94, 98, 109–10, 114, 117–18, 120–21, 127, 131
long-term contracts 55–6, 61, 88, 100–101, 112, 129

Maghreb 109, 111, 113
Malacca Straits 18, 28, 33, 36
Malaysia 8, 13, 28, 36–7, 54–5, 90, 121
Mashreq 113
Mexico 11, 27, 30, 54, 70
Middle East 13, 19, 21, 26–8, 30, 34–5, 37, 41, 45, 53, 55, 58, 67, 77–8, 90, 92, 95, 105, 114–15, 117–21, 130, 134–5
Moldova 71, 77, 87
monopoly 43, 60, 79, 81, 87, 99, 102, 128
monopsony 13, 36, 65

Nagorno-Karabakh 87, 115
national champions 56, 62–3, 65, 74, 112
NATO 91–5
neo-liberalism 55, 59, 64, 125
Netherlands 56, 79, 90
new Europe 80–81, 83, 91–3, 103, 105–6, 123–4; *see also* Eastern Europe
Nigeria 15–16, 35, 55, 57, 109–10
North Africa 41, 45, 49, 54, 71, 90, 95, 109, 111, 114, 120, 130, 135
North America 7, 10, 15, 28, 54–6, 121
North Europe 62, 64, 99
North Sea 15, 41, 46, 92, 106
Northwestern Europe 77
Norway 13, 21, 45, 54, 57, 58, 90, 95, 97, 105–9, 122
nuclear accident (Japan) 23, 29, 98, 135
nuclear power 2, 23, 26, 29, 31–2, 37–8, 45, 49, 98, 112, 119

Obama, Barack 11, 31, 88

OECD 15, 38, 86
oil prices 5–6, 9–11, 13, 15, 17, 19, 25, 27, 34, 56, 61
old Europe 81, 91–2; *see also* Western Europe; Central Europe

Partnership and Cooperation Agreement 72
peak theory 5
pipelines 12–14, 21, 29, 33–4, 36–7, 46–8, 51, 54–5, 57, 60, 62–3, 66–9, 71, 77, 79, 81–5, 87, 89, 91–6, 98, 99–101, 103, 105–7, 109–12, 115–19, 121, 124, 126–7, 130
    AGP 110
    AGRI 97, 120
    Baku–Supsa 46
    Baku–Tbilisi–Ceyhan 43, 46, 95
    Baltic 67–8
    Blue Stream 4, 84
    Druzhba 46, 77–8, 85
    Europipe I 106
    Europipe II 106
    Franpipe 106
    GALSI 67, 109, 111
    Greenstream 109, 111
    ITGI 67, 84, 95–7, 115, 120, 130
    Langeled 106
    Maghreb 109, 111
    Medgaz 109, 111
    Nabucco 67, 84, 94–7, 110, 116, 118, 128, 130
    NIGAL 110
    Nord Stream 81–6, 89, 93, 123–4
    South Caucasus 95
    South Stream 84–5, 94–5, 101
    Transadriatic (TAP) 96–7
    Transmed 109, 111
    Trans-Caspian 115–16, 119
    Vesterled 106
    Yamal–Europe 77–8, 85
    Zeepipe 106
Poland 53, 65, 67–8, 77–9, 81, 94–5, 98, 102, 106, 123–5
Portugal 49, 54, 67–8, 109
prevention and emergency mechanism 69, 75
privatization 60
protectionism 64–5, 93, 102–3, 128–9

Putin, Vladimir 12, 80, 93
Qatar 8, 25, 57, 117–18, 120–21

Realism (as an international relations theory) 103, 125
reciprocity 64, 102, 129
refining 9, 18, 24, 43
regulatory model (energy) 20, 59, 69, 71–2, 75, 135
renewables 1, 11–12, 16, 20, 23–4, 26, 29, 31, 37–8, 41, 45, 48, 52–3, 98, 112, 133–7
resource nationalism 14, 16, 41–2, 58
Romania 67–8, 71, 77, 79, 84, 95, 120
Royal Dutch Shell 118
rules of the game 13–14, 51, 64–5, 103, 105, 112
Russia 4, 8, 11–14, 16, 21, 28, 34, 36, 37, 41, 43, 45–7, 49–55, 57–8, 62, 64, 66, 72, 75, 77–105, 108–9, 113–19, 121–30, 136

Saudi Arabia 27, 30, 34, 44
Schröder, Gerhard 12, 93
Serbia 70, 84
security regulation (gas) 20, 67–9, 74
shale gas 7, 25
Single European Act 51, 59
Slovakia 67–8, 77, 79, 95
Slovenia 78–9, 84, 94
SOCAR 115
solar energy 1–2, 30, 37, 48, 134–5
solidarity 13, 21, 51, 53, 66, 68, 73, 93, 95, 123–5, 136
Sonatrach 50–51, 62, 64, 89, 112–13, 129
South Europe 112, 119
Southeast Asia 9, 17, 36
Southeast Europe 70, 84
Sovereignty 13, 35, 48–50, 106, 120
Soviet Union 46, 77, 115, 119, 126
Spain 67–8, 109, 111–12, 117, 120
spare capacity 9, 25
spot markets 11, 55–6, 61, 85, 88, 94, 101, 112
Statoil 51, 108
storage 29, 31, 61, 67, 85
Sudan 34–6
super cycles theory 5, 7

supranational 43, 48–50, 52–3, 58, 65–6,
   68, 74, 106, 123–5
Sweden 56, 61, 94, 106, 134
swing producer 27

Taiwan 33, 35, 117
third party access (TPA) 47, 61–3, 101
Total 118
trade-off 11–12, 117
transit 46–7, 59, 81–4, 89, 94, 109, 119–20,
   124, 130
Transneft 81
Transparency 17–18, 38, 71–2
Turkey 4, 13, 46, 67, 77, 84, 95–6, 110,
   120
Turkmenistan 34, 36–7, 43, 46, 115–17

UAE 8, 117–18
Union for the Mediterranean (UfM) 113
Ukraine 71, 77–8, 81–4, 87, 94, 114
unbundling 63, 70, 101–2, 112, 129
unconventional oil 24
underdevelopment 118, 136

US 4, 8, 11–15, 18–19, 20, 23, 25–31,
   33–6, 39, 43–4, 52, 54–5, 73, 77,
   81, 95, 100, 109–10, 116–19, 121
Congress 29
Senate 31
White House 29
utilities 63–4, 80, 101
Uzbekistan 43, 46, 115–17

Venezuela 12, 14, 16, 27, 30, 35
Chavez, Hugo 12, 16, 27, 36

welfare 18, 74, 118, 123, 131, 136
West, the 3, 8, 15–18, 20, 24, 34–5, 38–9,
   42–3, 46–7, 53, 80, 82, 95, 100,
   116–19, 136
Western Europe 80, 83, 92, 126
wind energy 1–2, 37–8, 48, 134
Wintershall 93
world economy 16–17
World Trade Organization (WTO) 43, 70,
   87, 125

Yamal region 77, 86